D1258038

The Collected Sermons of

Walter Brueggemann

Volume 2

The Collected Sermons of

Walter Brueggemann

Volume 2

Walter Brueggemann

WESTMINSTER
JOHN KNOX PRESS
LOUISVILLE · KENTUCKY

© 2015 Walter Brueggemann
Foreword © Westminster John Knox Press

First edition
Published by Westminster John Knox Press
Louisville, Kentucky

7|15   15 16 17 18 19 20 21 22 23 24—10 9 8 7 6 5 4 3 2 1

Unless otherwise indicated, Scripture quotations are from the New Revised Standard Version of the Bible, copyright © 1989 by the Division of Christian Education of the National Council of the Churches of Christ in the U.S.A., and are used by permission. Where scriptural translations depart from the NRSV, they are the author's own renderings, sometimes in liberal paraphrase. Scripture quotations marked CEB are from the Common English Bible, © 2011 Common English Bible, and are used by permission. Scripture quotations marked RSV are from the Revised Standard Version of the Bible, copyright © 1946, 1952, 1971, and 1973 by the Division of Christian Education of the National Council of the Churches of Christ in the U.S.A., and are used by permission.

Book design by Sharon Adams
Cover design by Dilu Nicholas
Cover photo by Bill Ecklund

Library of Congress Cataloging-in-Publication Data

Brueggemann, Walter.
  [Sermons]
  The collected sermons of Walter Brueggemann / Walter Brueggemann ; foreword by Samuel Wells.—1st ed.
    p. cm.
  Includes bibliographical references and index.
  ISBN 978-0-664-26041-5 (v. 2: alk. paper)
  ISBN 978-0-664-23445-4 (v. 1: alk. paper)
  1. Sermons, American—21st century. 2. Sermons, American—20th century. 3. United Church of Christ—Sermons. I. Title.
  BX9886.Z6B77 2011
  252'.05834—dc23

                                                        2011023740

∞ The paper used in this publication meets the minimum requirements of the American National Standard for Information Sciences—Permanence of Paper for Printed Library Materials, ANSI Z39.48–1992.

Most Westminster John Knox Press books are available at special quantity discounts when purchased in bulk by corporations, organizations, and special–interest groups. For more information, please e–mail SpecialSales@wjkbooks.com.

In Memory of Frederick W. Schroeder

Contents

Part 2: Sermons for Lent and Easter

Part 3: Sermons for Pentecost and Ordinary Time

Part 4: Sermons for Other Occasions

Foreword

The legendary Lutheran preacher and teacher of homiletics Edmund Steimle once said of a famous pulpiteer of a previous generation that his sermons were elegant and rhetorically brilliant, but they lacked specific context. "They could have been preached," said Steimle, "in New York or Toronto or the highlands of Scotland, could have been uttered in 1950 or 1850. They floated above circumstance. There was no grit of a particular time and place."

A lack of gritty context is by no means the case for these provocative and evocative sermons of Walter Brueggemann. Not only do they contain specific references to the locations in which they were preached—Chicago, Seattle, Houston, the coast of Florida, Boston, a small town in Georgia, and more— they even more significantly evoke the cultural moment in which they were spoken and to which they are addressed: the anxious, fearful, fevered, consumerist culture of the weary and declining American empire in the bottom of the ninth inning. These sermons in no way "float above circumstance," but instead they energize and illumine specific times and places with judgment, grace, and hope.

Brueggemann is well–recognized as a prophetic voice in our time, and these sermons will do everything to burnish that reputation. He shines a searching light on our society and does not shrink from naming "the power of chaos and death, of greed and brutality, of selfishness and hate" that festers among us. But it seems important to note that Brueggemann has been holding steady in this pulpit for several decades now. He is a prophet to be sure, but a resident prophet, one who buys a piece of real estate in Anathoth even as he weeps for the doomed city.

These sermons, therefore, are not "drive–by shootings" committed by a rootless activist preacher with nothing at stake. Brueggemann lives here and yearns for the restoration of a just community. He provides a sharp critique, but it is always on the way to proclaiming hope, hope engendered by the God who will not leave the people forlorn or the church forsaken, but who will always bring redemption out of despair.

Brueggemann's prophetic voice cannot be collapsed into partisan theological politics. He recognizes that all of us, regardless of position, are caught in the snare. "Conservatives among us," he observes, "do not want . . . change; and liberals among us only want change we can manage." The goal of these sermons is not persuasion to a particular political or theological posture. It is instead the opening up of for all of us the possibility of singing the doxology. "It might be an expensive doxology," he warns, because the very act of praise implies an unsettling of the status quo and a welcoming of God's transforming power. "When we praise," says Brueggemann, "we sign on. We are for sure invited to reach toward God's new world that is on its way . . . by the mercy of God!"

These sermons are themselves versions of that dangerous but longed-for doxology, and they move from ruthlessly honest cultural analysis to confident praise with such linguistic power that one can easily overlook the superb detail, the impressive craft, and the fine tooling employed by Brueggemann, the master preacher. The impact of these sermons comes not simply from the finished artwork but also from the artist's technique—the preparation of the homiletic canvas, the mix of pigment, and the brush strokes.

To begin with, these sermons are firmly biblical, in fact to be more specific, they are profoundly *textual*. They burrow deep into the marrow of biblical texts, exploring their contours, surveying their passageways, delighting in the interplay of their images and metaphors. They are a form of Christian *midrash*. Sometimes hearers attempt to compliment a preacher by saying, "You made the Bible come alive!" For Brueggemann, though, the Bible already is alive, humming with energy and power, and he attaches jumper cables from the text's dynamo to the sermon, springing it to life.

In his stimulating essay "The Preacher as Scribe," Brueggemann argues that the best way for today's parish preachers to "speak truth to power" is not to imagine themselves as Moses, raising the fist to Pharaoh, or as Nathan, dramatically pulling the mask of pretense off a wayward David, but as scribes—not the scribes who are the New Testament opponents of Jesus, of course, but the kind of scribes Jesus himself depicts when he says, "'Therefore every scribe who has been trained for the kingdom of heaven is like the master of a household who brings out of his treasure what is new and what is old'" (Matt. 13:52). Such scribes are alert both to the fluctuations, transitions, and shifts in the culture and to the primary task of *re-texting* God's people. Faithful scribes do for congregations what the sermons in this volume do: they refresh the memory and irrigate the parched imagination of the people of God with the streams of subversion and hope coursing through their own nearly forgotten scriptures.

These sermons, then, embody Bruggemann's own advice to preachers to hew closely to the biblical text—"to study it, to trust it, to engage it, to be led by it, to submit our modernist assumptions to it, and to have confidence that this text—despite all its vagaries and violence, its unbearable harshness and confounding cadences—is the one that merits our primal attention as a word of life." The preacher as "scribe" speaks powerfully to those in our time who have no text to guide them or who are living out of hollow and vapid cultural texts:

Some in the congregation are textless, believing that they can live out of their autonomous experience without any text, while others bring a weak, thin text of technological, therapeutic, military consumerism that is an odd mix or moralism, market ideology, self-congratulations and anxiety. The scribe, then, does not do text-work in a vacuum, but (a) in the face of resistance that rejects any text, or (b) in the face of thin text that claims excessive and disproportionate authority, or (c) in the presence of those who are inclined to this text but who have little clue about how to hear it so that it can function as identity-giving." ("The Preacher as Scribe" in *Inscribing the Text*, 13–14)

Part of Brueggemann's alertness to texts involves his savviness about genre. For him, the Bible is not an undifferentiated literary milkshake but a rich bundle of varying genres: poem and drama, story and chronicle, chant and hymn, antiphon and proverb, oracle and testimony. When Brueggemann enters a scriptural house, he knows both the neighborhood of the text and its architecture, and he allows the multiplicity of the biblical witness to find expression in his sermons.

Another mark of Brueggemann's fine sermonic craft is the freshness of his language. The more pedestrian preachers among us might say that "God is present in our world," but Brueggemann proclaims that "God is on the loose." For Brueggemann, we don't merely "do sinful things," we are instead "scavengers and cheats and corner cutters," and instead of just saying that "God will establish righteousness," Brueggemann has us wonder, "What would you do if you were God? And you saw the world you had made gone crazy?" For Brueggemann, the church is not simply the "recipient of the Holy Spirit" but is "the breathed-on church."

One could go on, placing chevron after chevron on these sermons to mark their excellence, but there is at least one more virtue that cries out to be named, and this one perhaps unexpected. These sermons are clear, simple, and profound all at once, or perhaps better, they are "simply profound." There is great depth of thought here and sophistication of exegesis, as one would anticipate from a scholar like Brueggemann. But having plunged many fathoms into these biblical texts, he resurfaces with prose accessible and inviting. In one sermon, for example, Brueggemann is explaining Jesus' call to discipleship:

Let me tell you what I think that means in the Gospel story and in our lives. Jesus calls people to believe that he saves and that he is saving and that we are saved . . . that we are safe and loved and cared for. To be a disciple means to know you are safe and loved and to live that way. Jesus calls people to trust that God is with us, that we are not alone even in the face of death and every kind of danger.

Those could almost be words from a children's sermon, and in a way they are, a sermon to all of us who are God's children and "little ones."

All readers of these sermons will be challenged and rewarded. Preachers will find much bread for the journey. The editors at Westminster John Knox Press have polished this already gleaming collection by arranging the sermons according to the liturgical year, thereby making them useful to the company of preachers who desire both to discern the times in which we live and to observe that countercultural shaping of time that is the Christian calendar.

Thomas G. Long
Candler School of Theology

Preface

For those of us who preach, the act of preaching and the craft of the sermon constitute an endless challenge and something of a puzzle, albeit a deeply serious puzzle. We keep at it but continue to wonder how the good news of God's love and the serious summons of God's will are transmitted, uttered, and received in our foolishness. Like most people of my generation, I have had much to unlearn about conventional modes of preaching and much to keep learning about contemporary possibilities of that art and that craft. In the presence of that ongoing unlearning and relearning, however, I continue to retain much of what I have been taught in seminary, what I have learned from my father-preacher, and much that continues to work in the strangeness of the church.

I am able to trace some patterned development in my way of preaching and can identify four accents that have become increasingly important to me:

First, I have come to believe that we may and must trust the biblical text more to do its own work, even given our best critical capacity over against the text. I certainly do not mean that the text should go uncriticized! I have no doubt that the text is recurringly more interesting and more compelling than anything we might talk about. It may be that I rely so much on the text because in my more-or-less itinerant ministry, I am almost always preaching with people whom I do not know, and the text is a point of reference in such a venue. In any case, I believe increasingly that the work of the sermon is to make the biblical text available to the church so that church folk can, if they choose, reimagine their lives according to the strange cadences of the text.

Second, my embrace of the practice of "imagination" has been a long study in my life, ever since I first read Paul Ricoeur. I take "imagination" to refer to the capacity to host ("image") a world other than the one taken for granted among us. I understand preaching to be a process of layered imagination. First of all, the biblical text itself is an act of imagination, not much illuminated by historical critical study of the kind fostered by the Jesus Seminar. The biblical writers and the long-term traditioning process are witnesses to a world other than the one practiced by the several empires that constituted the matrix for ancient Israel and the early church. In turn, the church tradition and the critical tradition of scholarship are practices of imagination that a preacher then takes up in her own imagination. It is this peculiar act of the preacher's imagination that permits a thousand different sermons to arise on the same Sunday on the same text. The finish of the project is the fact that the listening congregation also engages in an active process of imagination, as it does not hear what is spoken but what can be received. That is why the preachers are thanked and attacked after church for things they did not say. I suppose the process is not unlike the ancient game of "Rumor" in which there is a succession of whispers of the same message around the room, with the outcome at considerable variance from the beginning. Such imaginative preaching is an exercise in freedom that does not aim at precision, but at empowerment and generative possibility that are not possible or available until the word has been uttered.

Third, I have come to see that evangelical imagination is an offer, as best we can, of an alternative to what is otherwise available as a livable world. That means that in a variety of ways preaching is a contestation between the world given in the text as God's good rule and the world where we live otherwise when we are not listening. I am struck by the way in which the preaching in Deuteronomy, the prophets, and the apostles are always in contestation with the prevailing order of the day. I suggest that the preaching venue in the church is one of the few available venues for such contestation, because elsewhere the ideology of the world out there is so totalizing as to permit no contest.

Fourth, I have come to see that preaching is a performance of God's good rule that, in an act of utterance and receptive listening, mediates the truthful, joyous reality of that rule. By performance of course I do not mean anything theatrical per se, but the actual (*wirklich*) doing of the truth of the gospel. Thus preaching is not simply a reference to or remembrance of something from elsewhere, but it is here and now the offer of that news. Such a practice of re-presentation eschews any temptation to be didactic; it has taken me a long while to come to that realization.

Thus I imagine that the biblical text, rendered with all of the faithful imagination that we can muster or that is given us by the Spirit, is an offer of a world other than the world of weary anxiety that is everywhere among us. I have no doubt, moreover, that the offer of this alternative world that is always an elusive figment of faithful imagination will be all the more urgent in time to come in our society. As the grip of the ideology of military consumerism tightens among us, as it surely will in our anxiety, the utterance of an alternative is both urgent and high risk. The contestation consequently will be, perforce, more vigorous and the preacher placed more at risk.

I am greatly indebted to the folks at Westminster John Knox Press, notably David Dobson and Julie Tonini, who exercise great care, patience, and attentiveness to my work. And I am grateful to Tom Long for his generous foreword, as Tom remains for me one of the model preachers of our generation.

I am glad to dedicate this book to the memory of Frederick W. Schroeder, my first preaching teacher in Seminary, then teacher who in a preaching class gave me my lowest grade in seminary. He was also the president of the seminary who appointed me to my first teaching position at Eden Seminary, my alma mater. Earlier I had written of him: "These then are Schroder's guidelines: passionate churchmanship, disciplined intellect, deep faith, and open ecumenism." That list continues to be the guidance to which I try to adhere. Schroeder was austere and parsimonious in his humor. Occasionally he sent one of us home to "dress better" before we could preach in class He taught me about the deep urgency and seriousness of preaching that continue to summon me, and I am grateful.

Walter Brueggemann

PART ONE

Sermons for Advent, Christmas, and Epiphany

1

The *What* and the *When* of the Christ Child

PSALM 25:1–10

LUKE 21:25–36

People like us have careful work to do in Advent, to weave our way between two big dangers. On the one hand, there are dangerous people floating around the church who specialize in times and dates and schedules, who know with precision the time of Christ's coming and who speak confidently of millennia and pre-millennia and post-millennia. . . . They know too much and reduce God's freedom to the timetable of their ideology. On the other hand, there are dangerous people floating around the church who are offended by those people, and who in reaction are in love with their comfortable affluence and who imagine that it will not get any better than this, and who expect no gospel arrival at any time ever. People like us live in that awkward place amid those *who know too much* and those *who expect nothing.*

But we, in our theological tradition, occupy a different posture about Advent as we ready for Christmas. We are the ones who know *what* is coming but do not know *when.*

The *what* for which we wait at Christmas and for which we prepare in Advent is that God's rule of starchy justice and generous mercy will arise in the earth, and all that seek to negate abundant life will be overruled and nullified. That is how we pray every time we are together. We pray, "Thy kingdom come, thy will be done." We pray that God would show God's self so that the power of chaos and death, of greed and brutality, of selfishness and hate would end, for such negators cannot stay when God comes among us. We pray always in confidence, for we end and say, "For yours is the kingdom and the power and the glory": . . . it belongs to no one else.

3

But we do not know the *when*. We do not know when because the coming of God is not our doing. God's way is a mystery that has not been entrusted to us. It is hard for us to imagine that the regime of violent death will finally not prevail, and we do not know when or how it will end, because we trust all of that to God.

So we have this work before Christmas, to think deeply and pray hard and face passionately the "what" of God's way, without any anxiety about "when." We confess the "what" against those who expect nothing who are left in ultimate despair because they think it will finally not change at all. We confess no "when" against those who know too much and reduce the mystery to political ideology. We have passionate preparation to do in Advent so that we may be ready, and of course you know that that preparation has nothing to do with the consumer fever of American society. My modest gift to you today, as you gather around *what* and shun *when* is this Psalm 25, a delicate, passionately confident prayer that can give us a way to the "what" as we arrive at Christmas,

- Rested up for the "what,"
- Not exhausted with shopping,
- Not undone by too many parties,
- Not stressed by family quarrels over Christmas decorations, just on the alert!

The prayer of Psalm 25 is all about waiting:

Do not let those who *wait* for you be put to shame.
You are the God of my salvation,
For you I *wait* all the day long.
(v. 3, 5)

Thus the one who speaks the Psalm is waiting. But this waiting is not dormant, passive inactivity. It is being on active alert in hope, watching for signs, the kind you see at small airports where people gather to meet planes with big signs and flowers and happy waving, not knowing when the plane will arrive, but already elated well ahead of time, because it is someone we so want to see and hold and welcome. Advent is for getting our lives and our money and our energy and our time and our future and our outlook attuned to the one who is coming soon.

I.

What strikes me about this prayer in Psalm 25 is that it is so *God centered*. It begins:

To you, O Lord, I lift up my soul.
O my God, in you I trust . . .
You are the God of my salvation.

The life of the Psalmist is focused on the God who is a reality of faith and prayer and worship known in Israel's past for wonders of steadfast love and miracles of faithfulness.

Now all of that is obvious, except it is not an obvious practice for assertive, effective people like us. We are mostly preoccupied with the world, with the parade of crises that claim our energy and attention. And if we are too self-centered to focus there, we may focus more closely on ourselves, on our family, our money, our sexuality or whatever. The world is very much with us!

What this Psalmist knows, moreover, is that when the world is too much with us, we are talked out of hope, and the future feels like more of the same stuff that leaves us exhausted. But Christmas is not about us. It is about this God who erupted amid the Roman Empire. It is about the God who birthed this vulnerable Jesus just at the instant when a decree went out from Caesar Augustus to sign up for the taxes and the military draft of the empire. It turned out in Bethlehem that the world was not about Caesar's taxes or Caesar's draft or Caesar's war or Caesar's failed economic policies, but about the baby who confounded the powers of this age. Perhaps Christmas is about refocusing our lives away from all those forces that diminish us, to focus instead on this one who is our hope and our trust, our future and, indeed, our present.

II.

The Psalmist prays:

Do not let those who wait for you be put to shame.
(v. 3)

If you spend your time advocating the things of God, you will look like and sound like an innocent who does not know the ways of the world. The world is all about power and force and money and control. And those who live that way easily dismiss those who gather around the Christ child who specialize in neighborly love and unwanted children and needy widows and illegitimate outsiders of a dozen kinds. The people of the gospel keep up this alternative advocacy and we are left out of the main power games; it seems obvious that the rulers of this age will win, and our little gospel claim is so weak and so marginal and we ourselves doubt it sometimes. The "shame" is the impression that we back a loser when we bet on the future of the world.

This Psalmist prays that God should show God's hand, that God should appear in some sign and validate our faith and our advocacy. It is a good prayer to pray in Advent, to pray it before we lose hope and cease to trust.

III.

The Psalmist revels in God's mercy, goodness, and steadfast love:

> Be mindful of your mercy, O LORD and of your steadfast love.
> According to your steadfast love remember me.
> All the paths of the Lord are steadfast love and faithfulness.
> (vv. 6–8)

It is the same term three times, *steadfast love*, a term always on the lips of ancient Israel, a term that most fully characterizes the God of Christmas for whom we prepare in Advent. "Steadfast love" means solidarity in need enacted with transformative strength. It is the solidarity enacted with strength that Israel knows in the exodus and in a thousand other life-giving miracles. It is the solidarity in need offered by Jesus to the woman at the well, to the IRS man in the tree, to the blind beggar, to the woman with a bad back. What human persons and human community most need is abiding, committed, passionate *transformative solidarity*. This Psalmist waits for it in need and knows the place from where it comes.

Truth to tell, that kind of solidarity is not on offer in our world from the big players in power and money and authority. Israel knew that it was not on offer from Pharaoh who always demanded productivity. Jesus knew it was not on offer from Pilate who washed his hands of need. It is not on offer by most of the loud voices of ideology and propaganda among us.

But we are like the Psalmist. We know better; we are not seduced. So we wait with eager longing, for the one thing needful, for the one source that assures, and we will be in readiness.

IV.

But there is more about steadfast love from the God for whom we wait. I just gave you verse 10: "All the paths of the LORD are steadfast love and faithfulness." The word "path" in the Old Testament means the way of the Torah, the guidance of the covenant, the instruction of the tradition. It is the reason the first Christians were called "followers of the way," the way of Jesus, the way of the gospel, the way of steadfast love, mercy, and justice. The Psalmist prays:

Make me know . . . your ways;
Teach me . . . your paths;
Lead me . . . in your truth,
Teach me . . . Instruct me!

And then the Psalmist says in verses 8 and 9:

Good and upright is the LORD,
Therefore he *instructs* sinners in the way.
He *leads* the humble in what is right,
And *teaches* the humble his way.
                              (emphasis added)

The Psalmist is aware of the way of the world. The "sin" he talks about is not wild, distorted stuff. It is simply life against the Torah, pretending that God has no purpose for the world, or for us; we are on our own, autonomous agents who must make it all up as we go along. But the ones who wait know better. The ones who wait do not ask for a free lunch of mercy. They ask that we be educated in and for God's future. They ask to be humble and equipped for the new life of God's rule, to enact that justice and to enact it now.

So imagine, good church folk, imagine the Advent faith of the New York Avenue Presbyterian Church. Imagine a whole company of believers in this place rethinking their lives, redeploying their energy, reassessing their purposes.

The path is *to love God*,
not party, not ideology, not pet project,
but God's will for steadfast love that is not deterred by fear and anxiety.
The path is *to love neighbor*,
to love neighbor face-to-face,
to love neighbor in community action,
to love neighbor in systemic arrangements, in imaginative policies.

This Psalmist knows that if we do not prepare for and receive the future God will give, we will be left simply to cope on our own with the world of hurt and hate and violence and selfishness, without a hand to play in an alternative life.

Sometime during this Advent week, somebody will say to you in an open-ended, leading question:

You know what?!

And you can say, "Yes, the 'what' is that the gospel world is coming upon us; it will be a new world of well-being without fear." And they will ask, "When will that be?" And you will say, "I do not know 'when.'" But I am waiting for it, and already living it. I know the path into the future . . . loving God and loving neighbor.

The decrees of Caesar Augustus continue to go out for taxes and for draft and for frantic attempts to keep the world under our control. But the truth is found in the vulnerable village of Bethlehem outside the capital city, the village that disregarded the imperial decree. It will take a village to exhibit this alternative, and we are citizens of that coming society.

December 3, 2006
New York Avenue Presbyterian Church, Washington D.C.

2

The Poem

Subversion and Summons

ISAIAH 11:1–9
MATTHEW 3:1–12

Adults have always known that critical thinking is the best way to manage our life. Adults, since Plato, have learned to trust reason and proceed reasonably with their lives. Adults, since Aristotle, have preferred syllogistic logic that makes things certain. Adults, since the ancient Greeks have, by reason, logic, and critical thinking, been able to reduce reality to a memo, a syllogism, a syllabus, a brief. The Romans took over this Greek way to adulthood, and combined it with ruthless power to accomplish control and wealth and security.

In latter days, we in the United States have replicated Rome with our practice of memo, syllogism, syllabus, and brief . . . together with raw power. We have found our way to wealth, security and control. And to sustain that way in the world, we have founded great universities to champion critical thinking, reason, and logic. How is that for a quick summary of Western civilization?!

I.

Except this! Mostly unnoticed and not taken seriously, mostly under the radar in this adult world of control and order, there have been Jews. For the most part Jews have not committed to reason and logic and memo and syllogism and brief. Because the Jews came with their peculiar stories of odd moments of transformation, all about emancipation and healing and feeding and newness, all under the rubric of "miracle." And behind the stories there were poems . . . lyrical, elusive, eruptive, defiant. Jews have known from the outset that a commitment to memo and syllogism will not make things new. Jews have known

9

all along that in poetry we can do things not permitted by logic or reason, because poems never try to sound like memos. Poetry will break the claims of the memo. Poetry will open the world beyond reason. Poetry will give access to contradictions and tensions that logic must deny. Poetry will not only remember; it will propose and conjure and wonder and imagine and foretell.

So Jews, in their covenantal fidelity, did poems. Miriam did poetry when they crossed out of Egyptian slavery. Deborah did poetry when it dawned on them that the Canaanites were not so formidable. Hannah did poetry when little Samuel was born. Eventually Mary did poetry when she found out she was pregnant. All these mothers in Israel celebrated the impossible that was right before their eyes, even though they could explain none of it. They did poetry while the hard men were still parsing logic, and writing memos to each other, and drafting briefs. I propose that Advent is a time of struggle between the poem that opens the future that God will work and the memo that keeps control. Advent is a time for relinquishing some of the control in order to receive the impossible from God.

II.

Well, not just any poem. After the mothers in Israel there came the other poets, the ones we call "prophets." They turned the poetry toward the future, never doubting that God would give new futures out beyond our memos. The book of Isaiah, complex as it is, is framed by poetry. The poems of Isaiah are about the future God will yet give. At the beginning of Isaiah, in chapter 2, there is this poem:

> In days to come . . .
> They shall beat their swords into plowshares,
> and their spears into pruning hooks;
> nation shall not lift up sword against nation,
> neither shall they learn war any more.
> (Isaiah 2:2a, 4)

It is an imaging out beyond our posturing in power through which we will never prevail. At the end of Isaiah, in chapter 65, there is this poem:

> For I am about to create new heavens and a new earth;
> the former things shall not be remembered or come to mind.
> But be glad and rejoice forever in what I am creating;
> for I am about to create Jerusalem as a joy,
> and its people as a delight.
> (vv. 17–18)

The poet anticipates, against all the data, that there will be no more infant mortality and no more economic displacement:

> No more shall there be in it an infant that lives but a few days . . .
> They shall not build and another inhabit;
> they shall not plant and another eat.
>
> (vv. 20, 22)

And finally, a peaceable creation with no oil spills:

> The wolf and the lamb shall feed together,
> The lion shall eat straw like the ox . . .
> They shall not hurt or destroy
> on all my holy mountain, says the LORD.
>
> (v. 25)

It is promised! It is imagined! It is proposed! Surely the memo writers did not pause; but the poem lingered. The book of Isaiah moves from "not learn war any more" in chapter 2 to "not hurt or destroy" in chapter 65, a sweep of well-being that contradicts the facts on the ground.

III.

And right in the middle of this poetry, in chapter 11, is the poem entrusted to us on this Advent Sunday. It is a poem that refuses the facts on the ground, and invites us listeners to watch for newness outside our constricted, frightened logic. It begins with this that takes our breath away: "Out of the stump of Jesse." Jesse being David's father. David's family and dynasty run out in failure, no king, no future, no royal possibility, only a stump. But, says the poet, the stump will produce a shoot, a shoot of new life that was not expected. The memo writers no doubt were at work thinking how to honor the stump and close down that history. But the poet said, "Watch for the shoot," the new David, the new possibility of shalom. The poem that follows is about that shoot that cannot be explained by our reason.

What a shoot it will be, conjured by the poet! This new ruler to come, only imagined here, will have qualifications like you have never seen, wisdom (not mere knowledge), understanding (not just data), wisdom and understanding from the Lord, fear of the Lord, recognition of the holy mystery that is at the core of the power process. This new shoot will be glad to sign on for God's promises. Like every ruler, he must sort things out and make economic decisions. He will decide with righteousness on behalf of the poor. He will break the monopoly of the power elite and will notice that other neglected public.

He will rule for the meek, the ones who have no voice and no political clout and no smart lawyers. He will be all dressed up in robes of covenantal fidelity, and he will not forget what his vocation is.

The poem requires us to take a deep breath, because it is reality defining. What we usually have is authority with knowledge but no wisdom, with data but no understanding, the kind of power that governs on behalf of the billionaire club, so that the rich get richer. And now comes a poem of the new incursion of God's spirit that will break open the cabal of the critical control.

But there is more. The poet takes a long pause. Since we are already into God's impossibilities, the big impossibility is lined out:

> The wolf shall live with the lamb,
> the leopard shall lie down with the kid,
> the calf and the lion and the fatling together,
> and a little child shall lead them.
> The cow and the bear shall graze,
> their young shall lie down together;
> and the lion shall eat straw like the ox.
> (vv. 6–7)

The old enmities, the old appetites of the food chain, the old assumptions of the survival of the meanest, all of that is subverted. The wild will not stay vicious, because the coming one, marked by righteousness and justice, will overrule raw power in the interest of new possibility. Finally, the young child will toy with the asp and the adder; nobody will get hurt, because the poison will be removed from the world. The poison will be gone because the shoot will override all business as usual. All will be well, and all manner of thing will be well:

> They will not hurt or destroy on all my holy mountain;
> for the earth will be full of the knowledge of the LORD
> as the waters cover the sea.
> (v. 9)

The poem is about advent, about the coming one. And we dare to say, we confessing Christians, that the poem concerns the Christmas baby who refuses Rome's rule of force and religion's rule of code, opening the world to healing, freedom, forgiveness, and joy. So try this in advent. Depart from logic and memo and syllogism, and host the poem.

IV.

But there is an important caveat about the poem. Those who listened to John the Baptist, the big advent guy, loved the poem. They thought they owned the poem. They thought they had the poem as a special promise just to them. It is the temptation of entitled people to think we have privilege about the poem. So John addresses them, calls them seething, slippery, creepy reptiles, lowlifes. And he says to them: Don't just enjoy the poem. Do the poem. Sign on!

> Bear fruit worthy of repentance . . . every tree therefore that does not bear good fruit is cut down and thrown into the fire. (Matt. 3:8, 10)

This is the bite of advent. It is not just marveling at newness God will give. It is not about cozy, comfortable hope. It turns out, as always among Jews, that the poem is a summons to action. In these days of advent, then, imagine if the poem is true. Imagine if the poem is the true text of our life. What then?

> Well, be a carrier of wisdom and not just knowledge;
> be an agent of understanding, and not just data.
> Take on "the fear of the Lord," a sense that there is an out beyond us who
>   finally governs.
> Watch for the poor and make a difference with them;
> watch for the meek and be a voice for the voiceless.
> Embrace the lamb and summon the wolf to newness;
> enfold the kid and deal with the leopard;
> watch for the hissing snake and notice the end of the poison.

And watch for the child:

> The little child will lead them . . .
>   wolf and lamb,
>   leopard and kid,
>   calf and lion,
>   cow and bear,
>   lion and ox.
> The nursing child will play over the hole of the asp.

The poem anticipates the child. And when he is born, we should not be preoccupied with memos and logic and brief and critical thought. Because the child . . . and the poem . . . evoke a leap beyond our control. It is a leap to another world that requires daily obedience. And it ends . . . the poem ends . . . this way:

> They will not hurt or destroy on all my holy mountain; For the earth will be full of the knowledge of the LORD as the waters cover the sea. (v. 9)

That end of the poem is our beginning, beginning beyond memo and brief and syllogism. It is a world that began in the Jerusalem temple, ran through Bethlehem, and breaks open among us. Watch for the little child!

December 5, 2010

3

A Love Letter . . . concerning a Work in Progress

LUKE 1:68–79
LUKE 3:1–6
PHILIPPIANS 1:3–11

How would you like a love letter addressed to you in Advent, in anticipation of Christmas? That is what we have in the Epistle to the Philippians, Paul's love letter to his friends in the church in Philippi. He loves them dearly and writes to tell them so. Like a good love letter, he celebrates them with their best features, dreams of their future well-being, and uses elegant phrases about the ongoing process of their lives. If Paul had known about the church in Birmingham, he would no doubt have written us such a love letter. Since he did not know about us being the church here, we will read this letter as though it were for us.

I.

In his first paragraph, our reading, Paul sets out to frame the life of his beloved church in the large drama of God's purposes. He sketches out the beginning and the end of that great divine drama. His phrasing suggests a way for us to think about how our lives are situated in faith, so that there is a grid through which to perceive the everyday stuff differently.

First, the beginning of the drama: Paul writes of the God "who began a good work among you" (v. 6). Paul pushes clear back to the beginning of creation and imagines that from that first moment of creation God had a purpose and a hope for shape and well-being of our lives in faith. Presbyterians call that "providence," the slow, hidden resolve of God among us. Calvinists get tied up in knots over the claim. The point, in any case, is that there is a large

15

purpose derived from God's hope that has been surging through our lives from the beginning. The hope of God from the beginning is not control or coercion but positive, passionate expectation that we will get our lives fully in sync with God's intention. Try it this way: "Angels danced the day you were born." Angels danced at creation, danced in joy and doxology as they pondered the potential of lives that would cohere with God's good will.

And then Paul writes that the God of the beginning will bring our lives to completion by the day of Jesus Christ (v. 6). Paul has complete confidence that God's hope will prevail for us; it will end well because God is faithful. Paul and the early church had no doubt that the rule of Christ would be established in creation. The reason we read this text in Advent is that Christmas is not just about the birth of the baby. It is the full, visible assertion of the compassionate rule of Jesus, so that we can see and receive and celebrate God's fullness. We mark Christmas as the liturgical recognition that the fullness of our lives in God is a gift for the day.

Paul wants his friends to construe their lives as situated between the beginning *hopes of God* at creation and *the full culmination of God's gifts* (at Christmas). The stretch between beginning hope and full gift, between alpha and omega, is occupied by God's generous fidelity. Paul says to his beloved church, imagine your life caught up in the great divine drama in order that you may not imagine your life as a tale told by an idiot signifying nothing, in order that you may not imagine your life as an endless rat-race that no one can win, in order that you will not imagine your life as an endless series of accidents that amount to very little. Christians are people who imagine and receive their lives differently, bracketed and ordered by God's goodness and God's resolve for us. Advent is a chance to reflect on that framing of our life according to the truth of the Gospel. Advent is a wakeup call that we take some responsibility and some joy and some new, obedient freedom in the truth of God's claim on us. Like a good love letter, Paul wants us to imagine our best life, a life in God's faithful drama.

II.

And then Paul, in elegant phrasing, imagines the space between beginning hope and culminating gift, full of stuff to work on through the course of our life. I will lift up four of his wondrous phrases from his opening paragraph through which Paul invites his beloved to think and act again.

1. Paul urges "that your love may overflow more and more" (v. 9). The imagery is of a river of self-giving love that builds and builds, and knows no boundaries. There is no flood-control for self-giving love that is rooted

in God's love. Paul's term is of course *agape*, love that moves beyond the self to the other. If our lives are a meaningless tale, a rat-race, or a series of accidents, then self-preoccupation is appropriate, a self-preoccupation that leads to accumulation, selfishness, greed, and endless anxiety. But when our lives are grounded in God's fidelity, we are able, in gladness, to reach beyond ourselves, to give of ourselves and all that we have, to our best friends, to our neighbor, to our community, eventually to those who threaten us because they are not like us, and to our enemies. Paul imagines a great flow of generosity that has transformative power in the neighborhood. Advent is a time for thinking again about generous, forgiving, transformative love that reaches beyond self and can make a difference.

2. Paul hopes that his beloved church will have "knowledge and insight to help you determine what is best" (v. 9). Paul's sense of "knowledge" is tricky; you may remember in 1 Corinthians 13, in his great poem about love, he warns against knowledge that is self-regarding and elsewhere he calls it "puffed up," all of which adds up to nothing. Paul here is not concerned for the accumulation of data, or scientific breakthroughs, or technical advances. The knowledge about which he writes is defined by his next word "insight," the capacity to look beneath, to discern the meaning of things, to honor the mystery of love, mercy, compassion, and justice that enhance the human enterprise.

Our society, like every strong society, has gone haywire in our assumption that more controlling knowledge will make us safe and happy, so we have the wild pursuits of the "intelligence community." But what we now need is not more such learning. What we now need are mature folk who probe the mystery of God's world and the wonder of the human process that lives by generosity and hospitality. The purpose of such "knowledge and insight," if we have discipline and patience, is that we will learn what is best, not for ourselves, but for the world and the coming generations of the earth.

3. Paul urges that in "the day of Christ," that is for us, on Christmas day, you may be "pure and blameless" (v. 10). Paul knows that a life in sync with God's purposes requires the disciplines of holiness that give us power and energy and freedom. Paul is not speaking of being goody-goody or pious in showy ways. But he reaches back to the book of Leviticus where there are commands for offering animals in sacrifice to God that have no flaws. The same phrase "pure and blameless" (that is, no flaws) turns up in the story of Job, the man who is perfectly in sync with the hopes of God. When you are in the presence of such a person, you know that there is a calm not diseased by Christmas preparation, not impressed with the loud greed of the world, but quiet, grateful, alert, uncompromised in the neighborly conduct of money and sexuality and work and speech. Paul expects his beloved church to live a different life that is not defined by the pressures of his society.

4. Paul wants that on the day of culmination, for us Christmas day, that you may have produced "the harvest of righteousness" that comes through Jesus Christ (v. 11). Isn't that a wondrous phrase! "Righteousness" in the Bible does not mean moralistic acts. Rather it refers to acts of intervention whereby the strong with resources intervene on behalf of the weak who are without resources. The targets of such covenantal righteousness are characteristically the vulnerable and the needy, the poor, the widow, the orphan, the immigrant, the prisoner, all those who cannot fend for themselves. The imagery of "harvest" suggests long-term work over the growth season, so that such compassionate engagement produces visible outcomes. Paul imagines a life that has been mobilized for the well-being of the community.

III.

It occurs to me that this letter from Paul to his beloved is a marvelous guideline in Advent for Christmas preparation:

- It affirms that our lives are *bracketed by the big drama of God's purposes* and we do well to ponder such deep beginnings and such awesome culminations. Imagine God's large purposes hovering around your life.
- Paul becomes specific in his wondrous phrasing about the *"in between"* that is our Advent work. Clearly, in between we have unfinished business, we being a work in process. But this is the way with love letters; we always know that the one addressed is not yet finished, but still a work in process. And we intend to provide support along the way for a wondrous conclusion to the beloved. For us it goes like this:

  "Overflow in love" . . . boundless generosity;
  "Knowledge and insight" . . . the pondering of how God's governance works in our lives;
  "Pure and blameless" . . . a life simple enough to avoid pathological anxiety by holy discipline;
  "A harvest of righteousness" . . . a long history of interventions for the sake of the neighborhood.

- Paul finishes by affirming that *all this will converge* in "glory and praise of God" (v. 11).

This advent practice, in sum, is about ceding ourselves over to God in gladness, to refer our life back to God who has given it to us.

What strikes me about this Advent love letter is this. When Paul writes the church, he assumes that Christmas preparation is serious business. But it has nothing to do with how the world lives with that commercial orgy. It is rather that when our lives are set in God's great drama, we have a quite different agenda. It is a profound agenda, because it touches the deep reality of how we are to live in God's mercy. It will be a prayer we pray for each other that we have enough resolve not to get caught up in the orgy, but to create time and energy and space for serious Advent. The urgent question always in the final days of Advent is: "Are you ready yet?"

Are you ready with overflowing love?

Are you ready with knowledge and insight? Are you ready with purity and blamelessness? Are you ready with a harvest of righteousness?

No, not ready yet . . . but under way toward the great day of fullness. God will bring our life to completion. We may be glad and grateful as we wait.

December 6, 2009
First Presbyterian Church, Birmingham, Michigan

4

A New World Birthed

Have you ever wondered how you would have begun to tell the gospel story of Jesus? Each of the Gospel writers—Matthew, Mark, Luke, and John—did it differently. Today we have before us Matthew's beginning of the gospel story of Jesus. The text we have just read tells of the announcement and expectation of the new baby that is on the lips of an angel in a dream to Joseph. But before that, the part of Matthew 1 that I did not read, there are seventeen verses of "begats" that trace the lineage of Jesus all the way back to David in the Old Testament until his father Joseph. Matthew wants to show by this pedigree that Jesus is deeply rooted in the royal line of ancient Israel, for all the ancestors of Jesus are kings in Jerusalem.

Except that Matthew wants to play a trick on us that we notice when we read carefully. The royal pedigree is up until Joseph, but then Joseph is not the father of Jesus and so the pedigree doesn't really pertain. This trick by Matthew is made possible by a quote from Isaiah 7. Matthew loves to quote the Old Testament; in this verse it is about a young woman—perhaps a virgin—who will birth this new baby, the one we celebrate at Christmas. There are some important things to notice about this text from Matthew as we arrive at Christmas.

I.

Notice that the whole business whereby Joseph learns that Mary will have a baby is at night when he was relaxed and his guard was down. In the night of his vulnerability we are told:

20

> But just when he had resolved to do this, an angel of the Lord appeared to him in a dream and said, "Joseph, son of David, do not be afraid to take Mary as your wife, for the child conceived in her is from the Holy Spirit." (Matt. 1:20)

What a mouthful! It is, moreover, a mouthful from an angel, a messenger of God, one sent from heaven to earth, a message from the outside not given in human terms, not given in earthly terms, not given according to Joseph's normal assumptions. The angel spoke in a dream, not when Joseph could be awake and in control. So notice first, that the expectation of Jesus is outside all of our categories, given by God's rule in God's own way. Our way in response to this text is not to explain; it is, rather, to be dazzled that at Christmas something happens beyond all of our calculations. This is a baby and a wonder and a gift that are designed to move us beyond ourselves.

II.

Notice second, that the baby has no father. That could have been a scandal, as some babies seem not to have fathers. But that is not the point. Rather the accent is that the baby is from the *Holy Spirit*. We may set aside a lot of silly arguments and equally silly speculation about biological transactions and notice, rather, that newness comes, according to our faith, when God's spirit stirs beyond everything that has been settled:

- It is God's spirit that hovered in Genesis 1 to greet a new world, a new heaven and a new earth where there had been none;
- It is God's spirit, God's wind that blows the waters back in Egypt and lets our ancestors go free;
- It is God's spirit that called apostles and prophets and martyrs beyond themselves to do dangerous acts of obedience. They were indeed blown.
- It was God's spirit that came upon the disciples in the Book of Acts and created a new community of faith and power and obedience and mission.
- It is God's spirit that begins something new when the world is exhausted, when our imagination fails, and our lives shut down in silence and despair. That is what happened here; God's spirit stirred and caused something deeply new in the world. The healing, transforming, creating wind of God has caused a new baby who will change everything among us.

III.

Notice third, that the angel takes the trouble to tell the dreaming Joseph what to call the baby. Names matter, and the angel gives Joseph two names for the baby we celebrate at Christmas.

First, "you will call him *Jesus* for he will save his people." The Hebrew name Jesus is the verb "save." Imagine having a baby named "save." It is the same word that is given in the several names of Joshua, Isaiah, and Hosea. They all, each in a distinct way, saved Israel; and now Jesus will save. He will save from sin and guilt. He will save from death and destruction. He will save from despair and hopelessness. He will save from poverty and sickness and hunger. We can look at the many stories of Jesus that the early church remembered. And in most of them Jesus saves. That is what we prepare for in Advent, the one who saves us when we cannot any longer save ourselves.

The angel offers a second name for the baby, *Emmanuel*, that is, God is with us. It is the faith of the church that in Jesus, God was palpably, decisively present in the earth and came to be with us in the world in a way that makes us safe and beyond fear and threat and anxiety. Stories that we treasure most about Jesus evidence that he regularly shows up to be with people in need . . . lepers, the deaf, the blind, the lame, the hungry, the unclean, even the dead. His very presence makes new life possible. The church consists in all the people who have been dazzled by the powerful reality of God who has come to be with us in this season of need and of joy, all through this miraculous baby.

Well, I do not know how you might start the story of Jesus if you have to write it; but Matthew did pretty well for us:

- He grounded it in *an angel's message in a dream*, a point of contact that was beyond all of our control or expectation;
- He credited *God's own spirit* with the miracle of the new baby who will come and make all things new among us, the way God's spirit always makes all things new.
- He *named the baby twice*—
- *Save* from all that kills
- *God with us*, we are not alone!

Then the angel leaves. We are left with a baby with two names, "save" and "God with us." That is all! . . . except, of course, that the Gospel of Matthew continues. If you turn the page in the Gospel story, you will very soon come to the adult Jesus, just after the visit of the wise men. And what the adult Jesus does is to call people to discipleship and say to them, "Follow me." And he is still doing that by the work of the Spirit. He is still calling men and women and boys and girls to discipleship.

Let me tell you what I think that means in the Gospel story and in our lives. Jesus calls people to believe that he saves and that he is saving and that we are saved. . . . Not an abrupt Baptist way necessarily of being saved, but that we are safe and loved and cared for. To be a disciple means to know you are safe and loved and to live that way. Jesus calls people to trust that God is with us, that we are not alone even in the face of death and every kind of danger. That is why we say with the Psalmist, "I will fear no evil, for thou are with me." And if God is with us, that means that we have a sure companion and a resource to live healthy, loving, healing lives in the world.

I will tell you why I think this is important. There are, in the world and in the church, lots of people who think that there is no saving power in their lives and so they must manage for themselves. And when we manage for ourselves, we grow anxious and angry and greedy and hurtful. There are lots of people in the world who live as though God were not with us, as though we were alone in the world. And if we are alone in the world, we must have our own way, we must hit out at others who do not agree with us, and we become a destructive force in our communities and in our families.

There is a choice to be made at Christmas, whether the angel is telling the truth or not . . . whether there is a saving among us or whether we are unsaved . . . whether God is with us or whether we are alone and on our own hook. And what we decide makes a difference about how we live. There are lots of liberals among us who live as though they are unsafe and all alone. There are lots of conservatives who live as though they are unsafe and all alone. It need not be so! because the angel has spoken the truth about Jesus and, therefore, the truth about us. We are safe because of the baby named "Save." We are not alone because "God is with us." Christmas is not just a time for romantic joy and shopping. It is about a decision. And we are a people who trust the gospel and we are people who have become disciples of this baby, this adult, this Savior, God with us. And because we have signed on for this good news we live differently. That is the big time truth of Christmas!

As Christmas comes, rest up so that you have enough energy to be dazzled. The gift of Christmas contradicts everything we sense about our own life. Our world feels unsavable and here is the baby named "Save." Our world and our lives often feel abandoned and here is the baby named "God with us." Be ready to have your sense of the world contradicted by this gift from God. Rest upon the new promise from the angel that you may be safe and whole and generous.

Coming Son of God, blowing spirit of God, hovering Father God, we are very sure in these hope-filled days that neither life nor death nor angels nor rulers nor things present nor things to come nor powers nor heights nor depths nor anything else in all creation can separate us from you and your love for us. For this we are grateful. We give you thanks for your gift to us in the saving name of Jesus we pray. Amen.

December 19, 2004
Timberridge Presbyterian Church, McDonough, Georgia

5

What a Difference a Week Makes!

ISAIAH 63:7–9
HEBREWS 2:11–18
MATTHEW 2:13–23

A week is a long time. The week from Christmas to the next Sunday is a very long time, filled with tension, exhaustion, and extra business. Oh, I do not mean your week. I mean the week that has passed for the characters in the Bethlehem story, for they continue to be the main characters in this second gospel story, even though everything has changed for them. It is that startling, drastic change in the characters that I want you to focus on, for it is the story of our life as well as theirs.

I.

The cast of characters in the Christmas story is well known, even though we coalesce the stories of Matthew and Luke. There are Mary and Joseph. They are silent and obedient, and awed by what is happening. There are the wise men who have come and then gone, warned in a dream. There is Herod. He presents himself in the Christmas story as caring and attentive: "When you have found him, bring me word that I too may come and worship him." If we had only this, we might not know his statement is ironic. And there are angels, first one lone announcer, and then a heaven filled with a choir of singing voices. The story overflows with wonder and amazement. For an instant, our trains stop running, we stop running, we suspend our cynical judgment and are glad to be bathed in this narrative of innocence. It is the innocence of God's holy intrusion; it is the innocent power of God's love

25

and reconciliation. It is the desperate innocence of believing that we and our world can begin all over, anew.

For children, but not only for children, the story ends too soon. The wise men depart, the angels vanish, Herod has business to conduct. We forget and return to our ordinary weariness. We are modestly changed and warmed, but we go back to our tired lives.

II.

Well, linger; don't go back yet. Stay with the story and with the characters a while longer, because in one week everything has changed for them. The characters, like us, seem to have departed their trusting innocence and moved into real life. In this episode, they are very different.

Consider first Herod. If we had only his word to the wise men, we could imagine that Herod, like us, is prepared for the new king, prepared to submit to the new governance . . . "that I also may worship." But what a difference a week makes!—to Herod. Perhaps his intelligence has told him more; perhaps he has thought longer. Perhaps his word in the beginning was a ruse. In the time of one quick week, the narrative has transformed Herod into a desperate, frantic, ruthless killer, all for "reasons of state." Herod replicates the old way of Pharaoh back in the book of Exodus (Exod. 1:15–22). Herod is about to search for the child in order to destroy him (v. 13). He is in a "furious rage." In order to control the threatening little baby, Herod has to kill all the others. He is ready to "shoot into the crowd."

What a difference a week makes! The text is candid about the power of evil and fearfulness and brutality. Mild people can be transformed toward passionate rage when their life is disrupted, when their interest is jeopardized, when a treasured status quo is put at risk. In this story, we see the full play of evil. Oddly, the church's lectionary suggestion skips over these verses; too cruel. The church would like to skip over the evil, for the church prefers to stay romantic. A week after Christmas, however, the Bible brings us cold faced to the power of evil that takes socio-political, military, economic form. It implicates us in the brutality, for we are not so far removed from passionate rage that wants to eliminate the threatening baby.

III.

Linger in the story a little. Consider second, the baby. What a difference a week makes. The baby Jesus is largely passive, neither acting nor speaking.

The baby nonetheless is indeed the driving force of the story. Everything happens only because of the baby. At Christmas, the baby is honored, worshipped, adored, saluted—gifts and treasures of gold, and frankincense and myrrh. It is a lovely scene, which we rightly enhance with extra sheep and oxen.

In the next episode a week later, in our story, everything has changed. The music in the background has taken on a chill. The baby is still passive in speech and act. But the presence of the baby has intruded and now, everything is changed. From the beginning, the power of this Jesus changes everything. We can observe two things about this Jesus by the way the other characters have responded to him.

First, Jesus has become a threat to Herod and to the whole world organized in unjust, greedy, and brutal ways. Just one week after birth, Jesus threatens the destructive way the world is organized. As his life goes on into adulthood, Jesus keeps threatening our wrongly ordered worlds, because in his very person, Jesus unleashes power for goodness, dreams of freedom, passion for justice, miracles of healing. The testimony he evokes is that where he is present, the blind see, the lame walk, the poor rejoice, the dead live. In our tired, frightened status quo, in our lives of privilege and preference, Jesus scares us as much as he threatens Herod.

Second, Jesus is himself vulnerable and threatened. He is only a very little, helpless baby. Even when he becomes a man on the move, he continues to be resourceless, weaponless, defenseless. He is, as we know, occupied by another purpose, another power, one that the world does not respect, and thinks it can destroy. That vulnerability, culminating in the cross, of course is what his power is all about, perfect strength in weakness, perfect authority in gentleness, perfect sovereignty in grace. All the Herods of the world are turned into frightened, raving animals by this power of newness that they cannot penetrate or domesticate. The power the baby embodies is set in the very face of Herod!

IV.

One week later, the issue is joined. It is still our issue. The cunning Herod has become brutalizing power unleashed. Innocent Jesus has become both a threat and threatened. We are, in this narrative, drawn into this unequal conflict. In this conflict (and nowhere else) is where we must live and decide, and pick a winner. The world in which faith is confessed and practiced is an unequal world and we cannot have our faith in any other world.

Notice the odds, put your money down, and bet your life. The cunning power of Herod is massive on the way to brutality, the innocent presence of

Jesus is endlessly vulnerable. That is where the story puts us and where faith always must live. Herod spoke loudly, as if speaking loudly would matter. He voices the power of greed and fear, seeking self-sufficiency, imagining he can control his life, having his own way, fearful of trust, unable to risk its transformation, endlessly engaged in destruction of himself and all the others around him. Herod embodies resistance (which we all know), resistance to the movement of God and the coming of well-being in the earth. Against him there is this vulnerable, exposed Jesus who carries the dreams of the kingdom and the hopes of humanity. The face-off is so patently uneven and unequal.

V.

But linger with one other character. In the birth story (in Luke at least, though not in Matthew) the angels loom large and loud. They announce the new king, they assert that the world begins again, under new management. In our odd moment of credulity, we accept these angels as necessary to the drama. But then they leave. Having sung their anthem, they depart; and we depart to our controlled world, which excludes the angels, not giving them a second thought. We willingly entertain them in our innocence, but only briefly.

But what a difference a week makes! Did you wonder what happened to the angels? Well, it has been a very long week for them. In that dangerous week, the angels have been changed as much as has Herod and the baby. What sweet-voiced messengers become risk-taking political actors. We do not know how it happened. When we meet the angel again in this story, he is powerful and assertive, no longer willing to sing at the margin of the narrative.

This angel who must have soloed at Bethlehem appears twice in our story. First, "Behold, an angel of the Lord appeared and said, 'Get out of here with the baby, or Herod will kill him.'" And then the angel led the baby and the parents to the safety of Egypt, out of reach of Herod. The angel takes the initiative in keeping the vulnerable baby safe from the rage of the empire. Second, "When Herod died, behold an angel of the Lord appeared in a dream and said to Joseph, 'Take the child out of Egypt, back to the land.'" The angel leads another Exodus out of Egypt, just as the angel had long ago led Moses out of danger. The angel is a force to protect the blessed baby from the crazed king. The angel is an agent to bring the baby to the land of ministry and of promise. The angel is the wild card in the deck of God's history that makes all the other characters sit up and take notice. How different it is for the baby and for the king, because the angel has seized initiative in the story.

The angel is our narrative way of affirming that there is *an overplus of God's power and God's resolve and God's love at work* in our common life, upsetting all our equilibriums, overriding all other power arrangements, and making new things possible. To get this said, the story must go back to the old memories of angels who are bodyguards, who will guard you on the journey, let you float above dangerous paths, and biting snakes (Ps. 91:11–13). So the poet can say:

> The angel of his presence saved them, in his love and in his pity he redeemed them, he lifted them up and carried them all the days of old. (Isa. 63:9)

The Bible confesses that God's protective power keeps vulnerable love at work, keeps ready faithfulness safe, guards those who obey, keeps those who devote their life to the purposes of God.

You see, if our story had had only Herod and Jesus in it, Herod would have won and the baby would have been killed. That is predictable. What changes all that is that "an angel of the Lord appeared." The angel came, and the story is changed. Have you noticed how this same *overplus* of God's power and love keeps life open to newness where none seemed possible? Have you noticed the strange break points in the struggle for justice and brutality where, against all odds, freedom and justice and peace keep turning up, beyond defeat where we thought it not possible? Have you noticed in your life, and in life around you, that openings for humanness and newness and healing and wholeness come, even against all odds? This happens because there is more at work than our quantifying analysis will even acknowledge. This happens because there is power at work that the categories of Herod can never discern. You see, the event at Christmas was not a little pageant to be dismissed and from which we depart unscathed. The event of Christmas is an assertion about God's power in the world against the power of evil. For that reason the baby is safe, the promise is under way, the world is open, and we are available for change.

It is an odd and awkward assignment to speak of angels on a university campus, where we are so sure and see so well and explain so clearly. Indeed, the university is where we gather in celebration of our awesome control and our capacity to have life the way we want it. In our context, it sounds maudlin and romantic and fantastic to speak of angels. But consider, do you believe there is only cruel Herod and vulnerable Jesus? Do you think there are only brutalizing forces versus innocent love? The story says otherwise, "An angel of the Lord appeared and said . . ." The third character who had a long week is the strong, understated power of God's resilient purpose, an underestimated power on the loose in ways that we cannot predict or control. By the end of this narrative, Herod is gone, vanished from history; the baby has come home. The angel departs the story, perhaps back to singing at the throne. But that angel is not to be trifled with, tough, hard, powerful, determined. In the midst of "the slaughter of the innocents," God's powerful resolve is at work, not always visible, not always triumphant, but at work in the midst of Herod's insanity, and beyond. A long, long week, but a new beginning beyond the craziness and destructiveness, a new beginning wrought only by God's overplus of power and love. A new beginning that persists in vulnerable but resilient ways.

December 31, 1989

6

A Baptism about Which They Never Told Us

PSALM 29

MARK 1:4–11

ACTS 19:1–7

As you may know, Christmas stories occur only in the Gospels of Matthew and Luke, and we have now celebrated that.

As you may know, the wise men occur only in the Gospel of Matthew, and that is why we celebrate Epiphany, when Jesus is revealed to the nations outside Israel.

As you may know, the Gospel of Mark has no Christmas story, no shepherds, and no wise men. The first thing that happens in the Gospel of Mark is that Jesus is baptized. And so today, just after Christmas and just after Epiphany, we celebrate the baptism of Jesus.

As you may know, in all four Gospels the constant recurring element at the beginning of each Gospel narrative is always John the Baptist who comes to baptize.

As you may know, all four Gospels begin with John the Baptist quoting Isaiah:

> Prepare a way in the wilderness
> make straight his paths.

This is a quotation familiar to us from Handel's *Messiah*, poetic verses that anticipate a new superhighway so that the king can come in triumphal power.

All four Gospels, as different as they are, begin with John the Baptist and want to announce a quite new beginning of the life of the world. So today, we think for twenty minutes *about John* the Baptizer, *about the baptism of Jesus* according to the Gospel of Mark, and *about our own baptism.*

31

I.

In the story of Jesus' baptism, John and Jesus are twined together. They are linked as cousins in the narrative. While they shared many things, they may have been rival preachers, each with his own movement. The beginning point is with John; he is portrayed as a man from outside of society who wore rough clothing, who ate odd food, and who preached a demanding gospel in shrill and abrasive ways. He is placed first in the New Testament story, at the very beginning. But he is in fact an Old Testament figure, standing in continuity with the prophets of the Old Testament . . . abrupt, demanding, urgent, sharp, threatening.

John immerses people in the water and thereby lets them shed all that is old and failed in their lives. Thus he offers a baptism "for the forgiveness of sins." Forgiveness . . . and a chance to begin again . . . is a wondrous offer, a promise that one may become unburdened. That act is not, however, a baptism that is free and unconditional. It is a "baptism of repentance," a vigorous demand to admit failure and only then to begin again. The two themes of *forgiveness and repentance* are classic themes of Old Testament prophets. They saw that a new beginning is not cheap or easy; it requires a serious decision about living life in a new direction.

The wonder of the narrative at the beginning of Mark is that Jesus comes to John and submits to his baptism. This has been an awkwardness in the church, because it suggests that Jesus must be forgiven and Jesus must repent. We are not told why Jesus is baptized; it is, however, plausible that at the beginning of his public life Jesus takes upon himself the whole story of Israel. He relives the memory of Israel. As Israel begins by going into the waters of Exodus, being at risk and trusting only God, as Israel wades through the waters of the Jordan to enter a whole new life in the land of Canaan, so Jesus relives the Exodus of Israel and relives Israel's entry into the land of promise. In this way he begins again the story of Israel as the faithful people of God. This is indeed a new beginning, and Jesus takes his place as the initiator of a whole new history of faithfulness to God in the world.

But then, in Mark's account, something very strange happens to Jesus in the process of his baptism. It is something so odd that it must have surprised John and surely pushed beyond everything that John thought that he was doing. Perhaps it also surprised Jesus. It turns out that the baptism of Jesus by John is not just about forgiveness and not just about repentance. His baptism turns out to be a new beginning of God's life in the world, something John surely did not expect.

Two things happen that Mark can express only by poetic imagery. First,

> And just as he was coming up out of the water, he saw the heavens
> torn apart and the Spirit descending like a dove on him. (Mark 1:10)

The heavens—where God lives and from where God comes—break open.
It is as though the sky parted and *God's spirit came down into the world* and
settled upon the person of Jesus. Mark says it was "like a dove descending,"
not a dove, but like a dove, a free floating graceful energy from God that
changed everything. The New Testament thus has imaginative ways to speak
of the peculiarity of Jesus. He now is fully empowered and authorized to be
the new leader and ruler of all the earth. The coming of the spirit upon him
is like the spirit that came upon the boy, David, who became king in Israel
(1 Sam. 16:13). In David, and now in Jesus, this is no ordinary event; it rather
is the divine authorization of a new human initiative. This is the way the early
church understood God being publicly infused into Jesus' own life.

And then second:

> And a voice came from heaven, "You are my Son, the Beloved; with
> you I am well pleased. (Mark 1:11)

The heavens *opened for the spirit* and then the heavens *opened for a voice*, for
God's own declaration of God's new will for the world. The voice of heaven
quotes Psalm 2 with reference to David; but now the quote is the full authorization of Jesus as *God's special beloved agent* in the world, the one who brings
delight into God's own life.

There is a baptism of forgiveness based on repentance; but now this act
of baptism pushes beyond forgiveness and beyond repentance to the peculiar
recognition that Jesus is the edge of a new world when divine power is given
through him that will make all things new. From this moment Jesus is tested
in his new vocation (Mark 1:12–13); he then begins to recruit people as disciples to join him in his new movement in the world that carries the news of
God's love (Mark 1:14–20).

II.

Since that day with Jesus, the church has been baptizing in the name of this
same God in order to *sign people on* in dramatic ways to God's new way in the
world. We move then from the *baptism of Jesus* wherein he is empowered with
newness to the *baptism of the church*. In Acts 19, our second text for today, Paul
is at Ephesus where there was already a church. He begins to quiz church
members about their baptism; he asks them:

> Did you receive the Holy Spirit when you became believers?
> (Acts 19:2)

Did you share in the baptism of Jesus to make a radical new beginning with new power?

And they answered Paul, "What? Nobody every told us about that. Nobody ever said baptism was connected to God's powerful spirit." So Paul asked, "Into what were you baptized?" (v. 3). And they said, "Into the baptism of John, the baptism of *forgiveness* by way of *repentance*." Paul does not object to this answer nor does he reprimand the Christians at Ephesus. He also knows that baptism of forgiveness and repentance, which is the gift of prophetic faith, which permitted reconciliation with God.

But then Paul wants for them more than that. He wants them to know about *the surprise* of baptism in the name of Jesus that pushes beyond forgiveness that is grounded in repentance. He wants these church members to be as amazed and empowered by the gifts given through Jesus as John the Baptist was surprised by what happened. Paul takes the baptism of Jesus—that gave the Holy Spirit of God into the world—as the true mark of the church.

And so, says the narrator, the people at Ephesus were baptized again, this time in the name of Jesus who is the one through whom God's new life comes into the world. And as happened with Jesus, the Holy Spirit came upon them and they were taken up into the new reality where God's life in the world was committed to them. And the text says, the surprise of it all, as surprising as Jesus' own reception of the spirit, is that they spoke in tongues and prophesied. That is, they experienced the world in a wholly different way that is out beyond all of their usual categories and all of their usual capacity to control.

This capacity to prophesy and "speak in tongues" seems very odd to people like us, and perhaps even offensive. We are so settled, so bourgeois, so rational, and so sure of ourselves— perhaps so liberal—that we would not want such an invasion of the spirit to come upon us. I had a Pentecostal student recently explain to me a bit about speaking in tongues. Maxine said that that occurrence did not mean that one was necessarily made unconscious or out of control. Rather, it is a willingness to speak the *jabbering in a baby-like way* of any two-year-old, to jabber in ways that do not sound meaningful, to be as *weak* and *vulnerable* and *dependent* as a helpless child, presenting oneself to God so that God may care for us in new and amazing ways. Thus this baptismal narrative ends in vulnerability by which the church can experience the world in dangerously new ways, beyond all the old settlements that we have come to trust too much. This baptism gathers people into a new community of the vulnerable, the empowered, the ones ready for the new world that comes in Jesus.

III.

So consider:

Jesus' baptism pushed beyond forgiveness and repentance to a whole new life empowered by God's spirit.

In the church at Ephesus *folks were baptized* a second time in order to become vulnerable to God's leadership, and to be infused with God's spirit. They are now marked as people no longer contained in old categories that feature certitude and control. Now they are prepared for a new world of peace and healing that is fluid and unsettled.

We may think about *baptism in the church today.* For the most part we have not done well on baptism. For the most part, our understandings of baptism are still in terms of the old established church categories of Europe where one had to be baptized in order to be a respectable citizen in society. And because baptism has become simply an acceptable conventional thing to do in settled culture, it is mostly the practice—liberal and conservative—that we "do" babies when it is convenient for grandparents.

But do you know that there is in the world church *a vibrant new recovery of baptism,* a fresh awareness in the church that God's own presence does come among us to invite us to *new vulnerability* and *new power* for *new obedience* in the world. You know, do you not, that these are dangerous times in the world, when hate and war and greed and ambition are about to destroy us all with our commitments to consumerism and militarism, when the world is being reshaped according to the sweep of violence. And you know, do you not, that this is a dangerous time in the church because the church is so settled in its conventions of being liberals or in its conventions of being conservative, so sure of itself and so shut down without energy that it tends to become irrelevant in our society.

But the news is that God's spirit is at work in the church, recruiting people to become vulnerable like little babies, driven by God's spirit out beyond our control to think new thoughts and imagine new imaginings and sing new songs and do new deeds. The church is being gathered by God's spirit out beyond what is settled, so that it may commit acts of generosity and transformation and justice and reconciliation. When we do those deeds of generosity and transformation and justice and reconciliation, we sometimes wonder what has come over us and what has gotten into us. Well, what gets into us and what comes over us is exactly *God's spirit* that swept up Jesus and that continues to sweep up the church. By the spirit we are made to be a new people that stirs things for good in the world. It is God's spirit that causes us

to be outrageously generous,
to be daringly transformative,
to be wondrously engaged in healing.

Forgiveness and repentance are important, as John understood. Getting right with God is important; but there is more. Our faith is finally not about our being right with God. It is about being transformed by God's power so that we may be open and vulnerable and courageous enough to be at God's work of newness. Those who are open and vulnerable and powerful enough are indeed like Jesus " . . . well beloved with whom God is well pleased."

January 12, 2003
Plymouth Congregational United Church of Christ,
Coconut Grove, Florida

7

Talking and Walking with an Open Ear

PSALM 40:1–11

I CORINTHIANS 1:1–9

JOHN 1:29–42

Paul begins his letter to the church in Corinth with a strong affirmation about the church, its spiritual gifts, and its testimony, and then he says, "God is faithful" (1 Cor. 1:9). It is God's faithfulness that has called you into the fellowship of his Son, Jesus Christ our Lord. He just says it. We have a lot of arguments now about God and God's existence, and God's capacity in the world and will for the world. But here is no doubt or dispute! The faithfulness of God is not the conclusion drawn from an argument. It is rather a premise from which much follows for Paul. It is our assumption from which everything follows in the church. While our world comes unglued politically, economically, socially, morally and in every other way, we say, "God is faithful!" That is my topic for now. I want to talk about Psalm 40, because it is a forceful exploration of God's fidelity that has cropped up in the life of this Psalmist.

I.

The speaker begins with a memory of God's fidelity:

> I waited patiently for the LORD;
> he inclined to me and heard my cry.
> He drew me up from the desolate pit,
> out of the miry bog,
> and set my feet upon a rock,
> making my steps secure.

37

> He put a new song in my mouth,
> a song of praise to our God.
> Many will see and fear,
> and put their trust in the LORD.
>
> (vv. 1–3)

The speaker can remember being in a desolate pit, a miry bog. We all can! Some of that memory is quite personal, and people carry heavy, heavy stuff. Some of it is quite public about failed schools and vetoed food stamps that let children go hungry, and illness, and injustice, and death, and betrayal. This speaker can remember that in such unbearable circumstance, God was faithful, so faithful that there came to him a new song, a new song that matched his new well-being with new energy, and new courage, and new possibility. The Psalmist affirms,

> You have multiplied . . . wondrous deeds.
>
> (v. 5)

"Wondrous deeds" from God means inexplicable transformations and unexpected gifts. The church lives by such memories. We hold dear the old biblical memories of those wondrous deeds when the blind see, the lame walk, the deaf hear, the lepers are cleansed, the dead are raised, the poor rejoice (Luke 7:22). But such wonders are also contemporary, and it is important that we recite them because they are the main substance of faith. We ourselves in our own lives, personal and public, have seen God's faithful acts of transformation, a neighbor cared for, a school opened to all, a new law that provided food for the hungry, a new overture to peace, a parent forgiven, and on and on, because God's work goes on in the world. And we have seen it!

II.

Our reading of the Psalm ends in verse 11 with a hope for God's active presence now in a moment of need:

> Do not, O LORD, withhold your mercy from me;
> let your steadfast love and your faithfulness keep me safe forever.
>
> (v. 11)

The Psalmist asks for the three biggies of covenantal faith . . . *mercy, steadfast love, faithfulness,* all synonyms for the tenacious, transformative reality of God that we must have to live. The three terms . . . mercy, steadfast love, *faithfulness* . . . are like a mantra in faith, the self-giving of God for our well-being. The Psalmist does not know—the next time—if God will perform the wonders of transformation and rescue and healing. She has every reason to hope so. Israel had every reason to hope from God into the future. The church has ample reason for hope. But it is a hope. It is not a guarantee, because God is not an automaton. God is a free agent who in freedom cares intensely for us and acts for us. The Psalmist knows that after money and power and influence and force and pride and control . . . after all these things that our society values . . . what we must have to live is fidelity that can come only as God's gift. So our verses end in petition:

> Do not . . . withhold your mercy from me;
> let our steadfast love and your faithfulness
> keep me safe forever.

The Psalmist begins in *treasured memory* and ends in *vibrant hope*. The hope for now matches the memory from times past. Both the memory and the hope are shaped by God's active fidelity.

III.

We live our lives in faith between that memory and that hope. So does the Psalmist. I think the interesting question in this Psalm is, "What do people like us do between remembered wonders of fidelity and anticipated wonder of fidelity?" The Psalmist fills in that gap that is the business of our lives.

I find most interesting and suggestive in this space between remembered miracles and anticipated miracles, this awareness in the witness of the Psalmist:

> Sacrifice and offering you do not desire,
> but you have given me an open ear.
> Burnt offering and sin offering are not required.
> (v. 6)

The two lines that open and end the verse minimize the importance of big acts of piety and devotion: sacrifice, offering, burnt offering, sin offering. There is a whole catalogue of obligations. The worship of Israel had differentiated all of these different offerings, like the mission fund and the building fund and the orphans fund and the flower fund. Or in our secular society, there is a catalogue of requirements like soccer practice, and cell phones and Facebook, and better SATs and more cosmetic surgeries and manly drugs, etc., etc., etc., and buying, buying, buying . . . all required to keep up. And, says the Psalmist, none of that counts with God.

But you have been given an "open ear." Isn't that a wonderful phrase? Our ears are made ready and able to hear when addressed by God. Mostly our ears are closed to God. We don't really want to hear anything that rocks the boat. We do not want to hear from those who disagree with us. We do not want to be addressed or summoned or reminded. Or we are so tired of the din of ideology and propaganda and silly lies that we tune it all out. We become able to tune out everything except our own voice and our own conviction and our own vested interest and our own fears and hurts. Or as a woman in my church said recently, "I have made up my mind about everything."

But not here! Between *remembered miracles* and *anticipated miracles* is an *open ear*, a readiness to be addressed, an expectation to be summoned, to be called out of our old convictions and our prejudices and led toward newness.

And when we listen with open ears, says the Psalmist, we learn anew what is expected of us. So the Psalmist says (v. 7), "Here I am." Here I am, ready to be addressed and summoned and changed and made new. What follows, when situated between remembered wonders of verses 1–3 and anticipated wonders in verse 11 is a new talk and a new walk.

The **new talk** is the glad news:

> I have told the glad news of deliverance in the great congregation;
> see, I have not restrained my lips, as you know, O LORD.
> I have not hidden your saving help within my heart,
> I have spoken of your faithfulness and your salvation;
> I have not concealed your steadfast love and your faithfulness from the
>   great congregation.
>
> (vv. 9–10)

The Psalmist had already said in v. 5:

> Were I to proclaim and tell of your wondrous deeds,
> they would be more than can be counted.

The subject of conversation is not the best beer or the best football team or the best drug or the best political cause or the one we most love to hate. The best talk is talk of God's wondrous deeds that cannot be counted. Those wonderful deeds concern "your faithfulness" and "your steadfast love" and "your salvation." The best talk is to bear testimony to our kids and our neighbors, that the force of God's purpose is at work in the world, transforming all relationships and all public policies.

Such talk is an ongoing stream of gratitude because that to which we witness is free, unexpected, and beyond our explanation. The talk is in the great congregation. Now I am glad to say this because I am a Calvinist and Calvinists never want to say anything to anyone about the wonder of faith. But even we Calvinists in the UCC are summoned to such talk. Testimony must be a given that contradicts the phoniness of common chatter, the falseness of market ideology, the arrogance of excessive patriotism, the approval of greed and acquisitiveness, the erosion of anxiety, the small-mindedness of hate and resentment, because none of that will save us, heal us, or make us happy. What heals and saves and liberates is God's faithfulness. So we talk about it.

Along with the talk, there is **the walk:**

> "I delight to do your will, O my God;
> your law is within my heart."
>
> (v. 8)

I delight in responding to your requirements. Your Torah is in my heart. This does not mean moralistic religion. Rather the line uses the word "Torah." And most often the term "Torah" means specifically the book of Deuteronomy with its repeated talk about widows, orphans, and immigrants, the big three of vulnerability in that ancient world. I delight in obedience to reach out to those without resources or security or protection. And from that comes readiness to reshape the practices and policies of well-being and to share in generous and just ways the resources for life that have been given to us, to share them through generous actions and through just policies.

So we have it. Between *remembered miracle* and *anticipated miracle* we are a people with *open ears*. And what God asks of us is *honest talk* about new life with God, about thanks and a new song to sing. Along with honest talk is *bold walk* out beyond all that is conventional. There are other religious questions to be sure. But in this Psalm we get this address and summons about being different in the world. The talk tells an alternative truth that contradicts the world. The walk is a journey in deep, glad obedience. The talk and the walk are about God's fidelity that we do not doubt. Talk of infidelity and walk of cynical indifference are resistant to the mercy of God. So here we are, blessed with open ears, sure to be addressed, so that we may answer with the Psalmist, "Here I am."

January 19, 2014
Sylvania United Church of Christ
Sylvania, Ohio

8

Remembering Who We Are

The Temptation to Amnesia

DEUTERONOMY 26:1–11

LUKE 4:1–13

It is a great thing to have a name and an identity . . . to know who you are, whom to trust, whom to obey, how to hope, how to be in the world. Two things are clear about getting a name and an identity. On the one hand, it is the work of a lifetime; we are never finished with the work of settling our identity. On the other hand, it takes a village or a community or a family to give us our name and identity. We are endlessly negotiating with village, community, and family to work out trust and obedience and hope in the world.

In the Christian community, the great sign of name and identity is the mystery of baptism, that dramatic moment when we are signed by water, promised God's spirit, invited into the church, and named as one of Christ's own. It is our baptism that is the event and the continuing process of name and identity, whereby we know to trust Christ, to obey Christ, to hope for his promises, and to be his disciples in the world. Response to Jesus Christ who gives us name and identity is the task in which we Christians are all engaged.

I.

The Old Testament text we have today in Deuteronomy 26 has been regarded as the key Old Testament text for name and identity. It portrays people in Israel, all people in Israel in every generation, coming before the priest with an offering of gratitude in order to make a declaration of name and identity, a repeated liturgical process whereby Israelite boys and girls, women and men, publicly announce their name and identity as the people of God.

42

That declaration that is at the core of the Bible includes four affirmations that are central to biblical faith:

- First, my *father was a wandering Aramean*, a dying Syrian. I can remember back many generations when my family began. What I remember is that we were totally at risk. That is the beginning of my identity.
- Second, I can remember that we were poor people, cheap labor in Egypt, living on less than minimum wage, working in the brickyards under impossible quotas, exploited and taken advantage of. But I can remember, because my parents talked about it all the time, that God saw our pitiful situation and heard our pain and acted in power. *God brought us out of an impossible economic situation to begin a new life.* I can remember how we danced and sang as we left the unbearable labor pool.
- Third, I can remember that the God who led us away from exploitation and suffering is the God *who brought us into luxurious well-being and abundance* where we could live in prosperity and safety all our days. I can remember that long trek from abuse to abundance that I and my people have made many times, always because the God of emancipation and well-being noticed us and cared for us and acted in solidarity with us.
- Fourth, because this narrative defines my life:
    a narrative of risk;
    a narrative of deliverance;
    a narrative of incredible abundance,
- I gladly put my life down in this identity with this God. As a sign that this is my identity, I bring an offering of my best produce and pledge to live my life with and for this God, in obedience to the commands of this God because this is who I am and who I will be in all circumstances and in all times to come.

Israel, in ancient days, recited and reenacted this drama over and over, in each new generation, in each new circumstance. And so the young and the outsiders were incorporated into this identity; they could no longer be slotted as foreigners or as cheap labor. In this act and recital, Israel accepted an identity as the people of the God who saves and blesses.

II.

Many Israelites over the generations embraced this identity. Eventually Jesus, son of Israel, embraced this identity. We know that Jesus was circumcised as a Jewish baby. We know that as a young teenager he made the Jewish pilgrimage to Jerusalem and announced to his parents that he must be about his father's work. Everything about the narrative of Jesus makes clear that he had inhaled and embraced this same identity. We can imagine that he stood, as his many mothers and fathers had stood, to recite these same identity-giving statements:

We were at-risk Syrians;
We were exploited as cheap labor;
We were delivered by the wonder of God;
We were brought up to a place of abundance;
We enact our gratitude to the God who has saved us.

He had an identity with this God through this story.

It is this identity that is the taproot of Jesus' vocation. He was teacher, rabbi, healer, forgiver of sins, and eventually messiah who would obey God for the sake of the world. Even in his prayer in the Garden of Gethsemane and on that Friday cross, he kept to his identity. He remembered that this life was connected to the God who saves and blesses, who would be obeyed.

III.

But what I want to talk about is this narrative and temptation of Jesus in Luke 4, our Gospel reading. In that story Jesus is confronted, at the beginning of his public life, with temptations from the devil to give up his identity, to abandon his vocation, to forsake his calling, to have a better life outside his true identity.

The devil, that sneaky voice of seduction, offers him lots of alternatives:

- The alternative to perform miracles in order to exhibit his power;
- The alternative to have power and glory by giving in to seduction;
- The alternative to demonstrate his status by an act of daring.

Each of these temptations asks Jesus to contradict his identity as a child and servant of the true God to whom he belongs. Each of these temptations is an invitation to embrace an alternative identity that the world will celebrate, and to forget his true character.

The devil who comes to Jesus is not a guy with a pitchfork. He is, rather, the quiet voice of seduction that comes to us in the night and entertains us with scenarios of having a better life on other terms. Jesus knew that his life in obedience to this God was to be difficult—even inconvenient—and he must have dreamed of a safer life. He was nearly seduced into forgetting his true self.

But Jesus answers the devil of seduction like a true Israelite. He answers directly out of the Book of Deuteronomy, the same book from which we got our first text today:

- One does not live by bread alone (Deut. 8:3).
- Worship the Lord your God and serve only him (Deut. 6:4–5).
- Do not put the Lord your God to the test (Deut. 6:16).

The story exhibits Jesus as firm in his identity, rooted in his community, ready to live with his vocation from this God.

IV.

But of course the temptation narrative in Luke looks beyond Jesus . . . to the disciples . . . to the church . . . to us. After we see how Jesus resists the temptation to abandon his identity, Luke turns to us and asks, "What about you?" How are you doing on your identity as a follower of Jesus, as a child of Moses? Luke asks that question of us because Luke knows that we all face the tempter, the seduction in the middle of the night, when we are talked out of our identity and invited to forget our baptismal name.

I believe that the big issue in the U.S. church today is that we are tempted to amnesia and must take great care to remember who we are in our baptismal names and identities. The voice of seduction takes many forms among us, as it took many forms in the life of Jesus. I will name three forms of seduction that I believe address each of us in our culture:

- *The seduction of power* was a "biggie" for Jesus as it is for those of us who are U.S. citizens. We imagine we can flex our muscle and have our way, because we have such a sense of entitlement. As our military seduction talks us out of obedience to the gospel, so the drive for power and control and wealth and influence is a primal pursuit for many of us. And when we sign on for the effort to control, either public or personal, we may forget about the vulnerability of Jesus, the practice of mercy, until we give it all up in a kind of shameless habit without thinking about the cost of control.
- *The seduction of self-indulgence* is immense, fed as it is by market ideology and television consumerism, until we imagine that when we have more and better, somehow we will be made happier. The most elemental practices of face-to-face engagement disappear as we have many techniques for communication, but rarely say anything important to each other. We imagine that we should be on the receiving end of the fantasy world of youth and beauty and success, until we forget about the strange path of discipleship with its signposts of discipline, obedience, and sacrifice.
- *The seduction of anxiety* in which we give ourselves over to a thousand worries:
    that "outsiders" will take over our society and our economy;
    that our kids will not get into Harvard unless they do soccer and ballet;
    that people with different sexuality will erode the values of our society . . . until we become frantic, shrill advocates without the civility for neighborliness or the calmness of heart based in the sure rule of God, in the conviction that the world will hold.

What happens when our baptism is forgotten and we embrace the seductions of power, of self-indulgence, and of anxiety is that the church loses its edge for mission, forgets its capacity for generosity, and forfeits its passion for forgiveness. When we forget our identity, we can divide the world in red and blue, liberal and conservative, and imagine that it is our way or no way. The church is in crisis in the U.S. because we have given up on an identity that calls us to trust and obey, to love God with a singular passion, to love neighbor with compassion, and to entrust our own lives not to our weapons, our money, our beauty, our youth, or technology, or our smarts, but to the mercy of God.

Our task is to answer the voice of seduction . . .

To answer as did Jesus:

"We do not live by bread alone,"

to answer as did ancient Israel,

"My father was a wandering Aramean,"

to answer as does the church,

"My only comfort in life and in death is that I belong to my faithful savior Jesus Christ."

Our gift from God: To answer, to resist, to remember, to be on our way rejoicing, not talked out of our glorious vocation of freedom and obedience to God's truth in the world. It is a gift given out of which we, like Jesus, may live very differently . . . unafraid!

February 25, 2007
Memorial Drive United Methodist Church, Houston

9

Celebrating the Revolution

PSALM II3

LUKE 4:14–21

Epiphany is about God becoming visible in the world. Of all the words of Scripture that make God visible in the world, none is more dangerous or welcome—depending on who we are—than Psalm 113. My gift to you today is to line out this Psalm so that you may—in your several moods of danger or welcome—ponder the truth of the God of the Gospel. This is a song that ancient Israel must have sung that they put in their hymnal, the Psalter, and it still comes up in our lectionary.

I.

At the center of the Psalm, in verses 7–9a, are some of the most stunning words we have about God, lined out in lyrical fashion:

> God *raises* the poor from the dust;
> God *lifts* the needy from the ash heap;
> God *makes* them sit with princes;
> God *gives* the barren woman a home.

Through this series of active verbs God is said to be at work turning the world upside down, revamping the economy, reordering the values of domestic life. The words exhibit God as the prime mover in a revolutionary transformation of the way money and power work in the world. The text is an invitation for us to think again about the depth and power and seriousness of the news of the Gospel.

47

The Psalm undoubtedly reflects the joy and astonishment of people in that ancient world who were helpless and powerless and in despair. And then, in ways they do not explain, they found the world revised. And they credited that revision to God. This Psalm is the celebration voiced by the *poor* who are invited back into the economy. It is the voice of the *needy* on the ash heap who sound like ancient street people. It is the song of *barren women* who were shamed in the ancient world for not producing children. They all find a new lease on life, because the God of the Gospel would not let any of God's precious children— the needy, the poor, the barren—be second-class citizens who had to live in shame and poverty. People like us may find such a song a jolt, because we have settled for a more timid God; but this is the one shown us in the text!

II.

This song represents a significant piece of the biblical repertoire. It is a song that was picked up by old lady Hannah who in old age became the mother of Samuel. At the new birth she sang in amazement about social reversals:

> Those who were filled have hired themselves out for bread, But those who were hungry are now fat with food. . . . The Lord makes poor and makes rich, He brings low, he also exalts. (1 Sam. 2:5–8)

Hannah celebrates that God is at work turning the world so that it will be made new.

And after Hannah, Mary the mother of Jesus, at the news of her pregnancy, sang the same song:

> He has filled the hungry with good things,
> He has sent the rich empty away.
>   (Luke 1:53)

Mary reflects on the ways in which this revolutionary God has started a new movement that will continue in her son Jesus. It is in Jesus that the Psalm, the Song of Hannah and the Song Mary all converge. The songs must have been ringing in his ears as he grew in faith and began his ministry.

III.

In the Gospel reading of Luke 4, Jesus has come home to Nazareth for his first public visit at home. Luke tells us he read from Isaiah 61, yet another revolutionary text:

About good news to the *poor*;
About release of *prisoners*;
About recovery of sight to the *blind*;
About *oppressed people* being cared for and made free.

And then he said, this old text is what I am going to be doing with my life. My life is about giving concreteness to God's recovery of the world. These texts all converge around Jesus, but the hope is as old as the Old Testament, because the God of the Bible is always the same, always on the move in the world, always turning things upside down, always an advocate for those the world rejects, always calling the wealthy and the powerful to account on behalf of the others, always making things new.

IV.

These revolutionary verses in Psalm 113—only verses 7–9—are sandwiched in between wondrous acts of praise in which the gathered community of faith is summoned to celebrate the God of the transformation. Verses 1–4 are all praise, all exultation, all song of triumph and gladness and well-being. The community of faith sings the truth about the world, nothing glib, nothing rote, but a serious readiness to sign on for the truth of God:

Praise the LORD . . . (the Hebrew is Hallelu Yah);
Praise O servants,
Praise the *name of YHWH*, the God of the exodus liberation.
The *name of God*, the one who sets slaves free and who loves barren
    women and who releases prisoners,
The *name* is to be blessed and affirmed,
From East to West
from now to forever,
All times, all places, all life,
Above all rival gods.

The Psalm ends in verse 9 with one more summons to praise: "Hallelu Yah"; the praise at the beginning and praise at the end sandwich the verses about the revolution. The church at praise celebrates the God who turns the world toward wholeness.

Now a moment of candor before I finish. Likely you did not come to church as a revolutionary, nor did I. Likely you may find the news of this God working against your vested interest, for who among us wants the economy reordered or who among us wants the prisoners released or who among us wants family values revamped? Conservatives among us do not want such change; and liberals among us only want change we can manage.

The Psalm and the narrative of Jesus speak against our settled worlds. It would take practice to learn to sing this way, to sing about the revolution that God is undertaking that centers in Jesus; but unless we sing and live that song, we settle, against the Gospel, for the world the way it is. The news of Epiphany is that God is on the loose.

That news is dangerous, but it may also be welcome. God wants the world to be otherwise and we are invited to God's news of dignity, respect, and viability. It might be an expensive doxology, for when we praise, we sign on. We are for sure invited to reach toward God's new world that is on its way . . . by the mercy of God!

January 21, 2007
Saint Michael and All Angels Episcopal Church, Dallas

10

On Offer

Gospel Adults

ISAIAH 58:1–9A

PSALM 112:1–10

1 CORINTHIANS 2:1–12

MATTHEW 5:13–20

Jesus tells his disciples, in our Gospel reading, that they must have a "righteousness" that surpasses any punctilious moralism. And then Jesus intensifies the commandments of Sinai in the Sermon on the Mount to trace the way his followers are to give themselves over to the command of God that is their true destiny. Such terms as "righteousness" and "commandments" smack of rigorous requirements and ours is a society that resents and resists such requirements. So try it another way. Paul writes to his friends in the church and invites them to think about what it means to be "truly human" (1 Cor. 2:11). I suggest that in biblical rhetoric terms like "righteousness" and "commandment" are ways of talking about being "truly human" according to the mystery and purpose of God. Except of course that the Gospel has a very different notion of being human, for it has nothing to do with being "good" or being strong or being rich or being a winner. The notion of being truly human in the Gospel, that is, being "righteous," is remote from what our society thinks of as a "successful person." We have two sketches in our reading of that "truly human" that are worth pondering.

I.

Psalm 112 sketches out "righteous persons" as those who have power and influence and gravitas to make a positive difference in the life of the community:

- They are said to be "merciful and gracious," having a healing, restorative capacity with their neighbors;
- They deal generously, lend readily to the poor, and conduct their business affairs with justice, that is, without advancing their own interest. They act with economic generosity and use their resources for the well-being of all their neighbors; likely they support programs and systems that enhance the common good;
- Their hearts are steady; they are not afraid of evil tidings. They are unflappable and do not participate in the Orange Alert anxiety of the fearful society around them;
- They distribute freely and give to the poor on a sustained basis.

In sum, they are the kind of people who are attentive to need around them; they make a difference. They are the ones we call in need or in an emergency; they keep their cool and enact a restorative buoyancy in the neighborhood. And because of their way in the neighborhood, the psalm says, they are blessed and their legacy endures.

II.

The second sketch we have in our reading of such righteous persons is the poem of Isaiah 58. The poetry comes from a time when the Jews are having a big argument about what constitutes authentic worship. They had "worship wars" back then, likely arguments between people who wanted it "traditional" and those who yearned for "contemporary" and "experimental." They count on God's promises and know how to fast and what counts as a proper fast and proper sacrifices and offerings, no doubt which way to turn at the altar. Sound familiar? It turns out, in this poem, that neither advocates for the traditional or the contemporary carry the day.

Right in the middle of the dispute, the kind that churches love to have, the poet says, "None of the above." He says, "Let me tell you about real religious discipline. Let me tell you about authentic worship. Let me lay out for you the discipline of fasting that matters." And then comes the big surprise, right in the middle of the argument:

Is not this the fast that I choose [says God]:
to loose the bonds of injustice,
to undo the thongs of the yoke,
to let the oppressed go free,
and to break every yoke?

(v. 6)

The poet is talking about oppressive, exploitative social and economic practices, for already in verse 3 there is mention of "oppressing workers," surely with a bad minimum wage.

> Is it not to share your bread with the hungry
> and bring the homeless poor into your house;
> when you see the naked, to cover them,
> and not to hide yourself from your own kin?
> (v. 7)

Real religious discipline, real worship, real righteousness before the throne of God has to do with economic justice and solidarity between haves and have-nots. It is to let the people out from under hopeless debt. The focus is on bread (food) and clothing, and housing. Real righteousness concerns the bodily existence and well-being of the neighbors who are without resources but who, because they are there, are entitled to a share in the life of the community. There must have come as stillness in the argument, a stunning summons to a different righteousness, a notion of what it means to be truly human in God's world. Now I am sensitive to the fact that I do not know any of you and my mandate is not to provoke. But these texts sit in front of us today; these sketches make me think we are having the wrong conversation in our society, and the church knows better. The question of the truly human refocuses our thought and our action. I assume you are like me in front of these texts, knowing and hoping and resisting, all at the same time.

III.

If we take the sketches of the Psalm and the poem in Isaiah, we have a completely different notion of what it means to be "righteous." That is what Jesus is talking about. The Pharisees, his opponents, had a careful notion of being righteous, how often to pray, how many sacrifices to offer, what oaths to keep, the kind of close disciplines that keep life tidy. So Jesus says, "I have in mind a different kind of human person. I have in mind a kind of adult who is rooted in the promises of God and who is tuned to the neighbor."

When Jesus, in our reading, goes over the old commandments, the first one is about anger. If you come to God angry, says Jesus, don't go there first:

> "When you are offering your gift at the altar, if you remember that your brother or sister has something against you, leave your gift there before the altar and go; first be reconciled to your brother or sister, and then come and offer your gift." (Matt. 5:23–24)

He ends his long teaching by his most radical thought:

> "But I say to you, Love your enemies and pray for those who perse-
> cute you, so that you may be children of your Father in heaven; for
> he makes his sun rise on the evil and on the good, and sends rain on
> the righteous and on the unrighteous. For if you love those who love
> you, what reward do you have? . . . Do not even the Gentiles do the
> same?" (vv. 44–47)

The truly human person Jesus has in mind has the freedom of God to override petty promoting of self so that neither anger nor dismissal of those who
threaten us counts for anything. He ends his instruction this way: "Be perfect,
therefore, as your heavenly father is perfect. (v. 48)"

Not "be perfect." Be integrated; be whole. Get yourself together and live
one thing in this world as a child of God. Be more like the God of mercy and
generosity and forgiveness and abundance. Be like that!

IV.

God wills . . . and the world . . . needs righteous people. God wills and the
world needs authentic adults who can take responsibility for the well-being
of society. Our society is not big on growing adults who refuse self-indulgent,
self-preoccupied narcissism, who get their minds off themselves and their
interests. Our society evokes a different sort of adult who is mentioned in
the final verse of the Psalm, a verse we usually do not read. The verse goes
like this:

> The wicked [the opposite of the righteous] see it and are angry;
> they gnash their teeth and melt away;
> the desire of the wicked comes to nothing.
>
> (Ps. 112:10)

The "wicked" are not people who do sex and drink all the time. They are,
rather, people who do not care or notice. It drives them crazy, says the Psalm,
to see the generous and compassionate at work in the neighborhood, because
it is such a sharp contrast and contradiction. And, says the Psalm, their desire
comes to nothing. The self-preoccupied can never be satisfied.

I always wonder about the ads for "adult movies or "adult books stores."
Our society takes "adult" to mean lavishly self-indulgent and irresponsible.
But they are not the real adults. The authentic adults are the ones who,
according to the summons of the Gospel, give their life away for the neighborhood. So imagine such adults alive to the world. Paul says that "we have

the mind of Christ" (1 Cor. 2:16). The adulthood of the gospel toward which we grow is to become truly human, to slough off the indifference, and to be gracious, unflappable, compassionate, to care about justice in the world, to love the world in God's way of love. That is why we eat and drink here, a meal for the truly human toward which we grow.

February 6, 2011
Indian Hill Episcopal Presbyterian Church, Cincinnati, Ohio

11

Life Together . . . in the World

DEUTERONOMY 30:15–20

PSALM 119:1–8

I CORINTHIANS 3:12–19

MATTHEW 5:21–37

This is a hard time in the church. These texts suggest to me two big decisions that the church now faces if it is to live a Gospel life. One big decision is an internal decision about how we will live together in the church. The other big decision is how to be present in our culture in faithful ways. The two decisions are related to each other, but they are not the same.

I.

The big decision about living together in the church is signaled in Paul's letter to the church at Corinth. Paul spends a lot of energy advising that congregation that he had founded, because the church had a lot of intense problems. Indeed, it sounds like most congregations that I know. They were choosing up sides. They picked the leader they liked, and trusted—Paul himself or Apollos, and we have been picking sides ever since. There are many ways to divide the church over our preferences and our convictions and our prejudices and our settled certitudes and our biases. It strikes me that now the main picking of sides is ideological. A few years ago I got invited to address the Episcopal House of Bishops. And the leaders told me that the great threat to the church, as they saw it, is that we are divided as conservatives and liberals, we have red and blue congregations and red and blue bishops and pastors. Of course, it is not different in any of our churches, and certainly not among Presbyterians.

Paul regards such quarreling over preferences to be a mark of immaturity in faith. He says, "You are still on milk and not ready for solid food, the real

56

stuff of the gospel." He says, "You are of the flesh," by which he means, propelled by self-serving desire.

So Paul invites his congregation in Corinth to rethink its way of being the church. His appeal is that we are all in this together. Using the figure of a seedling that is to be planted and watered, he says that one leader planted it and another watered it, and everybody's work was necessary. He ends his appeal by saying that we are God's servants, coworkers signed on together.

Now this appeal is not to compromise or pretend that we all like and trust each other, we liberals and we conservatives. It is rather an insistence that church people act and live differently because we are not only bound to each other in faith. We are bound to Christ who is the full performance of God's deep love for the world. As "coworkers" in the work of Christ, our task is to exhibit and enact God's deep love for the world, that is, to get our minds off ourselves and our biases and our particular passions enough to situate ourselves in the big picture of Christ's work in the world. When we act in immature ways and of the flesh, propelled by our self-serving desires, we simply imitate the society around us that does not know Christ. But Jesus goes beneath all of our ideologies, all party labels, all partisan ideologies. Jesus sees the world human, and sees human persons in need and loved by God. I believe the big crisis in the church in our society is that we have forgotten what is distinctive in the missional identity of the church. And then it is as though we live in the church but act like everyone else who is not caught up in God's love.

So here is a piece of good news. Young evangelicals, it is now clear, have little interest in mega churches and no interest at all in culture wars. They rather want to gather in communities that are engaged in the mission of loving the world. It could be that we mainline folk could be instructed by young evangelicals who want to get on with the work of the church to which they have been called. So Paul says, You are God's field . . . expect to be cultivated;

You are God's building . . . expect to be occupied.

Cultivated and occupied by love that calls us beyond ourselves!

II.

The second big decision that the church now faces—when we are coworkers and we order our internal life according to the Gospel—is that to think again about our relationship to the culture around us. The other readings, along with Paul's letter, are all about the church being under a different discipline and a different mandate that are not just an echo of culture. So the decision we face is to consider what disciplines and mandates will best exhibit our baptism as a different people in the world:

The reading from Deuteronomy—I set before you the ways of life and death, therefore choose life—is an old reflection on being God's people in a Canaanite culture. "Canaanite culture," as faced by ancient Israel, was a culture of commodities in which everything and everyone was reduced to a usable, tradable, own-able commodity. And Moses calls Israel to covenantal relationships that are not dominated by a hunger for "things." Well, it is an easy connection for us, because we live in a culture where we are taught, over and over, that another electronic connection, another drug, another car, another surgery will make us safe and happy. But Moses knows better than that. He knows that love of God and love of neighbor in quite concrete ways is the only source of well-being.

The reading from Psalm 119, an echo of Deuteronomy, is an affirmation of Torah commandments and statutes, that is, guidelines for being in sync with God's purpose for the world. For a long time we Christians have so feared "Jewish legalism" that we did not want to consider Torah requirements. But as you know, Jesus summarized the whole of Torah as love of God and love of neighbor, that is, order our life around relationships and policies of fidelity and generosity, and that will bring happiness. What we can see is that society ordered around money, control, consumer goods and concentrated wealth, and military violence does not make us safe and does not make us happy. Choosing life is choosing, in our churches, in our families, in our neighborhoods, in public policy a different way of practice that resists the seductions of private security and domination at the expense of others.

And Jesus, Torah teacher that he is, reviews the old Torah requirements, about murder, about adultery, divorce, false swearing, and enacting retaliation. Lover of the world that he is, he does not ease Torah requirements. Rather he tightens them up, makes them more rigorous, and urges actions and policies that refuse violence, betrayal, vengeance, and facile, deceptive interactions. Jesus will end his radical interpretation of Israel's Torah by a command to "love your enemies." And finally he will say at the end of the chapter, "Be perfect"—be whole—have integrity—be about one thing in your life. Be in sync with God. But such being in sync requires, as serious Jews have always known, swimming upstream against ordinary social practices. And we have a mandate to nurture our children and grandchildren to swim upstream against a culture that is on its way to death.

So we have in these texts three testimonies that all make the same accent in the same cadence:

Deuteronomy: choose covenant instead of commodity;
Psalm 119: Torah obedience is a way to happiness;

Jesus: be reconciled to your brother and sister;
> Don't lust in anxiety;
> Stay faithful;
> Just say yes or no, don't equivocate.
> Be perfect, not morally pure but fully committed to a Gospel way of life.

- Moses knows of the Canaanite pressure that is interrupted by the Torah;
- Psalm 119 knows that foolish self-indulgence is a path to death and we need not go there;
- Jesus knows about the seductions of self-indulgence, and we know about a culture that wants to talk us out of our baptism.

Along with Moses, and the Psalm, and Jesus, we know better! And we have that big decision in front of us in the church.

III.

So imagine the church here and everywhere in our society:

- Deciding to order our life around the love of Christ and not around our quarrelsome fearful practices of red or blue, liberal or conservative. Imagine the church as a body of coworkers so drawn to Christ that we can be cultivated as Christ's field, and occupied as Christ's building.
- Deciding to walk a different path in the world, under discipline, the neighborly concern that the fast world around us regards as passé and old-fashioned.

These two decisions together are the answer, I believe, to the crisis of the church. More than that, in our society that has committed to a way of greed, anxiety, and violence, this in fact is that for which our culture hungers. If you want to know about Hunger Games, this is the food of life, the body broken, the blood poured out, the self given over to the brother, the sister, the enemy. That is how we live together . . . for the sake of the world that God loves! Imagine you (and all of us) this week, as coworkers precisely with those who think differently. Imagine you (and all of us) this week, upstream against our culture of death. We know better, but it requires of us sustained attentiveness. We cannot be the church by accident, but only with obedient intentionality.

February 16, 2014
Central Presbyterian Church, Anderson, South Carolina

12

Orphans Come Home

ISAIAH 49:8–16A

PSALM 131

I CORINTHIANS 4:1–5

MATTHEW 6:24–34

I am the one who gets to remind you of your real family and your real parents, your awesome father and your remembering mother.

I.

The Isaiah text is addressed to people in severe displacement who judge that they have been forgotten and neglected by God. As a result they cower in despair at being abandoned by the God who had made promises to them. And then the poet comes at them with a word from God. He asks them a rhetorical question: Do you think that a mother who nurses a child will forget that child? Well, no, because her breasts would hurt from fullness of milk. But the poet says, Well, in extreme cases such a mother might forget the child if she is distracted enough.

But says God through the poet, even if such a mother might in extreme circumstance forget such a suckling child, I will not forget you. I am your mother God who is more reliable and more faithful and more dependable than any mother you can imagine. The poet dares to present God as mother God with tender mercies like a nursing mother who pays attention, who always remembers, who never abandons. And then, just to make sure we do not miss the point, God says, "I will not forget you, because I have written your name on my hand." God, even before Sarah Palin did it, wrote the important stuff so that God would remember. The most important stuff for any child is our name, now written so that it is in front of God. And then, in verse 16, where

60

we Episcopalians are not supposed to read the second line, God says, "Your walls are continually before me." God remembers destroyed Jerusalem. And we dare to extrapolate that God remembers all the places of abandonment, suffering, and war, the places where people are in danger of being forgotten. This is a mother who gathers all the children like a hen gathers the chicks and brings them all home to well-being.

II.

But let me tell you about our real father. Jesus addresses his disciples. They are worried about traveling with him, because he travels light and does not have many resources. They worried about what they would eat and drink, and what they would wear and where they would stay. In their anxiety, the disciples constitute a microcosm of an anxious world that is worried about running out and not having enough, and being vulnerable and exposed.

And Jesus says to them, do not worry about that stuff, because your heavenly father knows what you need, and you will get it from that father who will give it to you. The father God is the creator who has arranged the world in abundance; because of that, the world keeps producing and generating, the gift that keeps on giving. As a result there is enough food for the whole world, if and when we cease the anxious hoarding and the extravagant standard of living and the war and the violence, all signs of endless anxiety. And the father says to the children, "Do not be anxious about how you will live."

III.

On offer here at this table is the mother God who will never forget and the father God who always provides. But unless we have some intentionality, we begin to think that we are alone. We begin to imagine that we are orphans, fatherless and motherless. We begin to worry about having enough stuff as if we were fatherless, about being forgotten as if we were motherless. And we begin to think only of ourselves, and we readily become scavengers and cheats and corner cutters; we take what belongs to others, doing damage to the body politic because we think only of ourselves and our survival and well-being. It occurs to me that our society now is a place of anxiety and threat and selfishness and narcissism and self-indulgence, as though we were fatherless without resources and motherless and forgotten. Consequently we leverage and muscle and calculate in the hope that our self-centered efforts will make us safe and happy; and it never does!

Well, this is the news. We are not orphans in the world! And here is the mandate for us and our society. We can quit acting like motherless, fatherless people in the world. The poem in Isaiah (through which we have access to the remembering mother) is addressed to ancient exiles who thought they were abandoned in their displacement. It is to them that God has declared:

> I have kept you and given you as a covenant to the people. (Isa. 49:8)

Imagine that, these people (and we as their heirs) are given by God as a covenant. We are given by God as the connectors, as a pledge of loyalty, as an act of solidarity. The mandate of being a covenant goes like this in the poem:

- "to establish the land," that is, to recover the social turf and make it livable again;
- "to apportion the desolate heritages," that is, to redistribute the resources so that all may live;
- "to say to prisoners, 'Come out,'" for as we all know, in that ancient world and in our contemporary world, it is the poor who fill the prisons, who have no other chance for rehabilitation.
- "to say to those in darkness," (the ones who have disappeared from the social screen), "Show yourselves," make an appearance.

This is an extraordinary mandate given to the sons and daughters of the mother-father God, to break the vicious cycles of orphanness in the world, to reconfigure social goods and social power and social access, so that those who have dropped out in failure can reengage the prospect of a human life in a human community.

It occurs to me that those who have mother and father, those who have been honored, beloved, remembered, and resourced as sons and daughters are able to get their minds off themselves and care about the whole family and the whole neighborhood and the whole sweep of the community. The news is that God will gather the family, and gather us among those who do the gathering work of God.

IV.

This summons is to act on behalf of the mother/father God in the world. That summons is wondrously situated in the assurance of the Psalm. Did you notice it when we said it?

> I do not occupy myself with things
> too great and too marvelous for me.

But I have calmed and quieted my life
like a weaned child with its mother;
My life is like the weaned child that is with me.
                                        (Ps. 131:1–2)

I have this image of a child who lies down at night safe, beloved, at rest, remembered by mother, protected by father, unanxious. Such a child awakens the next morning rested, with energy and freedom and courage for the family. Such a child has the "self issues" enough in hand, and is free to think about others. And so Jesus says at the end of his lesson on not being anxious:

Seek God's governance and seek God's neighborliness, and the rest will be given to you. (Matt. 6:33)

Think of the table, all of you who have traces of orphan-like feeling about your life. Here is homecoming. Here is the gracious mother God, the self-giving father God who meets us. We depart the table fully loved and sent back, with our names written down, sent again to be a covenant to the peoples.

February 27, 2011
St. Michael and All Angels Episcopal Church, Mission, Kansas

PART TWO

Sermons for Lent and Easter

13

Flooded with Fidelity

GENESIS 9:8–17
PSALM 25:1–10
I PETER 3:18–22
MARK 1:9–15

What would you do if you were God? And you saw the world you had made gone crazy? You could see how the rich devour the poor and reduce more and more folk to poverty. You could observe how the great nations use up precious resources with war efforts, and call killing "patriotism." You could watch while the lead creatures . . . man and woman . . . defile and pollute the earth and make it unlivable. Well, if you were the God of the philosophers— all knowing, all mighty, all present, you might not respond at all, as all this is surely only a blip on your large, unchanging screen.

I.

But if you were the God of the Bible who loves the world, what you would do is engage that world that has gone crazy. You would engage at some deep emotional level that matched your love and concern for such a self-destructive operation. And so the Bible imagines God, back in Genesis. God is deeply upset with the world gone crazy. God is sorry that the project of creation was ever started at all. In an emotional frenzy over betrayed love, God decided to drown his sorrows. All the spigots of heaven and earth were opened to full blast. And in order to trace the emotional extremity of God, the story traces the coming of raging floodwaters:

67

Forty days and forty nights!
The waters swelled and increased greatly!
The waters swelled so mightily that all the high mountains were
    covered!
The mountains were covered fifteen cubits deep!
Everything died!
All were blotted out, human beings, animals, creeping things, birds!
. . . for one hundred and fifty days!

Understand: this story is not about the water. It is about God's emotional attachment to the earth. It is about God the way it is about a parent of a teenager who loses it in a frenzy over teenage insanity and recalcitrance. The waters come up to match the rising affront that God felt with a failed earth, the same failed earth we observe all around us,

Of the rich eating the poor;
Of war using up resources;
Of lethal violation of the environment.

This is a God who cares in frenzied ways about the earth!

II.

And then, in a jarring moment of recognition, we are told, "God remembered." God remembered the faithful who had not joined the insanity. God is stopped short in the frenzy of emotion the way a parent of a teenager is stopped short when one remembers that this object of rage is a well-beloved daughter . . . or son. God comes to God's sense, after having lost the way:

The waters subsided;
They gradually receded;
The waters abated;
The waters continued to abate and the dry land appeared, a tool of God's
    remembering resolve.

The story is not about water. It is about God and God's deep way with the earth, God's raging anger at betrayal, and God's abrupt about-face when God remembered what God had forgotten, had forgotten about loving the earth and the creatures in it.

III.

So what would you do if you were this God,

> When you saw the rich eating the poor into more poverty;
> When you observed killing wars in the name of patriotism;
> When you watched while the earth was carelessly abused?

Well, what this God did was to make a "second effort," the kind Bud Wilkinson used to talk about. The first effort was an emotive punishment that was to drown God's sorrow as the earth was drowned. But the second effort comes with new resolve when God remembered.

We are told that God did four new things:

First, God came to a new realism about the earth and its creatures. God came to see that human persons are indeed bent on self-destruction with an "evil imagination" that will not change. God decided, in that awareness, to lower expectations for human creatures; God decided to rise above such self-destructiveness, not ever again to act in such uncontrolled rage. Thus the Psalmist can say:

> He knows how we are made;
> He remembers our frame;
> He knows we are dust.

God does not expect more of us than we can deliver in response to God's goodness.

Second, God issues an amazing decree:

> As long as the earth endures,
> Seedtime and harvest, cold and heat,
> Summer and winter, day and night,
> Shall not cease.
>   (Gen. 8:22)

This is a decree only a competent creator can issue. It is a divine guarantee that the world will work in all its seasons, in all its agricultural cycles, in all its reliable rhythms. God promises to guarantee a productive food system that the earth will be sustained, that creation will be fruitful and blessed with generosity that is not interrupted, even by our craziness.

Third, God assured that all human life shall be honored and protected,

The lives of the poor,
The lives of criminals,
The lives of Muslims,
The lives of old people and babies.

God prohibits the kind of violence that this crazy world continues to perpetrate.

These three acts constitute God's generous second effort:

- a realism about human capacity;
- a guarantee of food-bearing creation;
- a protection of all of human life.

The world is under new governance, the same new regime that Jesus came to enact when he said, "Repent, for the Kingdom of God is at hand." Because the rule of God is at hand, we can stop and must stop the craziness

Of the rich eating the poor,
Of war in the name of patriotism,
Of deathliness for the environment.

We can stop that . . . because it does not fit with the new governance!

IV.

But then we come to the fourth big response of God's second effort in the text we read today in Genesis 9. The whole of verses 9–17 is one long utterance by God, because God has much that must be said. It is a divine declaration of God's readiness to relate to the world differently. It is a promise on God's part to be faithfully the creator God who upholds the world and generates its life. We notice in this divine declaration of divine fidelity that there is no command on God's part to the creatures, no condition, just a resolve to uphold the world, to keep it safe, to make it function.

The term used for this fidelity on God's part is "covenant." The term for this storytelling is perhaps borrowed from Mt. Sinai and God's covenant with Israel. It is an anticipation of the church's Holy Communion in which we drink the cup of the new covenant. Only here the covenant, the promise of abiding fidelity, is not with Israel at Sinai; it is not with the church as in Holy Communion. It is now covenant:

> . . . with you and your descendants after you, and with every living creature that is with you, the birds, the domestic animals and every animal of the earth with you. (vv. 9–10)

Imagine God has sworn fidelity to birds, every finch and every blue jay and every buzzard. God has sworn fidelity to every animal, every squirrel, every hippo, and every cricket. God has sworn fidelity to every person, every Christian, every Jew, every Muslim, every Hindu, every disabled person, every street person, every white male, every gay person, every and all and each! A huge second effort! God promises that God will never go into a raging flood again. Indeed the only flood that will happen in time to come is that we be flooded with God's defining fidelity.

But God now has a good bit of self-awareness; God can remember back a couple chapters when God, in God's deep regret, became emotively destructive. God now figures, in this moment of utterance, that God might forget this oath and fall back into emotive extremity. And so God provides a vehicle for remembering the oath. The rainbow at the end of the rain is a reminder to God that is strewn across the sky so that God cannot miss it. And when God sees it, God remembers:

> God remembers God's resolve about us;
> God remembers to lower expectations for us;
> God remembers the guarantee of a reliable creation;
> God remembers the commitment of a viable rhythm of food
>   production;
> God remembers the vow of protection for every human creature.

God remembers twice, once with Noah to stop the waters, once now to sustain the creation of the world. The covenant is God's deep self-commitment to the world, the kind a parent makes to a wayward teenager after a wild binge of anger.

This is not about water. It is about God. It is about the God who emotes in anger, but who circles back with a second effort to flood us with fidelity. And because it is about God, it is about us. And because it is about us, it is about you . . . and me. It is about the world being flooded with fidelity that is the divine antidote to the craziness all around us. It is a witness to God's second effort, God's new sanity after a moment of divine craziness. It is an invitation to respond in sanity to our present special craziness.

So consider,

> We are flooded with the gifts of neighborliness; the economy of the rich
>   devouring the poor is now inappropriate;
> We are now flooded with peaceable possibility; the old lust for war and
>   violence is now out of sync;
> We are flooded with fruitfulness; the technological destruction that seeks to
>   sustain our unsustainable standard of living is now passé.

God does not here demand that we stop the craziness in which we are presently enmeshed. But God's great second effort makes our present craziness inappropriate, out of sync, and passé. The rainbow is aimed at God. But it would not hurt if we noticed it as well, as a reminder of the ocean of fidelity in which we live our lives.

> We are left dazzled by a God who has made a new resolve about creation;
> We are left aware enough to notice the regularity of gift-giving creation;
> We are left grateful that God gives and gives and gives, in keeping with God's own pledge of fidelity.

Imagine what it was like that day, to step off the ark into a peaceable land. And now the work is toward a new life that matches God's new promise. It is our proper work. We are inundated by God's loyalty. God remembers . . . and so we may not forget.

February 26, 2012
Boston Avenue Church (UMC), Tulsa, Oklahoma

14

Boundary-Crossing Generosity

DEUTERONOMY 26:1–11
PSALM 91:1–2, 9–16
ROMANS 10:8B–13
LUKE 4:1–13

We are invited, in this Epistle reading, to watch Paul while he thinks again about the Gospel, about the old exclusionary practices of faith, and about the news that all our categories have been shattered by Jesus. Specifically, how Jews can follow Jesus, and how Gentiles can follow Jesus, and how Jews and Gentiles can come to terms, *together*, with the newness of Jesus.

I.

Paul makes an argument about the prerequisites of faith that we may ponder in Lent. Here there are only two such prerequisites for following Jesus:

First, confess that *Jesus is Lord*. Do that with your lips. Believe that in your heart. That does not include all the authoritarian baggage we have accumulated in our several church traditions. Only the claim that Jesus, not the emperor, not the system, not our class or our nation state, can claim our loyalty. It's hard, but it is not complicated.

Second, affirm that *God raised Jesus from the dead*. Lent is on the way to Easter. There is no discussion here about whether it is a physical or spiritual resurrection, about historical realism or metaphor. Simply the lean claim that the executioners did not and could not keep him dead. Because God, that deep power for life, has shattered the system of death and made all things new. The Easter claim is not simply about resuscitation, but about a new reality in the world that is unrestrained by the force of fear or violence or privilege. Paul must become lyrical about this claim, because the reality outruns all

73

of our explanations. And we may situate our lives in this most elemental claim of the living Lord who opens new reality to us.

II.

From that Easter claim Paul draws a deep and decisive conviction upon which everything is based: The Lord is the Lord of all, and is *generous to all who call upon him.* The defining mark of the Easter world is *divine, cosmic generosity* that outruns our need and our want and our hope and our desire, to endow us with every good gift, most wondrously the gift of new possibility.

We have almost no categories for that! Every idol we can construct is grasping and controlling and accumulating. With almost no exceptions, gifts given in the world are quid pro quo, always a bargain, a bribe, a debt, a retainer, a footnote, a tacit demand, an expectation of a return. But generous to all! To the deserving, the undeserving, only one requirement: call upon him. Ask; sign on; look to him. Look nowhere else. This is the Lord who multiplies the loaves until they reach this table. This is the one who willingly forgives, the one who touches to heal, the one who imagines a world with a longing father. This is the one who reaches back into old memory about manna in the wilderness with enough for all and baskets of bread to spare. Easter is the summit of cosmic generosity wherein new life bubbles over for all.

III.

From that wild, limitless generosity, Paul exclaims:

There is no distinction! (v. 12)

There is no class structure. There is no exceptional tenure or entitlement, no riding in the back of the bus, no exclusion of Gentiles . . . women or conservatives, or progressives, or gays . . . or whomever we fear and want to exclude. The syllogism whereby Paul argues is coherent:

Jesus is Lord . . . Jesus is raised . . . The Lord is generous . . . no distinction.

I suggest that this logic, this evangelical logic of the Gospel, is a great pondering for us at Lent. God is bringing the world to a new inclusiveness on the basis of God's own generosity. And God is now calling the church to engage that inclusiveness, because all of our preferred distinctions are vetoed at Easter.

This is an awesome vision in Paul's ancient world where tribalism of a hundred kinds had been justified. And it is still an awesome vision. Because we can all name the ones who frighten and repel us the most. We want some of the ancient protections for our own kind, our own class, our own race, our own persuasion. We do indeed want the world on our own terms. Much of the turmoil and anxiety among us now is no doubt that it is dawning on us that we will not much longer have the world on our own terms, even as the ancient Jews and ancient Gentiles in the church had that dawning from Paul. I propose that the Lenten invitation is to identify the others who are toughest for us, and set them down, in our imagination, in the generosity of God. Paul was indeed such a troublemaker in the church, because his Gentile allies resisted the old Jewish restraints; and his Jewish companions in the church could not compute that it was "free for all" without restraint. Paul declares that the Easter goodness of God has blown away our categories of control and resistance. And what Paul expects from his churches, here the church in Rome, is a generosity that imitates the generosity of God, done through the private sector, done through the government, done through charity, done through legislation, done through justice, done in all those zones where the new governance of God operates. Imagine a God so rich in self that there is to need to claim or grasp or protect self. Imagine a church so rich in gifts with baskets and baskets of bread and cups and cups of wine for all whom God loves. And eventually, imagine a neighborhood so rich in things that it need not be poor in soul.

IV.

Jesus himself had to learn that reach beyond the familiar through the course of his ministry. He had to learn the reach of the Father out beyond the comfort zone his own tribe, as in the parable of the woman who wanted his crumbs (Matt. 15:22–28). And we may imagine that he cringed, sometimes, from his vocation of endless Easter generosity. For that reason we have this temptation narrative as a gospel reading, a drama in which Jesus is addressed in the wilderness by a voice that offers him an easier vision of his life. The "tempter" tries to talk him out of his vocation, so that he will settle into a life of majesty and power and honor . . . without self-risk. As you know, he resists that temptation and gets on with his proper vocation.

But what if the narrative is not about Jesus? What if the story is about the church in Lent, the church that faces the temptation to turn away from such self-risking generosity and contemplates an easier vocation? The tempter is always trying to talk the church out of its identity as adherent to the Easter God to an easier way in the world:

If only we had a God who lets us be as we want.
If only we had an Easter that was more domesticated.
If only we had a Lent that focused on petty disciplines instead of deep issues.

But we don't! What we have is a vocation of generosity to the others that defines us as it defines the God of the Gospel.

The good news for the Lenten journey to which Jesus summons us is the word in the Psalm for this day:

> For he will command his angels concerning you
> To guard you in all your ways.
> On their hands they will bear you up,
> So that you will not dash your foot against a stone.
> You will tread on the lion and the adder,
> The young lion and the serpent you will trample under foot.
> (Ps. 91:11–13)

Lent is a risky journey. But we are on the way toward the others, toward new life, toward inexplicable generosity, all in sync with the one who is Lord of Easter . . . out beyond all of our reluctances.

February 21, 2010
Church of the Redeemer, Cincinnati, Ohio

15

On the Road Again!

PSALM 121

ROMANS 4:1–5, 13–17

JOHN 3:1–17

We are on the road again! As followers of Jesus, we are on the road again in Lent, walking the way of obedience to Jerusalem for the big showdown with the authorities of church and state. It turns out, every time, to be a hazardous journey, full of toils and snares, potholes and adversaries, ending in a rigged trial. But women and men of faith are always on the road again, departing safe places, running risks, and hoping for well-being on the journey. So here are some thoughts about our travel, where we go, how we go, and with whom we travel.

I.

The defining journey of biblical faith begins in the departure of Abraham and Sarah back in the book of Genesis. They were dispatched by God to leave their safe place, to go to a new land yet to be given, to get a new name, to be blessed by God, and to be a blessing to the others around them. They went! And their family, generation after generation, has gone. And we, finally in their wake, must also travel beyond safe places to the gifted end that God intends, hopefully to be blessed and a blessing on the way.

Paul, in our Romans reading, casts the entire life of faith in terms of Abraham's travel. Abraham did not stay in a place he could manage or control or have on his own terms. Abraham trusted himself to God so completely that he acted in great freedom. As he went he found that the God he trusted was indeed totally reliable. Paul turns our attention from Abraham who trusted to

77

the God who traveled with him, whom Paul characterizes in the most stunning doxological language:

> who gives life to the dead and calls into existence the things that do not exit. (v. 17)

This God is the only self-starter and can make newness for us as the God who presides over Easter and makes newness for the whole world. Faith, like that of Abraham, consists in moving into the generative newness given by God.

II.

Jesus, in his instruction to Nicodemus, makes the summons to a journey as radical as can be. He says to this well-established intellectual in the Jewish tradition that we can and may journey to a new self, to a new life. He uses the language of "born again," or better, "born from above," born of God, birthed by God's goodness, recreated with a new identity by God's generous mercy. Of course Nicodemus does not get it. Unlike father Abraham, Nicodemus does not want to go. As a result, by the time Jesus gets to verse 16, the famous John 3:16, Nicodemus has disappeared from the narrative. He is a dropout, suggesting that if we linger with our old self, our old identity, our old world, we drop out of the narrative of God's merciful governance.

III.

So here we are, children of Abraham and Sarah, addressed by the God of all travel, companions of Nicodemus who was interrupted by Jesus who says that a new self and a new life are offered, grounded in the God who loves the world so much that God gives God's own self for the world. As children of Abraham and Sarah and companion of Nicodemus, accompanied by the God of all mercy, we may consider where we are summoned to go on our Lenten journey. The matter is in dispute among us. But if we think that a journey in God's love and mercy away from the world we know and love and control—the world that Abraham left and that Nicodemus could not leave—then it may be that our departure concerns the world of privilege, entitlement, power, and wealth that we simply take for granted in our conventional Euro-Caucasian chosenness. And if we ponder our destination, perhaps it is to be to the neighborhood of *shalom*, the neighborhood of shared resources, of inclusive politics, of random acts of hospitality and intentional acts of justice, of fearless neighborliness that is not propelled by greed or anxiety or excessive self-preoccupation. The big departure now required for the faithful in the US and the big arrival for the faithful in the US is an evangelical wake-up call that moves past our usual Lenten pieties to the ways in which our society and our world political economy is at a life-or-death stage of development. The issue before us is not partisan or liberal or conservative. It is rather an awareness that our conventional way of life in the US is organized so that we do not love the neighbor whom we have seen, and can hardly come to love God whom we have not seen. Thus we are situated, I suggest, for our Lenten journey between the willingness of Abraham and the stubborn refusal of Nicodemus, and we are left to decide to stay or to go, for participation or dropping out, eventually for life or for death.

IV.

So here is a good word. Psalm 121 is designed exactly for travelers who face a demanding, risky journey. It is a Psalm that has been used over and over by travelers, and now is available for us.

This traveler in the Psalm knows about being exposed and thinks cosmically about being safe:

> The LORD is your keeper;
> the LORD is your shade at your right hand.
> The sun shall not strike you by day,
> nor the moon by night.
> (vv. 5–6)

This traveler knows about stumbling on the way:

> He will not let your foot be moved.
> (v. 3a)

This traveler knows about being weary and being afraid to fall asleep and not on guard, and then remembers we can rest safely on the way, because:

> He who keeps you will not slumber.
> He who keeps Israel
> Will neither slumber nor sleep.
> (vv. 3b–4)

This traveler does not sense so much risk in a world that threatens, but is kept safe by the guardian of life:

The Lord will keep you from all evil;
He will keep your life.
The Lord will keep your going out and your coming in
from this time on and forevermore.

(vv. 7–8)

This traveler knows about being self-sufficient and wonders about assistance from elsewhere. The traveler asks:

From where will my help come?

And then promptly answers:

My help comes from the Lord,
who made heaven and earth.
(vv. 1–2)

This Psalm is an assurance and an affirmation that the journey we now undertake is not by ourselves alone. We are surrounded on the way by the God of all trust, the God who kept Abraham and Sarah safely, the one who walked all the way to Jerusalem with Jesus, all the way to Friday and on through to Sunday.

I imagine Lent for you and for me as a great departure from the greedy, anxious anti-neighborliness of our economy, a great departure from our exclusionary politics that fears the other, a great departure from self-indulgent consumerism that devours creation. And then an arrival in a new neighborhood, because it is a gift to be simple, it is a gift to be free; it is a gift to come down where we ought to be.

Imagine, the journey staged by the self-giving God who calls into existence the things that do not exist, a new you and me, a new society, a new world, one neighbor at time. At the table today, we will receive gestures of that self-giving God. We will be given the daily provision for the journey. It is an old Scottish blessing, "May you have traveling mercies," all the days of Lent.

March 20, 2011
Trinity Church, Boston, Massachusetts

16

The Future

Trust but Verify

GENESIS 17:1–7, 15–16
PSALM 22:23–31
ROMANS 4:16–21
MARK 8:31–38

In dealing with the Soviet Union, Ronald Reagan skillfully used the phrase "trust, but verify." He was pressed to "trust" by people who were passionate for some restraint on the arms race that was eating us alive. But he did not want to be soft, so he qualified "trust" by requiring inspections, evidence, and verification. That combination worked for him, and maybe for us in our Lenten journey of faith.

I.

Paul writes this lyrical chapter, Romans 4, to the church in Rome. He writes to the church as it is deciding how to move forward, not a bad text for a church that is between pastors, that must think about its future. There are hints that some in that church in Rome did not want to think about the future.

Maybe they preferred to think about the present in ways that generated quibbles and quarrels or debates about what was required in order to pass muster about faith and about conduct and about who was best and the most qualified to be in leadership. Or maybe they were preoccupied with their celebrated past. The Jewish Christians liked to think about how they had kept all the requirements of Torah; the Gentile members of the church liked to brag about their freedom that was grounded in the reasonableness of their thinking. They debated past and present, with all their pride and their scruples, and their passion for control, and perhaps they debated about what to give up for Lent in order to be more intentionally people of faith.

81

II.

But Paul abruptly changes the subject on the church in Rome. He tells them that their past . . . Jewish or Gentile . . . is not very interesting, because no one is really qualified because of their past, because all have sinned and fallen short. He tells them that the present measuring up to requirements for faith in the present tense should not be absolutized. So do not, he says, linger over a proud past or a reoccupying present tense. Because it is all about the future to which God is summoning us, the future that God is creating before our very eyes. Trust that future and walk into it.

III.

Paul reaches back to Father Abraham, the oldest guy in the memory of Israel, as a harbinger of God's future. You remember Abraham from our reading in Genesis. He was ninety-nine years old and he had no heir and no way to get an heir. Paul says he was "as good as dead," which means he had no chance for a son. This preoccupation with "reproductive possibility" indicates how contemporary the Bible is! Without an heir in that ancient patriarchal world, life was a total dead end. But God comes into his cul-de-sac and announces a future that required incredible trust on Abraham's part. A son would be given!

> You shall be the ancestor of a multitude of nations . . . I have made you the ancestor of a multitude of nations; I will make you exceedingly fruitful; and I will make nations of you, and kings shall come from you. I will establish my covenant between me and you, and your offspring after you throughout their generations, for an everlasting covenant, to be God to you and to your offspring after you. And I will give to you, and to your offspring after you, the land where you are now an alien, all the land of Canaan. (Gen. 17:4–8)

What a mouthful! The one with no future will have a full and rich and glorious future, all because of the gift of God.

Paul takes up this old memory and transposes it into the church's future. And Paul, with his uncommon imagination, magnifies this strange gift of an heir with other lyrical claims. He says,

> It depends on faith, in order that the promise rests on grace and be guaranteed to all his descendants, not only to the adherents of the law but also to those who share the faith of Abraham. (Rom. 4:16)

It all rests on grace, the inexplicable gift of God's grace in God's generosity that shatters all of our categories. It requires only faith, only trust, only readiness to receive.

And if that is not impressive enough, try these two extrapolations that Paul offers:

(a) "Who gives life to the dead." It's all about God's capacity to create new life and new possibility beyond all of our control and explanation. It turns on the resurrection of Jesus, just as Jesus promised his disciples in our gospel reading. It is this newness that is sung in our Psalm. The Psalm we read begins, "My God, my God, why have you forsaken me?" But the Psalm ends in wild praise and thanks, because God has raised this desolate Psalmist to new life. On the same way the church lives in the wake of Easter, celebrating that God overcomes the power of death and refuses to let Jesus be negated by the power of the empire. Talk about a future!

(b) But Paul goes further with the chill-bump producing affirmation:

[W]ho . . . calls into existence the things that do not exist. (v. 17)

This is a summoning of creation out of nothing, this God who has said, "Let there be light," "Let there be life," "Let there be dry land," "Let there be new possibility." Talk about a future!

The lyric of Paul is outrageous in its extravagance; but it is the ground of faith. Paul links these three claims for God's future:

- a baby born to this aged couple;
- a dead man raised to Easter life;
- a world made out of nothing.

A family, a life, a world! All things new by the good generous work of God who refuses to let us remain in a failed past or in a mesmerizing present.

The church lives by the surprises of God, and we situate our modest daily newnesses in that big lyric . . . a life changed, a sinner forgiven, a meal served, a garden planted, a mission undertaken, a friendship that transforms, and before we know it, we say, after the gospel and with great exuberance:

The blind see,
The deaf hear,
Lepers are cleansed,
The lame walk.
The dead are raised,
The poor rejoice,
because this is the gift of God in which we trust.

IV.

All this required is trust. All that is needed is to give ourselves over to the strange, inexplicable power for life that breaks all the old resistances of fear, anger, anxiety, and despair. So it is with our father, Abraham. He trusted. His trust was taken by God as full obedience. Such trust is not such an easy matter. We hold ourselves back. We calculate. We wait to see. We are suspicious. But that is the plunge of love when we risk ourselves into the power of bottomless love. That is what we do when we fall in love. Abraham, in that instant of promise, fell in love with God. And so he reached into the future given by God. Genesis says only that "he went."

But Paul says more:

- verse 20: No distrust made him waver concerning the promise of God;
- verse 20: He grew strong in his faith;
- verse 21: He was fully convinced that God was able to do what he had promised.

The long history of faith, with all the saints, is the story of walking into the future given by God. Lent is a time for sorting this out. Popular Lent is too much preoccupied with guilt and repentance. But not here. Lent is rather seeing how to take steps into God's future so that we are no longer defined by what is past and no longer distracted by what we have treasured or feared about the present. Lent is for embracing:

- the baby given to old people;
- resurrection to new life in Easter;
- the offer of a new world made by God from nothing.

And so in this great church, a new future of gospel possibility.

V.

But I have not yet come to "verify." Not just trust: verify . . . seek evidence . . . require facts. Faith around evidence that comes in narrative form:

Abraham's faith came to verification with Isaac:

> By faith he received power of procreation, even though he was too old—and Sarah herself was barren—because he considered him faithful who had promised. Therefore from one person, and this one as good as dead, descendants were born, "as many as the stars

of heaven and as the innumerable grains of sand by the seashore."
(Heb. 11:11–12)

The faith of the church is received by testimony. So Paul writes

> that he appeared to Cephas, then to the twelve. Then he appeared
> to more than five hundred brothers and sisters at one time, most of
> whom are still alive, though some have died. Then he appeared to
> James, then to all the apostles. Last of all, as to one untimely born, he
> appeared also to me. (1 Cor. 15:5–8)

If you want verification that God's promises are kept, you will not find that
verification among the new atheists who have reduced everything to a tight
little package of reasonableness that easily explains everything away. Nor will
we find verification among the fundamentalists who have God in such a box
that there can be no room for inexplicable gifts. You will find verification
among the daily performances of the trusting ones who live out their trust in
ways that the world terms foolish:

- The verification is in a church ready to be venturesome into God's future;
- The verification is in a church that pays attention to those disqualified by
  the capitalist system;
- The verification is in the acceptance of those who are unacceptable;
- The verification is in the commitment of time to neighbors when we
  prefer to have that time for ourselves;
- The verification is in the telling of hard truth about the world, and that
  in a culture of denial;
- The verification is in the slant toward justice and peacemaking in a world
  that loves violence and exploitation too much;
- The verification is in footing the bill for neighborliness and mercy when
  we have many other bills to pay;
- The verification is in lives that give testimony before the authorities who
  want to silence and intimidate and render irrelevant.

It turns out that the world teems with verification, concerning babies
from the barren ones, lives that have surged in the midst of death, hurts that
have been healed, estrangements that have been reconciled, enslavements
that have turned to freedom, all around us, particular, concrete, specific, for
people like us.

Ronald Reagan's move insisting on "trust and verify" was in fact a complex,
complicated, partial accomplishment, much less clear than his simple rhetoric
might have suggested. And so the church's invitation to "trust and verify" is
also complex, complicated, and partial. But it is decisive for us. So imagine in
this Lenten season, moving beyond treasured pasts, moving beyond precious

present tense arrangements to new God-given prospects. It is no wonder that the Psalmist can at the end sing:

> From you comes my praise in the great congregation;
> My vows I will pay before those who fear him.
> The poor shall eat and be satisfied;
> These who seek him shall praise the LORD.
> May your hearts live forever!
> All the ends of the earth shall remember
> and turn to the LORD;
> and all the families of the nations shall worship before him.
> For dominion belongs to the LORD,
> And he rules over the nations.
>
> (Ps. 22:25–28)

It is our song too. We are on our way rejoicing . . . into God's future.

March 4, 2012
Fourth Presbyterian Church, Chicago, Illinois

17

Lent as Alternative to Empire

ISAIAH 55:1–8
PSALM 63:1–9
I CORINTHIANS 10:1–13
LUKE 13:1–9

Some of you will remember the TV ads from AT&T a bit ago. They featured a winsome young teacher or librarian, sitting at a table with young children. He engaged them in friendly talk through a series of questions. The questions of course led to the conclusion that we should buy AT&T products. But the teaching addressed to the viewer through the children was this:

It is better to do two things at once, rather than only one thing at a time.
Or other lessons:

Big is better.
Faster is better.
More is better.

This is the standard line of corporate insistence. If we have better equipment and investment of high energy, we can succeed and expand and grow and take control and make our lives completely secure and prosperous. It all depends on being productive and the products will help us to be productive.

Well, I am a productive guy and I am glad to be among you, you company of productive people:

Because Presbyterians are productive people.
And Fourth Presbyterian types are productive types.
And Magnificent Mile people are productive.

And back in ancient Babylon, the Jewish exiles were productive. They wanted to get ahead in the Babylonian Empire, and the way we get ahead in the empire is to *do two things at once* and *dream of bigger as better* and *faster is better* and *more is better*. So they hustled and learned and invested and hustled some more. They were willing to participate in the greed, the anxiety, and the systemic violence of the empire in order to get ahead and make a good life for themselves.

I.

And then, right in the middle of their busyness with "Big is better" and "Doing two things at once is better," Isaiah disrupts with his poem:

> Why do you spend your money on that which is not bread?
> Why do you labor for that which does not satisfy? (Isa. 55:2)
> Why do you use your energy on the seductions of the empire?
> Why do you pursue greed and anxiety that will never make you happy?

In a word he stops them up short:

> What are you doing?
> How have you been seduced?
> Have you lost your mind? Or your identity?

Not a bad question for us in Lent. What are we doing with our endless pursuit, to get ahead, not to fall behind, and make our life an endless chase?
And then Isaiah offers an alternative:

> Anyone who thirsts, come to the waters,
> You who have no money, come buy and eat;
> Come buy wine and milk without money and without price. (v. 1)

It is all free! It is all a gift. It is all a sacramental offer of God's goodness in our faith tradition. So quit accommodating the empire; stop the endless cycle of greed and anxiety and the rat-race.

> Because big is not better,
> Because doing two things at once is not better,
> Because faster is not better,
> Because more is not better,
> Because such a pursuit will talk you out of your faith and out of your true identity, and will leave you busy and exhausted and unthinking and anxious and running endlessly.

Says the poet:

> Return to your roots; seek the Lord.
> Be a Jew, not a Babylonian;
> Be a Christian, not a rat-raced consumer;
> Be a gospel person, and not a rat-race producer. Act baptized!

II.

Because, says the poet, says God:

> My ways are not your ways,
> My intention is not your intention.

Because I have another life in mind for you for which you are destined and to which you are summoned. The news is that we are not fated to the endless compulsion of production and consumption. This alternative is a life grounded in *pardon* and marked by *mercy*:

> Let them return to the Lord, that he may have mercy on them,
> and to our God, for he will abundantly pardon. (v. 7b)

> Seek God: quit the mindless practice of anxiety;
> Quit the endless collusion in greed;
> Stop the eager readiness to win and control.

Because our God will abundantly pardon and take you as you are. There is no other venue for *pardon* like the venue of faith with this God who gives free gifts. Our God shows mercy; the gospel is the only place in which *mercy* is given in the midst of our fear and our inadequacy for which we can never compensate enough.

So I thought about Fourth Church, of what little I know of it. I thought of its budget and its programs, its urban presence and its clout as you are about to begin a new ministry. And then I thought that Fourth Church is a carrier of this stunning poem, and a venue

> For return to faith,
> For recovery of faith identity,
> For the practice of mercy,
> For the truth of pardon,
> For the free wine and free milk and free water and free bread.

Fourth Church is that reference point for this God in the season of Lent who disrupts our life with a question and a summons and an invitation. Lent is a summons for us to focus on this mercy that is given nowhere else and this pardon that is offered in no other venue.

This poem of Isaiah is a wake-up call for us when we have been nearly talked out of faith by the force of empire, when we have wanted to prevail instead of trust mercy, when we have decided to gut it out rather than let the pardon come, when we have bought in on the phoniness of the AT&T ad rather than the God of the gospel who gives free gifts.

III.

So Lent is for free gifts. But then there is this abrasive Gospel lesson with its hard sayings:

Jesus says to his hearers:

> Unless you repent, you will all perish. (Luke 13:3)

Jesus says a second time:

> Unless you repent, you will all perish.

We can believe in a punishing God if we want. But Isaiah suggests, rather, that if we do not change, our faith will evaporate and we will disappear into the woodwork of the empire. We will eventually forfeit our faith and our identity by trading out the mercy of God for "big is better" and the pardon of God for "Doing two things at once."

And then Jesus takes up a fig tree as a life lesson: If it does not bear fruit, cut it down!

> If it bears fruit next year, well and good. (v. 9)

Fig trees have the task of bearing figs. If it cannot produce figs, cut it down. If you do not bear the fruit appropriate to your life, your Jewishness will vanish; your baptism will disappear. So with us, the fruit of mercy and pardon are our true vocation without which we die.

The summons of Lent is not just to stop what we are doing that marks us by greed, anxiety, or systemic violence. The summons is to *stop* that . . . and then *start again* this other way with new resolve. Do the first fruit of the new life that consists in pardon and mercy and compassion and generosity and hospitality and justice.

IV.

I am left with this thought: Lent is a question, a gift and a summons:
The question of Lent is:

What are we doing?
Are we working for that which does not satisfy?
Are we spending for that which is not bread?

The gift of Lent is free gifts in the gospel that sustain life:

Free wine and milk,
Free water and bread,
All the markings of sacrament that refuse our thin attempts at empire.

The summons of Lent is to bear new fruit:

Do what is in sync with the God of the gospel, the God who has another intention for our lives, who wants us out of the rat-race of "big is better" and so has mercy, who gives us pardon when we do not do enough by doing two things at once.

We are left with a new sense of ourselves as God's people:

No longer working for that which does not satisfy; Receiving good gifts that we need for life; Engaging in a new productivity of that which heals and transforms.

This could be, for any one of us, a return to our true self after almost being talked of it. So the Psalm for the day ends in trusting satisfaction:

My soul is satisfied as with a rich feast,
and my mouth praises you with joyful lips
when I think of you on my bed,
and meditate on you in the watches of the night;
for you have been my help
and in the shadow of your wings I sing for joy.
My soul clings to you;
your right hand upholds me.
                                        (Ps. 63:5–8)

'Tis a gift to come down where we ought to be!

March 3, 2013
Fourth Presbyterian Church, Chicago

18

Seeing Clearly, Loving Dearly, Following Nearly

1 SAMUEL 16:1–13
PSALM 23
JOHN 9:1–41

It is all about seeing or not seeing, or refusing to see, or being unable to see, or being nurtured not to see. It is all about noticing or not noticing, or refusing to notice, or being unable to notice, or being nurtured not to notice.

I.

The man born blind is a witness. He testifies about his own transformation from blindness to sight. But he cannot testify about his changed condition without bearing witness about Jesus, because his new sight is a gift given by Jesus. So he answers his curious neighbors:

> I am the man who was born blind.
> The man called Jesus made mud, spread it on my eyes and said to me, "Go to Siloam and wash." Then I went and washed and received my sight.
> When they asked him where Jesus was, he said,
> "I do not know."

That conversation was simply low-key neighborly gossip.

II.

But you do not get a witness unless matters are in dispute. The narrative moves from gossip to a trial conducted by the local elite who are introduced into the story with this curious note:

92

Now it was a sabbath day when Jesus made the mud and opened his eyes. (John 9:14)

The elite do a thorough investigation with extended interrogation, because they wanted to get to the bottom of this strange occurrence; it is not every day that a blind person comes to sight! The reason they want to get to the bottom of this is that it did not fit their categories of understanding and control. They could not explain it or manage it, so it was a threat to them. They quizzed the man and he gave them the same story:

"He put mud on my eyes; I washed and now I see." (v. 15b)

The authorities make a surprising response to the testimony of the man who now can see. They do not respond to the wonder of new sight. Rather they focus on the time table, rather like "What did he do and when did he do it?" And they draw a damning conclusion:
Jesus does not observe sabbath!
He healed on the sabbath. He did not respect the old regulations. He refused the commands of his religion. They neglected the wonder and focused on a detail of holy time, of church calendar, that did not interest the man at all. He could care less about a religious calendar, because now he could see!
What follows is an attempt by the authorities to reframe the case around sabbath requirements rather than the miracle. They want to defuse the miracle. They extend the interrogation to the parents of the blind man who can see. But the parents are scared to death of the authorities. They say,

"We do not know who opened his eyes. Ask him, he can speak for himself."

The parents never mention the name of Jesus. Maybe they did not know. More likely they could not risk his name, because his name, as his presence, was a threat that called into question all status quo arrangements.
As a result of that questioning that led nowhere, the interrogators go back to the man himself. But he will not change his story. He is impatient and irritated with them because the matter is not at all ambiguous to him.

"I already told you. If you would not listen the first time, why do you want to hear my testimony again?"

He taunts them.

"Do you want to become his disciples? Are you about to trust my testimony?"

That would be a real breakthrough. He mocks them. You are so smart. But you cannot explain this because what has happened outruns all of your controlling explanations. And they respond with their high-handed indignation, like a cat arches its back under threat:

> "Are you trying to instruct us?"

III.

The confrontation between the authorities and the man who can now see is a dramatic one. It is a contrast between *old established truth* that keeps everything in place that has all the answers, that keeps everything under control and assures certain entitlements, and on the other hand *new inexplicable possibility* by Jesus and eventually by his people. The contrast is clear and dramatic. This story in the Gospel of John is addressed to the reader. It asks the reader to decide about the old way of management and the new inexplicable possibility that goes out beyond our control. It asks, are you on the side of managed truth that keeps the world settled? Or have you signed on with the new possibility that comes when Jesus is present?

After this long commentary and exchange in the text in which the authorities are shown to be losing the argument, Jesus reengages the narrative. He has not spoken for twenty-nine verses, not since he urged mud on the man's eyes. Now he addresses both the man who can see and the authorities. He speaks first to the man who now can see:

> "Do you like believe in the Son of Man, this strange figure beyond our management?"

The man answers,

> "Who is he, sir?"

Jesus says,

> "The one speaking to you is he."

That is: It's me! I am this Son of Man. I am the strange surge of God in the world beyond all old management. And the man replies,

> "I believe."

Or better, "I trust." And then he worshipped him! The man has the subject of his life changed. Now there is no looking back, no more argument with the authorities, no intimidation that catches his parents. Now there is only sub-mission to Jesus, the one who has the capacity to bring sight out of blindness, life out of death, and hope out of despair. In saying "I believe, I trust," the man defied the authorities and embraced the new possibility in Jesus.

And then Jesus addresses the obdurate authorities:

> "I came into the world for judgment (that is, for adjudicating the truth so that—get this—) so that those who do not see may see, and those who do see may become blind." (v. 39)

Jesus comes to scramble old categories so that that old assurances are placed under acute scrutiny. I came into the world to redefine what it means to see. And they, in their self-confidence said,

> "Surely we are not blind."

But they now begin to doubt themselves and their certitudes in Jesus' pres-ence, for they say,

> "Surely we are not blind, are we?" (v. 40)

And Jesus ends the story by saying,

> You say we see and your sin remains because the one thing you do not see is me.

The one thing not in their purview is Jesus. The one thing they miss is the defining power of Jesus that violates all of our assumptions about our life in the world.

IV.

So imagine us as participants in this great drama. Standing before Jesus is the one with new life who worships him and the defenders of old truth who refuse him. They each and all must decide about Jesus. It turns out that seeing is to accept Jesus and blindness is to refuse him.

And now we stand before the new chance of gospel possibility and old managed truth. Old managed truth, like the rule on the sabbath, takes many forms. It can be the old world of privilege and power and control. It can be the old truth of settled church orthodoxy. It can be the old mantras of market ideology that reduce life to owning and having and eating. It can be the old paralysis of privilege according to race, class, gender. It can be an old image given you by your mother or your father that has kept you from the freedom and joy of God's love.

And over against all of that old managed truth is this man who testified to new bodily possibility because Jesus has moved him into a new life that he did not even expect for himself. Jesus is an invitation and a chance and a summons to a different way of life. And we are always deciding.

This text strikes me as especially pertinent to us now. Because we are watching new reality being given us that does not fit old orders, now new possibilities,

> about a redefined social reality and neighborly economy,
> about a new church that is open to the real world,
> about a new social fabric in which generosity and justice are the order of the day.

We watch those emergents even while we see that the old world is in free fall.

We do not need to decide everything. What we need to decide concerns Jesus, the point person through whom God has unleashed well-being into the world. It is all about seeing or not seeing, or refusing to see, or being unable to see, or being nurtured not to see. It is all about noticing or not noticing, or refusing to notice, or being unable to notice, or being nurtured not to notice. And we are the ones who decide, who know enough about Jesus and about ourselves to say,

> "I was blind and now I see."

And we worship and give thanks and obey and bear witness. We say, I am the one who was blind. I have no explanation, but I received my sight. We see more clearly; then we love more dearly the one who gives sight. And then we follow more nearly, giving sight to others. Clearly, dearly, nearly. This does not make the old authorities happy; but it is the truth of our life.

March 30, 2014
Trinity Episcopal Church, Boston, Massachusetts

19

God's Easter Offer of Newness

JEREMIAH 31:31–34
PSALM 119:9–16
JOHN 12:20–33

The core truth of our faith is this: The God of the gospel brings life out of death. We can line out the move from death to life physically, historically, literally, metaphorically, symbolically . . . any way you want. But the truth is a rock bottom acknowledgement that God can probe into our deepest negations and create new possibility, new space for life, new energy for obedience, new waves of joy.

In the Christian tradition, the seal of the deal is Easter. On that dread Sunday morning the earliest church discovered that the Jesus who had been executed by the state was alive and on the loose; death had no power over God's will for life. The deathly systems of the empire had no grip on him even through his execution. It is an Easter mouthful!

I.

But in truth, the God of the gospel has been doing this forever:

It is this God of the gospel who took primordial *chaos* in hand, who said, "Let there be light," and formed a dry, ordered, fruitful land in which to live. And since that first moment, this God has been taking our dismal modes of chaos and forming them into launching pads for new life. That is life out of death!

It is this God of the gospel who came to that *barren*, hopeless couple, Abraham and Sarah in their old age, and gave them a child, an heir, and opened a future for them. And since then, the God of the gospel has been giving people

97

futures when they thought there was no possibility for newness. That is life out of death!

It is this God of the gospel who came to the *slaves* in Egypt, weary of being cheap labor in a harsh production system. God heard their cry under exploitation, saw their abuse, and came down to deliver them. And since that awesome moment, this emancipatory God has been hearing the cries of exploited people, and has been causing exploitative systems of cheap labor to collapse so that people can sing and dance in freedom. That is life out of death!

Everywhere we look in our memory of faith, we see this God who does these wonders of life where none was thought possible, into the hopelessness of chaos, the despair of barrenness, the abuse of enslavement that seemed like dead ends. This God makes a way out of no way!

II.

And now this text in Jeremiah 31. God speaks to the Israelites who ended up in the Babylonian imperial system; they were in despair of their life and their faith. God abruptly broke the despairing silence with a new declaration:

I will make *a new covenant* with you. I will establish a new relationship of fidelity with you. You will be able to count on my promise and my presence and my power for your life. As a result, the harsh reality of the imperial system of Babylon will no longer define your life, because it is my way of fidelity that will create new possibilities for you. That is why Handel, in his *Messiah*, could have us sing, "Comfort, comfort my people." The new covenant is new life out of the death of despair.

In this new covenant, God will *engraft God's Torah into their hearts.* The old Torah had been written on scrolls and they had resisted the scroll. They did not welcome the Torah in their lives. It was foreign to them and they wanted no part of it, and it ended for them in destructive recalcitrance, thinking they could have life on their own terms. But now, says the oracle, you will inhale the Torah, breathe in the commandments, so that they will become second nature to you; you will find in them a guide and a source for a different life in the world. You will be grateful for this icon of sanity in an insane world.

And, says the oracle of God, the basis for this new life will be the transformative declaration of God: "I will *forgive your iniquity* and remember your sin no more." Imagine that, this God holds no grudge. This God keeps no score. This God, in a plunge into self-giving, intends to break the cycle of death and despair and enslavement to begin again . . . fresh!

It is no wonder that the church took up this oracle from Jeremiah and claimed the new covenant of God for the New Testament and the new beginning and the new assertion of God's readiness for us in Christ. This newness is what God has been doing for a long time, self-giving fidelity on God's part that permits beginning again. This is indeed the stuff of resurrection to new life.

III.

The move from the prophetic oracle to the Psalm is a direct one. Psalm 119 is our longest Psalm. It goes on so long that we never read it all; we read about eight verses at a time. In our reading today, all eight verses in Hebrew begin with the letter Beth, "B." That is why we read eight verses, to get all the "Bees." It's all about the way to walk with God, the way of Torah; commandments are, in this Psalm, a source of delight. And when the Psalm refers to Torah (that we translate as "law"), it undoubtedly refers to the book Deuteronomy that is all about care for widows, orphans, immigrants, and poor people. It turns out that the new life in God's fidelity is a life for the neighborhood, a life devoted to the vulnerable, a life that includes all the others who are unlike us who are left behind by the imperial system of economics in which we live. Thus fidelity turns out to be solidarity between rich and poor, between the strong and the weak.

This is a life about changed priorities, new policies, new practices, new commitments of time and money, new initiatives of life for all our neighbors, away from the old ideologies of death that pervade our own imperial system. Resurrection life, here and now, is about resonance with the Lord of new life, with the freshness of forgiveness, with the inhaling of his commandments, and finding joy in the will and purpose of the God of new life.

IV.

When Jesus teaches his disciples, he tells them that he will die and be raised to new life. But he not only tells them of his destiny. He invites his disciples to walk that same way with him. He uses the image of grains of wheat being planted in the soil and being buried, so that it may sprout new life. The image is of dying to what is old to be surprised by what is new growth. The image is about "give it up." Give up what is old and deathly and greedy and anxious and hopeless. Give it up. Lose that old life.

And then he promises a new life given by God. He uses such imagery and teaching as a way of speaking of dying and being raised to newness. In the life of ancient Israel, such an image concerned displacement to exile, and homecoming to new covenant, new obedience, and new joy.

I do not need to tell you that in our society now, we must die to many old assumptions about wealth and power and control that have turned out to be a way of death. This is the drama of Lent, is it not? It is the journey of relinquishment of old visions of reality that are failed and being surprised by new life given in glad, inconvenient obedience. It is to this move that the God of the gospel invites us, again and again. This God is ready to give new life, more ready, as we say, to give than we are to receive.

March 25, 2012
Saint Michael and All Angels Episcopal Church, Dallas, Texas

20

On Changing Our Minds

PSALM 31:9–16
PHILIPPIANS 2:5–11
MATTHEW 27:11–54

Two things make Holy Week interesting and problematic for people of faith. On the one hand, as we move from Palm Sunday to Easter, we know how the week ends. It ends in Easter astonishment, Easter fear, Easter joy, Easter new life. But on the other hand, we also know we cannot leap from Palm Sunday to Easter. We have to go day by day through the week of denial and betrayal to the Last Supper to arrest and trial and execution. That is the only road to Easter, and that is our work this week.

I.

The long Gospel narrative is about that week. Matthew moves from the trial before Pilate to the mocking by the soldiers to the long detailed account of Jesus on the cross. It may strike you as odd that our reading is not about "the triumphal entry" on Palm Sunday with all of those palm branches. But that is because people do not much go to church on Thursday or Friday, and so we have to get the whole story in today. The Matthew narrative brings us to the abyss with Jesus' cry on the cross, "My God, my God, why have you forsaken me?" (Matt. 27:46) This is a moment of cosmic abandonment when Jesus is cut off from the life support of the Father. We linger there because Jesus dares to accuse the Father of infidelity and abandonment. There is no move in this story yet toward Easter, except the astonishing affirmation by the Roman soldier, one of the executioners. He said at the end of the story, "This man was God's Son." He said "This is the guy!" He must have thought, as he

101

recognized him, "What have we done?" Because the empire is always executing and eliminating those sent by God who are judged to be too dangerous and too subversive.

II.

But the narrative account is hyped by Paul who in Philippians quotes the most treasured, most pivotal hymn that was sung in the early church. It is a lyrical recital of Jesus' life and death. At the outset the hymn characterizes Jesus in the most exalted way as "in the form of God." But then second, it moves quickly to say that Jesus willingly and readily surrendered equality with God. He made himself vulnerable in human form and became obedient. He became an obedient human person and because of his passion for God's will for him, he collided with the will and purpose of the Roman Empire and with the Jews who colluded with the empire. He is not crucified because of some theory of the atonement. He is crucified because the empire cannot tolerate such a transformative, subversive force set loose in the world. Jesus' uncompromising commitment to the purpose of God contradicted the empire that lives against the grain of God's intention.

Then there is a pause in the poetry. It is a pause over Saturday. And then the hymn continues, "Therefore . . . " Consequently, as a result of his obedience . . . God has highly exalted. God has given him Easter honor and dominion and power as the Lord of the creation, as the ruler of all creation. This is indeed the "Fairest Lord Jesus, ruler of all nature." And we worship him!

The church recites this lyrical poetry of his *equality with God* . . . that he *emptied himself* in obedience . . . and then *exalted in honor.* This is the move from Palm Sunday through Friday emptiness to Sunday glory. It is the story of our faith and the work of this week.

III.

But there is a surprise in the letter of Paul. We move from the Matthew narrative to the lyrical hymn; both are all about Jesus. Except that in Philippians, Paul introduces the hymn with this preface:

Let the same mind be in you that was in Christ Jesus. (Phil. 2:5)

Have the same opinion that Jesus did. Then he describes the mind or the opinion of Jesus who emptied himself in obedience. Paul says to the church, be like that, think like that, have a mind like that, have a sense of self in the world like that. Think of yourselves in the way that Christ thought of himself.

And then, as a lead-in to the hymn, Paul teaches the church what that "same mind" would be like:

> Be of the same mind, having the same love, being in full accord and of one mind. Do nothing from selfish ambition or conceit, but in humility regard others as better than yourselves. Let each of you look not to your own interests, but to the interests of others. (vv. 2–4)

Paul summons the church and its members to exhibit in their common life the self-emptying that is congruent with Jesus. Paul knew about churches and about church people and the way we tend to act, concerned for self and our pet ideas and our intentions and our vested interests that bruise other people. And he said, do not look to your own interests.

So imagine the church, in this week of Friday and Sunday, in this drama of humiliation and exaltation, getting a new mind, a new opinion, a new readiness, a new heart in which church people do not pursue their own interests, but look to the interests of others:

> The old for the young and the young for the old,
> The wealthy for the poor and the poor for the wealthy,
> Liberals for conservatives and conservatives for liberals,
> Gays for straights and straights for gays,
> The included for the excluded, and on and on.

IV.

I assume you are enough like me for me to say this. This would require on our part a big change of mind, a renewed mind, a different opinion than the one we "normally" have. The mind we usually have, the mind that reflects the values and passions and fears of our society,

> Is to have our way as the only way,
> Is to exercise control,
> Is to be endlessly on the make,
> Is to imagine that those unlike us are a threat to us.

As a result the church becomes a mirror of the world in which we live.

The world in which we live, the world of self-serving preoccupation and greedy accumulation and fearful tensions and divisions is premised on a rat-race of competition, on the turmoil of ruthless individualism, and the collection of commodities, of rude social interaction and crude survival shows and toxic public life. And Paul says to the church, do not be so mindless. Do not be like sheep that imitate the world. Do not act like fearful citizens of the Roman Empire or of the American empire. Paul calls the church to be deeply and intentionally different. Paul does not do that so that the church can be the snug, comfortable happy place in town. Rather Paul intends that the church should be an exhibit to the world how our common life can be ordered differently, of rich and poor, gay and straight, liberal and conservative, even when we come to the great public questions of welfare and health and education and housing. All of that requires a different mind of obedience. The community gathered around Jesus is called to be as odd in the world as he himself was such an odd Messiah.

So here is my bid to you for Holy Week. As we walk the walk from Palm Sunday to Easter through the Thursday arrest and the Friday execution and the long Saturday wait in the void, imagine all of us, in the wake of Jesus, changing our minds, renewing our minds, altering our opinions concerning self and neighbor and world. The clue to the new mind of Christ is emptying of our need to control and our anxious passion for security. And as our minds change, we come to new freedom. It is Easter freedom, unburdened and fearless, freed for the interest of the neighbor. So we worship this Jesus who was dead and is alive, who was humbled and is exalted. But we also replicate his life in our own life. We find ourselves with Easter liberty to be our true selves as he himself was his true self. We know this very well: 'Tis a gift to be simple, 'tis a gift to be free, 'tis a gift to come down where we ought to be. And where we ought to be is right next to him in self-emptying obedience.

April 17, 2011
Highland Baptist Church, Louisville, Kentucky

21

Authorized for Risk

PSALM 150
JOHN 20:19–31
ACTS 5:27–32

Imagine the Roman Empire, its endless ambition and its endless wars. Imagine its troops always again going out to the fringes to stop the dissent, and word coming home always again of another violent death in "harm's way." Imagine the rat-race to pay taxes and 24/7 work to stay on top of the heap in the empire. Sound familiar? It was like that. And then, right in the middle of it, while his followers met where the doors were "locked for fear," he came. He stood there in the midst of the violent restless empire, and he said, "Peace be with you." They recognized him when they saw the scars on his body as he had been executed by the empire. This was the same Jesus of whom they despaired! And when they recognized him, he said a second time, "Peace be with you." The story exhibits the contradiction between the empire of death and the Living One whom the empire could not keep dead. We meet on this Easter Sunday to ponder that contradiction between *empire death* and *Easter life*, to consider our own faith amid the empire, and to be dazzled by the one who said then and who says now, "Peace."

I.

And then, "He breathed on them." In the Bible the notion of "breath" is the same word as "spirit." He gave them spirit. He performed artificial respiration on his bedraggled followers. He said, "Receive the Holy Spirit," which is the spirit of Jesus. He gave them the surging gift of surprising life, so unlike the lifeless charade of the empire that only knows about violence and control, but nothing about giving life.

Imagine a world of life come amid the destructiveness of empire. It is this life-carrier who said to his followers, "I give you the power to forgive sin." I recruit you for the forgiveness business. I charge you with healing, transformative reconciliation. It was then, and always is, a hard work for the church, because in the empire there is no free lunch, no open hand, no breaking of the vicious cycles of fear and violence and failure.

He said "peace." He gave spirit. He called to a ministry of forgiveness. And they knew it was the one they had trusted, for they saw the scars in his body left by the violence of the empire. They knew this was the real thing. They got it . . . except for Thomas. A week later he was still not convinced. But Jesus came again to them and said to them one more time: "Peace be with you." And Thomas touched the scars left by the empire. And then he is convinced enough to say, "My Lord and my God." Maybe that response is a big theological affirmation as the church has taken it to be. Maybe it is only an exclamation: "Oh my God!" Oh my God, it's him! Oh my God, he's alive! Oh my God, we are in the forgiveness business. He gave them breath; but he also took their breath away by his mandate.

II.

And then, it is reported, the followers of Jesus were touched with the power for life, summoned all around the empire, singing and dancing, healing and forgiving . . . all acts that contradicted the claims of the empire. In the story of the Book of Acts, we are told that the earliest church cured all sorts of people and cleansed folk of evil spirits, and it upset the empire that feared its loss of control. They arrested the apostles to curb this passionate movement of new life, but the jail did not hold them. It was reported to the authorities: "Look, the ones whom you put in prison are standing in the temple teaching the people" (Acts 5:25). They apostles were resilient and irresistible. And the high priest who had colluded with the empire confronted them in court:

> We gave you strict orders not to teach in this name, yet here you have filled Jerusalem with your teaching and you are determined to bring this man's blood on us. (v. 28)

The authorities did not even bother to argue about the claim of Easter resurrection. They just tried to shut them up about it.

So here is a first truth we get on this Second Sunday of Easter. The empire is scared to death of Easter. It does not want to know about God's power for life that is loosed in the world, because it does not want the world to change. It is like that with status quo power. It maintains itself by silencing voices to the contrary. It resists the power of transformation. It vetoes the thought of new possibility. It covers over the surging of the spirit with the tired ideologies of fear and intimidation. It recognizes that Easter is a threat to the old weary ways in the world and it does its best on Friday by executing him.

III.

But the story in Acts offers a second learning. The surging power of the Easter church is not throttled by the stifling of the empire. You can see that on every page of the Book of Acts. The Book of Acts is the account of that breathed-on church. Time after time, the Roman authorities . . . Felix, Festus, Agrippa . . . bring the Easter Christians into court and try to stop them, or silence them, or intimidate them, or imprison then. And time after time, the Easter church gives an account of itself and refuses the disciplines of the empire.

In our text in Acts 5, Peter speaks up for the church in perhaps the most breathtaking phrase we dare to imagine. He says to the imperial authorities, "We must obey God rather than any human authority." Or in the original patriarchal formulation, "We must obey God rather than man." The "man," the "human authority," not to be obeyed by the church is the Roman Empire. But beyond Rome, it is any form of the power of death that wants to shut down God's gift of life. And the God to be obeyed is the God who raised Jesus from the dead, the God who gives the spirit of life to the world, the God who calls the church into the forgiveness business. It is this God who must be obeyed rather than the old weary forms of death.

I submit to you, sisters and brothers, that the issue joined in the courtroom scene that day in the Book of Acts is no abstract or remote question. It was, and is, clearly a life-or-death decision that we are always making about the truth of Easter. We are always deciding whether we will succumb to despair as if the world were closed, or whether the world is permeated with healing powers. We are always deciding whether we shall be in denial in order to keep things as they are, or face the truth of our life and offer it to God. We are always deciding whether me-first consumerism is the way to well-being or whether outrageous generosity is a better route to real life.

The church in the narrative of Acts goes on to say:

We are witnesses to these things. (v. 32)

We are witnesses to the truth of Easter, to the power of life that God gives in the world. So imagine the Easter church in this place deciding afresh about contradicting the empire. The church, since the Book of Acts, bears witness to new Easter life, bears witness by generosity, by compassion, by hospitality, by justice and mercy. In a thousand ways, the church is restless for God's call to life.

IV.

The faith of the church culminates in praise. It ends, as does the Book of Psalms in Psalm 150, in full voiced exuberance, dancing for the news of new life given in the scarred body of Jesus:

> Praise the Lord!
> Praise God in his sanctuary;
>   praise him in his mighty firmament!
> Praise him for his mighty deeds;
>   praise him according to his surpassing greatness!
> Praise him with trumpet sound;
>   praise him with lute and harp!
> Praise him with tambourine and dance;
>   praise him with strings and pipe!
> Praise him with clanging cymbals;
>   praise him with loud clashing cymbals!
> Let everything that breathes praise the Lord!
> Praise the Lord!

Doxology is the outcome of Easter, referring our life over to God's goodness. I think the antithesis of doxology is a memo, the communication of clear, one-dimensional, unambiguous, controlling truth that fixes reality and keeps everything in its place. A memo is an instrument of control whether it is the "rules for engagement," or a complex tax code, or a settled catechism. But doxology is open, propelled by the spirit.

Well, it is a long way from Thomas who doubts to Peter who defies empire. But both of them, both Thomas in his doubt and Peter in his courage, speak for us. Thomas is skeptical and unsure. Peter is ready and overeager. Some of us are skeptical about the rush to civil disobedience. Some of us with abandon say, "Go for it." Or perhaps most of us know the mix of reluctance and eagerness in our own life.

So what should we do? Well, in the next paragraph in the Book of Acts, they argue in the Jewish council. Some want to kill the Easter folk and be done with it. But Gamaliel, shrewd rabbi that he is, says, "Let's give it more time and see what happens." Let's give the Easter movement some time and let's see if it will run beyond stifling empire in good ways.

So here is my pitch. Imagine that you and I, today, are a part of the Easter movement of civil disobedience that contradicts the empire. We are like Gamaliel: Let's see what happens. Let's see if life is longer than death. Some will never move, but will keep trusting in the empire. But we know this much: we have been breathed on. We have been addressed. To us he said, "Peace be with you." He said it three times, and then he charged us with forgiveness. We are on the receiving end from him of his offer of life . . . praise God!

April 11, 2010
University Congregational UCC, Seattle, Washington

22

Following the Sunday Guy

JOHN 21:1–19
ACTS 9:1–20

Nobody knew how long Saturday would last. Nobody knew if Saturday would ever end. So it is now as well. Nobody knows how long Saturday will last or if it will ever end. Saturday is that in-between day of stillness and doubt and despair when time stands still in lethal flatness. The old Saturday was about abandonment and disappointment at the far edge of the crucifixion. And then came all the Saturdays of fear and abusiveness, of the Crusades and the ovens and genocides in too many places. And then came our particular Saturdays of Katrina and 9/11 and economic collapse, Saturdays of overwhelming failure with no adequate resources. That is the mood of the drama in our gospel narrative.

I.

In the midst of that desperate stillness, the church listens yet again to another narrative that interrupts and intrudes and summons and haunts. The key character of this other narrative around which we gather is the Friday guy done in by the rulers of this age. That much they knew on Saturday; but that did not comfort them at all on Saturday. The wonder of the narrative around which we gather is that the Friday guy did not linger long on Saturday, but turns out to be the Sunday guy—not good clothes and proper behavior and much piety—but the first day of the week . . . the first day of the new world, and for those who engage, the first day of new life in the world. The way our texts are arranged today in the lectionary we have the ultimate story about

110

Jesus, and then a sidebar about Paul as a case study, the latter to show that the Jesus narrative touches down concretely in lived reality.

So consider this Sunday narrative that may interrupt your shadowed reality of Saturday. The disciples were out fishing; they had returned to their pre-Jesus existence, as though he had never been there. Then, at daybreak, he asked them about their work. He instructed them about where to fish . . . which worked! In that moment of his effectiveness, John had an instant of recognition: "It is the Lord," unexpected, inexplicable, full of life. They were not sure, but they could not ask him about his identity, because he had already told them. They did know . . . but they could not compute it. They were dazzled, but also baffled.

This story has always taken away the breath of the church, because church people are the ones who have found their Saturday life abruptly interrupted by a transformative presence who interrogates and instructs and then feeds. The background is to find out how it is for you on the Saturday of disappointment and abandonment. The interruption is an offer of an alternative. And then breakfast, because Jesus is known in the church as the one who nourishes and feeds and restores.

The abruptness of the Sunday guy is echoed in the Damascus Road story of Saul. He had been a persecutor of the church, an angry guy trying to keep the lid on God's newness, trying to keep things the way they had always been. He hears this voice query him: "What are you doing? Why are you doing it?" Saul of course does not recognize him. So he announces his identity to Saul: "I am Jesus." And then everything was changed: his name, his identity, his vocation, his sense of himself, because he had moved out of his frantic holding action of Saturday when the Sunday guy came upon him. The word from John and Saul is: expect to be interrupted in the midst of your Saturday dismay.

II.

After Jesus had provided this inexplicable breakfast, he begins to interrogate his disciples. He wants to know the lay of the land after the pain and fear of Friday. Three times he asks, "Do you love me?" Do you still love me the way you thought you did before Friday? Do you love me after the long Saturday you have faced? Do you love me enough to change your life? Do you trust me? Are you ready to commit to me? And three times Peter answers:

Yes, Lord; you know that I love you.
Yes, Lord, you know that I love you.
Lord, you know everything; you know that I love you.
(John 21:15–17)

The narrator reports that Peter was hurt because he had asked him three times. But that is how serious love is. It is probing and demanding, and unwilling to settle for flip answers.

And then Jesus says, "Don't talk of love . . . show me!" Show me by your actions; show me by your changed conduct:

> Feed my lambs.
> Tend my sheep.
> Feed my sheep.

"Sheep and lambs" are those entrusted to the Good Shepherd. We know about the good shepherd, the one who leads beside still waters, the one who restores my life, the one who lays down his life for the sheep, the one who goes out to find the lost sheep. Indeed, back in the prophet Ezekiel God exhibits all the qualities of the Good Shepherd:

> I myself will be the shepherd of my sheep, and I will make them lie down, says the LORD GOD. I will seek the lost, and I will bring back the strayed, and I will bind up the injured, and I will strengthen the weak, but the fat and strong I will destroy. I will feed them with justice. (Ezek. 34:15–16)

But now, says Jesus to the disciples whose life he has interrupted: "You do it!" You be the shepherd. You restore life. You lay down your life for the sheep. You go and find the lost and bring them home. You bring back the strayed. You bind up the injured. You strengthen the weak. You feed them with justice.

The Sunday guy speaks in an imperative, and the disciples are under mandate. It is the same with Paul en route to Damascus. Jesus says to him, "Get up and enter the city and do what you are told." And then Jesus commands Ananias: "Get up and go." Ananias resists, because Saul has been a bad guy and he does not much like or trust him. But Jesus says to him:

> "Go, for he is an instrument whom I have chosen to bring my name before Gentiles and kings and before the people of Israel." (Acts 9:15)

The Sunday guy has in mind active love on a big scale, a love that is to reach the Gentiles (the unacceptable "other") and even to reach kings and summon them to another way of life in the world. Paul will do this, under mandate; and Ananias, against his own better judgment, is to help this happen.

Nothing here about a mandate to purity. Nothing about pure teaching. Nothing here about putting the wagons in a circle. Nothing here about maintenance of or custodial care of the status quo. But also nothing here of shrill ideological sureness. All an extension of the food-gift of the creator God to all those who are hungry. It is a big mandate to the disciples. They had gotten a free breakfast. From now on, they have work to do, as we say, providing *Bread for the World*.

III.

And then Jesus knows that they wonder how the future will turn out for them if they are obedient to the mandate to feed the sheep. The disciples of course always worry about their own skin. Well, the Sunday guy says, I will tell about your future with me. And then he takes up a familiar narrative about what happens in old age. When you lose control of your life, and other people tell you what to do and how fast to do it. When you reach that point, they will take your driver's license away from you. And they will move you into a "care facility" where you do not want to go. He says:

> When you are younger, you used to fasten your own belt and to go where you wished.
>   But when you get old: You will stretch out your hands, and someone else will fasten a belt around you and take you where you do not wish to go. (John 21:18)

Because you will end up powerless. It sounds like "Grow old along with me." And it could be that, if it ended there. But the next sentence makes clear that this is not really a comment about old age. This is what will happen because you are in conflict with the authorities. You will be arrested because the status quo cannot tolerate the Sunday guy who contradicts the status quo. The authorities will take you where you do not want to go; eventually they will crucify you because you are allied with the Easter guy. That is, the mandate to feed the sheep out of divine abundance is a countercultural act against the authorities who thrive on scarcity, and so you will be deeply at risk.

It is not different with Paul. Jesus tells Ananias with reference to Paul:

> "I myself will show him how much he must suffer for the sake of my name." (Acts 9:16)

The new life given Paul is a life of deep risk. So far as the tradition tells us, he ended his life by being executed by the authorities in Rome. In Paul's case, he was baptized into the community of Jesus. And he spent the rest of the book of Acts in court, on trial for his faith. The narrative of Jesus is more terse. Just this:

Follow me!

That is all. Follow me into the new life of Easter. Follow me into the transformative feeding of the world. Follow me into daring countercultural activity. Follow me in offering the world an alternative life of justice and compassion and mercy and generosity that is not otherwise given. Follow me in the story of baptism and conversion and new obedience.

In the gospel narrative, we can track the entire work of Easter:

- He surprised them by his presence; he interrupted and changed their lives.
- He gave them a mandate to act out their love in concrete ways in the world.
- He anticipated that their obedience to him would put them at risk.

It is the same with Paul:

- He was interrupted: "I am Jesus."
- He was dispatched to Gentiles and kings with a mandate for new life.
- He was put at risk before the authorities.

This narrative about the Sunday guy is urgent among us because it is clear that the old narratives of money and power and violence and control have failed. There is among us a wonderment about another way in the world. This is it! It is discipleship after the guy who started the world again. And now in the church, all of us—conservatives and progressives—are wondering about this alternative.

We are not sure
But we expect to be interrupted;
We expect to be given a mandate;
We expect to be put at risk.

We are not sure; but we are haunted at the thought of it.

April 18, 2009
Church of the Covenant, Cleveland, Ohio

23

Voices against Monologue

PSALM 4
ACTS 3:12–19
I JOHN 3:1–7
JOHN 24:36B–48

Monologue—one person doing all the talking—is almost always top-down. Sometimes monologue is coercive and the top-down is authoritarian. Sometimes monologue is violent, when the top-down is a dictator or a totalitarian regime. Sometimes monologue is welcome as a way of giving certitude when one voice settles everything, and there is no debate or interpretation or uncertainty. Monologue can be a temptation or a seduction in which we collude or it may be a heavy imposition and a burden.

I.

We are watching now the breakup of many monologues, and I think that breakup leaves many of us uneasy and uncertain, because voices that have been long silenced are now breaking that silence:

> We have watched that in the civil rights moment as some African Americans spoke in abrasive ways about the rights of citizenship and the abuse of those rights.
> We have watched as some women have found voice and refused to stay in the kitchen.
> We are watching as gays and lesbians find their voice, and it makes some people very nervous.
> We are watching young people in the Arab world find their voices, and they shake up old patterns of order and power, to say nothing of our own Occupy Wall Street Movement.

And if or when we go for pastoral counseling we often discover in ourselves that there are many voices of the self that have been silenced and now will speak out. Sometimes those voices are shrill and filled with anger; sometimes they make sounds of loneliness and sadness and loss that we did not know we could speak, sometimes they are fresh statements of hope that have been suppressed for too long.

We live much of our life in a world where "father knows best" or teacher knows best or doctor knows best. But we are, each of us, a collage of voices, and we are deciding, yet again, which voices are to be allowed and which voices are too upsetting, and which voices are better off silenced, even if it takes coercion or threat to maintain that silence.

II.

I thought about monologue and the many voices of our lives as I considered Psalm 4, the assigned Psalm for the day. In fact the book of Psalms is a script of many voices coming to speech, all of them permitted, all of them addressed to God, all of them with freedom to say what must be said, even if it is awkward or offensive. As you may know, the Episcopalians have a collect prayer that addresses God as the one from whom no secret can be hid. Well, the Psalms tell all of our secrets to God. The Psalms take God very seriously; they engage in dialogic conversation with God that is, itself, a map and a generator for health and healing. For we know that silence kills. And when some voices of our lives are silenced or discredited, we are diminished by that much. My purpose now is to invite you to hear the many voices in the Psalm and then to think about how these voices swirl around in our lives, and how they may be brought before the throne of God as a way of telling the secrets of our lives that must be told if we are to be free in the gospel.

III.

This Psalm that tells one's whole life to God includes six distinct accents about which we all know:

1. Faith is the voice of *urgent asking from God*:

> Answer me when I call, O God of my right!
> You gave me room when I was in distress.
> Be gracious to me, and hear my prayer.
> (Ps. 4:1)

Imagine addressing God with imperatives. There are three of them:

Answer me;
Be gracious to me;
Hear my prayer.

The prayer is simple, direct, and urgent. The speaker can remember a time past in distress when God rescued; the Psalmist was in a tight place and God "gave room." But this, now, is a new time of crisis. The speaker knows more is needed from God than he can muster for himself.

2. Faith is the voice of *scolding conflict*:

How long, you people, shall my honor suffer shame?
How long will you love vain words, and seek after lies?
(v. 2)

The verse has two questions. But they are rhetorical questions that are in fact accusations that "you people," that is, my neighbors, have dishonored me and spoken lies about me. In any intense community, gossip and slander are most destructive practices. So right in the middle of this prayer to God, the Psalmist looks away long enough and is distracted enough to express anger toward neighbor. But our prayers are like that. We think and feel many things while we pray, even when we are in God's presence.

3. Faith is the voice of complete confidence in God:

But know that the LORD has set apart the faithful for himself;
the LORD hears when I call to him.
(v. 3)

This speaker knows that this is a God who pays attention. More than that, the speaker has a conviction that he himself is very special to God. Others may also be special to God. But I am! God has set me apart by God's attentiveness and love. God has marked me as a special object of love and care. This verse seems to offset the previous voice of anger. While my neighbors abuse me, God cherishes me. But that does not lessen the sting of the abuse I just mentioned in the last verse, but that is not the last word I will speak.

4. Faith is the voice of *nighttime resolve*. When we have the quiet and dark of the night on our beds, we feel and think all kinds of things that do not occur during the day. That is because our guard is down; we are vulnerable, and hidden things in our lives surface to us for which we had no time during the day. Thus verses 4–5 of this Psalm are a report on what happens to this Psalmist

in the night. He decided, right in the middle of the night, not to spend the night in anxiety:

> When you are disturbed, do not sin;
> ponder it on your beds, and be silent.
> (v. 4)

He recognizes that it will not do any good to toss and turn in anxiety or in anger through the night. And so he decides how to handle this distress he feels:

> Offer right sacrifices,
> And put your trust in the Lord.
> (v. 5)

He decides that instead of worry to bring an offering to God. We can imagine that when he decided to give his life over to God by way of an offering, he could roll over and sleep, and find undisturbed rest. But that rest required of him self-giving to God, something of value that is an act of love toward God, a yielding of self.

5. Faith is the voice of *satisfied praise*. The Psalmist praises God because he has more than a good farm crop, more than a generous yield of grain or wine:

> You have put gladness in my heart
> more than when their grain and wine abound.
> (v. 7)

This gladness is contrasted in verse 6 with those who are restless and always hope for a richer revelation:

> There are many who say,
> "O that we might see some good!
> Let the light of your face shine on us, O Lord".
> (v. 6)

The Psalmist is not that greedy or grasping for more from God. He has enough. He can recognize the gifts he has received from God and is grateful. He is not in competition for a better spirituality.

6. Faith is the voice of peaceable companionship:

> I will lie down and sleep in peace;
> for you alone, O Lord, make me lie down in safety.
> (v. 8)

Now, at the end of the Psalm, he is at rest, undisturbed. He has found rest for his life in the presence and faithfulness of God. He has come to see that his rest can come only from God: "You alone." You alone keep me safe and glad. He has not found such well-being anywhere else, but now treasures intimacy with God that he has received because he has voiced all his secrets to God.

III.

What becomes clear in this Psalm, as in many of the Psalms, is that this speaker is a cacophony of many voices, all of which are to be said out loud to God. The Psalmist exhibits his own depth and complexity, as he lines out for God his need, his anger, his anxiety, his hope, his faith, all in the midst of his abusive neighbors. He is a self of many voices, many secrets that do not need to be silenced before God.

This is the wonderful thing about the Psalms, that they give voice to our complexity. This is the wonderful thing about the God of the Gospel, that this God allows, attends to, and honors all the voices of our life and engages in dialogue with us, hearing and answering and caring. No secrets are withheld from this God who knows and hears all of our secrets.

So imagine that this human person in the Psalm is a collage of many voices that do not all fit together, but all are honored by God. And in the church there is exactly such a collage of voices that do not all fit together but all must be heard. And beyond that, our society, the city, the neighborhood is a collage of many voices that do not all fit together, but all are permitted and all are heard and honored.

There is great pressure among us to silence voices, to stop the dialogue and reduce life to a monologue of approved speech, of those who think just the way I do. Against that, imagine that in your dealing with your neighbor, with your adversary, or with those in your own family, or those who upset you the most they, like you, are a collage of many voices that for the sake of life and health, must be heard and honored.

Every time we speak or every time we listen, the world changes. Such conversation always feels like risk and always makes things new. The Psalm shows that the God of good news is a party to our conversations; that is the way in which we live the full life that God gives us. Did you notice that the last line of this Psalm, "You make me lie down in safety," echoes Psalm 23 about the one who is our shepherd? This is good news for us in a world filled with risk and possibility.

April 22, 2012
Asbury First United Methodist Church, Rochester, New York

24

Little Resurrections

After the Big One

PSALM 23
ACTS 4:5–12
1 JOHN 3:16–24
JOHN 10:11–18

In the book of Acts, the apostles and witnesses and preachers and church folk were running loose in the Roman Empire. They were talking gospel talk and they were walking the walk of empowered obedience to the gospel. As a result they were drawing big crowds of people who were taken with their talk and were mesmerized by their walk of empowered obedience.

I.

It will not surprise you that the managers of the Roman Empire were made nervous by this unauthorized movement. The authorities who were in charge of money, power, and control were, we are told, "amazed" by what they saw and heard. The wanted, at all costs, to maintain order and stability and control, so that their own privileged status could be maintained. We are told, in verse 1, that "priests, captain of the temple, the Sadducees" joined the crowd to listen to those who gathered to the talk for the church. These are the religious leaders who were in collusion with the status quo of the superpower, Rome. They no doubt took notes on the teaching of the apostles. And in verse 5, we are told, the assembly of heavyweights included elders and scribes, Annas the high priest, John and Alexander and all who were of the high priestly family. This is the local power structure that owed its life and its status to the authority of the empire. They brought the apostles in for questioning. They asked them the core question that nervous authorities always ask those who threaten:

By what authority or by what name do you do this?

You clearly are not acting from our authority because we never authorized you; and if we did not authorize you, you must claim some other authority that is a threat to our authority. They wanted to understand and control and limit this counter authority. The question they asked is an act of intimidation that the empire always speaks to dissenters.

II.

They did not ask, "By what authority do you teach?" They said, "By what authority did you *do* this?" The reference is back to the beginning of chapter 3 when Peter and John, on their way to the temple, saw the lame beggar. The beggar asked them for money. But they told him,

"We will do better than that. In the name of Jesus, stand up and walk."

And immediately, we are told, the lame beggar stood up and walked and leapt for joy.

His feet and ankles were made strong.

The apostles have performed *a mini-resurrection*. They have rehabilitated a disabled guy and invited him back into the stream of social life.

This mini-resurrection constituted a huge threat to the authorities who ran the superpower, because they imagined and claimed to have a monopoly on all life-giving resources and procedures. It was a cause for alarm for them to think that some other power for life was loose among them that they could not limit or administer. So they asked,

By what power and by what name did you do this?

Because it was not in the name of Caesar or any of the recognized authorities of government, or corporate life, or any of the normal accrediting agencies.

III.

The church leaders are questioned by the authorities. And then Peter answered them. He was "filled with the Holy Spirit," which means he had a surge of energy out beyond explanation. He was permeated with energy and courage, not at all cowed by or intimidated by imperial surveillance. He addressed the court that had sent him to jail:

Rulers of the people and elders.

Dear power Structure! We did a good deed to a man who is sick. Does a good deed make you nervous because you did not authorize it? He mocks the authorities, because he is not intimidated. Well, I will answer your question about the source of our action:

The man before you in good health is standing there by the name of Jesus Christ of Nazareth.

Talk about health care! If you want to talk about health care and health reform and extension of benefits to the unqualified with pre-existing conditions, this is the Jesus whom you executed as an enemy of the state, because he threatened your status quo. This is the one whom God raised from the dead. This is the Easter guy whom imperial execution could not limit. This is the one through whom God has unleashed into the world the juices of life and health and well-being. Easter resurrection is an act that defies the control of the superpower.

And what we have done is to take this *big resurrection* of Jesus that transforms the world into a venue for life, and on that basis we have performed this *little resurrection* for this disabled beggar by restoring him to life.

The bold statement of Peter accomplished two things at the same time. It is a declaration about Jesus who is the source of new life in the world. It is also a negative declaration about the empire of money, power, and control, that it has no power for life. It cannot give life; nor can it preclude life when the Jesus people get under way.

When they heard Peter, the authorities were stunned into silence, because this was a reality that fit none of their categories, the notion that well-being is given by the bold followers of Jesus who live outside the approved systems of power. The speech of Peter took their breath away, as it might take our breath away as well.

IV.

What might alert us in this story is the way in which *the big resurrection* of Jesus eventuates in *a mini-resurrection* of the disabled beggar that is enacted by the followers of Jesus. Thus I invite you to think about this:

First, the big resurrection is the basic truth of the church. It is all about the wonder of Easter that defied the control of the dominant system.

Second, on the basis of that big Easter, the church has power to enact mini-resurrections, for the poor, the lame, the disabled, the marginal, all acts of restoration that disturb and disrupt the status quo.

Third, the status quo power system can never understand or control or fully allow that power for life to be enacted.

As we come to this table of life, imagine that it is also a venue for resurrection:

> You also are a child of the big wonder of Easter;
> You also are authorized to perform mini-resurrections that restore life;
> You also are invited to defy settled status quo arrangements, because this power for life surges among us.

This is an ancient story; it is at the same time a contemporary story. It turns out to be our story of the big resurrection and the many mini-resurrections that are enacted in its wake. It is no wonder that the authorities had their breath taken away.

April 29, 2012
St. Thomas Episcopal Church, Fort Washington, Pennsylvania

25

Beyond the Ordeal

PSALM 23
JOHN 10:22–30
ACTS 9:31–43
REVELATION 7:9–17

I am about to commit an act of great risk. I am about to comment on this text from the book of Revelation. I do so because it is the appointed text for the day. It is a risk because I do not know any of you. I do not know how literal or imaginative any of you may be. It is a risk because every religious nut takes up the book of Revelation with time lines and schedules and explanations. And the book of Revelation is very accommodating; it is so pliable and open that it lets us all have our way with it. So here is my way.

The text moves in three dramatic scenes. It is, altogether, a vision or a dream or an imagination about what goes on eternally in the presence of God. Of course we do not know at all what goes on there; so we are free, along with the book of Revelation, to engage in poetic fantasy that may have a twinge of concrete reality to it.

I.

The opening scene of this text is *a great panorama of the gathering of heaven*, a multitude of folk all dressed in the innocence of white with palm branches and singing at the top of their lungs. I suspect there are a lot of Disciples of Christ there, because Disciples of Christ are among the best singers in the church. These are the ones who are known to be fit for heaven, suitable for the presence of God, engaged in long term voicing of doxology, for they have long known that the chief purpose of human persons is "to glorify God and enjoy God forever." The outcome of a well-lived life in the presence of God is not

124

the rat-race of producing and consuming; it is singing, praising, celebrating, and rejoicing in the wonder of God who is beyond all of our anxieties and our needs. All of that praise is addressed to God along with the Lamb, Jesus, who sits with God in that glorious realm. It is a fantasy of every nation, tribe, people, and language in peaceable company, no racial divide, no ethnic privilege, no national arrogance, all together in gladness before God, the recipient of all we can offer.

They sing their whole life back to God:

> Blessing, glory, wisdom, thanksgiving, honor, power, might . . . forever and ever.

What else is there? All to God, nothing held back! All to God in gladness, the offer of our best, healed, loved whole selves, our true destiny.

II.

The singing is interrupted by one of the elders. You know, elders are the wise careful ones who make sure that nobody gets by with anything. This elder has observed this glorious singing and wonders what is going on. Maybe he thought they were having too much fun. Or maybe he thought such a performance to all eternity was too much for God, because it does not seem like normal conduct, even in heaven. So *the elder asks about these singers*. He asks what we always wonder when there is an intrusion of people who seem a bit unlike us:

> Who are they, robed in white?
> Where do they come from?

And answer is given:

> They are the ones who have been through the great ordeal.

This answer is the pivot point in the text on which everything turns. A lot of craziness has been written about "the end of the world," but in fact the term here, ordeal, refers to the persecution of Christians by the Roman Empire. These are the ones who did not flinch about their faith, but remained true to their faith, honored their confession of Christ, and kept their identity. For some, this faith led to suffering and martyrdom. The phrasing, "They cleansed their robes" is an allusion to their baptism. Many others did not stand fast, and so never made it to the awesome sing-fest in heaven. The book of Revelation is an urging to keep our baptismal identity when it is not easy to do so.

Now this pivot point in the text does not concern us. Because in our society we face no such anguish of suffering or threat of martyrdom. So I asked myself, where is there a connection between this poetry of the ordeal and the life we now live? I believe it is this: Our society now faces the anguish of turning loose of a world that some of us have loved a lot, from which we have benefitted a lot, and in which some of us have suffered a lot. It has been a world of privilege and entitlement and prosperity for those of us who have been white and male and heterosexual. And many others have been "left behind" and excluded. And we did not much notice or care.

And now we face the anguish of that world dying. Much of our privilege in the world is under serious challenge and much of our entitlement is disappearing. We are now finding many other people in our society who want a slice of the pie that makes for smaller slices. We are facing the reality of loss of domination in the world, and we cannot any longer pay for it to keep it going with a limitless defense budget. We are learning, moreover, that the undisciplined exploitative use of the environment to our advantage is unsustainable, and now requires more regulation in order to protect what we can for our children after us, that God's creation should be honored, loved, and cherished. Thus we face the diminishment of old patterns of racial superiority, of national domination, of environmental indifference, and of economic mastery. The loss is huge, enough to cause anguish.

Given all of this, there is considerable anguish among us. The loss produces fear and anxiety, very often anger, sometimes hate, and eventually violence. We now live in a society of resentment and alienation in which there is greed to get a full share while there are still shares available, and neighbors are seen as rivals, competitors, or threats. Or instead of facing the reality of the anguish, we divert our energy to the chase for more commodities, or the illusions of cosmetics or the macho of sports.

In the midst of that anguish, however, there are those who made it through to the singing. In the words of the text, they are those who washed their robes and have been made white (pure) in the blood of the lamb. That old phrasing is a reference to baptism. These are the ones who have been baptized in the gospel who now participate in the anguish in a different way, in a way that is healing, transformative, generative, and hospitable. We never really know about our Christian vocation in baptism until we get to the anguish. And then, in the anguish of the old world ending, we are aware that we are called to live and act differently:

- Instead of refusing "the other"—gays, immigrants, Muslims—as threats, we take them as neighbors.

- Instead of greedy economics that serve our privilege, where all the others, especially prisoners and the disabled, are treated with dignity.
- Instead of environmental self-indulgence that pollutes and destroys, we are committed to ecological responsibility, to accept discipline, limit, and regulation, even if they inconvenience us and lead to a revised standard of living.
- Instead of strident nationalism, we take seriously the community of nations, knowing that peace and justice is a shared task that requires participation rather than domination.

What the anguish does is summon us to exercise our baptismal identity and live out our identity in Christ. The anguish causes us to decide. We can fall out of our baptism and join the parade of greed and fear and anxiety, and embrace the outcomes of alienation and violence. That is what happened to those Christians in the Roman Empire who fell out of their baptism. But we need not. These old saints imagined in white robes gathered around the throne of God in a song-fest are models of choosing another way in the world. We follow after them, entering the anguish in faithful ways and joining in the glad doxology.

III.

So the text says of their courageous obedience to the Gospel:

For this reason they are before the throne of God.
For this reason, for keeping baptismal faith through the anguish.
For this reason not giving up baptismal identity.
For this reason of knowing that the Gospel matters in the crush of real dismay.
For this reason the future of glad worship of the true God, in this age and in the age to come.

And then the poetry imagines the well-being to be given to those who have been steadfast amid the anguish:

They will hunger no more and thirst no more. (Rev. 7:16)

Already Jesus had said:

"Blessed are those who hunger and thirst for righteousness, for they shall be filled." (Matt. 5:6)

This same Jesus said,

"I am the bread of life. Whoever comes to me will never be hungry, and whoever believes in me will never be thirsty." (John 6:35)

"Do not be anxious about what you shall eat or where you shall live or what you shall wear, because your heavenly father knows you need all these things." (Matt. 6:25)

Already the Psalmist had affirmed:

The sun will not smite you by day nor the moon by night.

As though to reassure even in the face of global warming. Because steadfastness in anguish may turn back the unbearable heat.

He will guide them to springs of living water. (v. 17a)

Already the Psalmist had asserted in our Psalm of the day:

He leads me beside still waters, he restores my soul.

Not a bad promise in the midst of the arid Southwest.

God will wipe away every tear from their eyes. (v. 17b)

You will enter the future engaged in endless singing beyond sadness. They are to be in the presence of the God of life and do not face grief anymore.
This four-fold promise—of no hunger or thirst, no threat from the sun, no lack of living water, no tears—is a wondrous vision of a future given beyond the anguish for those who do not blink or fold. It is daring poetry as fulfillment of God's provision

of food,
of environmental protection,
of water,
of joy beyond every sadness.

It is poetry, an act of daring imagination. And each of us takes the part that rings true, as both summons and as assurance.

IV.

This is the move of the text and it is the move of our life in Christ:

- to be present in the anguish of the day in generative ways;
- to move through the ordeal to a new God-given well-being.

It is promised and it is imagined. Not all made that move through. Some succumbed to the anguish and were devoured by fear, anxiety, and hate. But when we hold this vision of glad singing around the throne, we can entertain the thought that the path to such joy is the path of baptismal action as courageous obedience. We are a people equipped for such a hard time as this and for such joy in the midst of it. This is indeed our time for glad obedience!

April 21, 2013
First Christian Church, Norman, Oklahoma

26

The Snares of Death and the Drama of Good News

PSALM 116:1–3, 10–17
ACTS 2:14, 36–41
I PETER 1:17–23
LUKE 24:13–25

Did you know that the classic Reformation sermon had three accent points? Some preachers of the old school thought it was any old three points, and Methodists thought it was three points and a poem. Many preachers believed it was three points and an illustration, even if the illustration did not really illustrate anything.

I.

But in truth, the three points that shaped the classic evangelical sermon were three crucial theological claims,

- that we are caught in the snares of death;
- that we have been rescued by the power of God;
- that we are released to a new life of gratitude.

That is the sum of the Gospel. And we can, if we are not vigilant, default on any of these three claims:

We can *refuse* to recognize that we are caught in the snares of death.
We can *deny* the saving power of God who changes everything.
We can *reject* a new life of gratitude.

But the accent for us is not on our possible refusal, or our possible denial or our possible rejection. It is, rather, on our willingness to walk through this

130

drama that, because of the goodness of God, keeps being re-performed again and again, in the life of the world. We baptized people are witnesses to the claim that this drama is real and valid and transformative.

II.

That drama is performed in all of our readings for today.

The drama is lined out *in the Psalm* that we have sung, a classic formulation of the truth of the gospel:

> verse 3: The snares of death encompassed me;
> verse 8: For you have delivered my soul from death;
> verse 17: I will offer to you a thanksgiving sacrifice and call on the name of the Lord.

The Psalmist touches all the bases:

- caught in death;
- delivered from death;
- energetic thanksgiving and gratitude.

The Psalm lines out the life and faith and experience of ancient Israel, and it must have been sung with exuberant music when Israel celebrated the drama of its life with God.

There is, as you know, a strong and deep tradition in the church that the real singer of the Psalm is Jesus, so we can hear his voice here:

> *It is Jesus* who on Friday knew all about the snares of death, the death sentence of the empire because he was taken to be a dangerous subversive;
> *It is Jesus* who walked out into new life on Easter morning in a way that is astonishing and inexplicable, having been freed from death by God;
> *It is Jesus* who gives thanks to God and who shapes his life and the life of his people as a Eucharist, that is, as a great thanksgiving.

Or in the book of Acts that we read in the second service:

> *It is the human community*, addressed by the Apostles, that is caught in "this corrupt generation."
> *It is the human community*, addressed by the preaching of the Apostles, that comes to be baptized and embraces the good news of deliverance by God;

> *It is the human community*, gathered by the Apostles, who enter a new life of fellowship and prayer, and we may believe of generative energy for the new future.

The book of Acts echoes and replicates the exuberance of the Psalm. We see the drama in ancient Israel in the Psalm, in the life of Jesus, and in the life of the world in the book of Acts. The three accent points turn out to be the truth of the world when it is seen in the presence of God.

III.

Our work in front of these texts, I imagine, is to make the dangerous contemporary move to ask how this same evangelical drama is being *re-performed in our lives* in the life of the contemporary church. I line it out this way:

1. We know about the "snares of death." You can take that phrase as ontological and metaphysical, or as poetic and imaginative as we sing from *Amazing Grace* "through many toils and snares I have already come." The "snares" are the powers or the forces or the social realities that box us in and immobilize us and negate our best selves and skew our future that God wants us to have.

So what if, in imaginative fashion, the snares of death are the rat-race of fear and anxiety that keep us always on Orange Alert, that draw us into greed because we are mesmerized by our felt and sensed deficits, that set us against the neighborhood and that eventually narcoticize us about the violence that is all around us, violence as neighborhood failure, as state policy, as fearful self-assertion in spite of everything to the contrary. Death is not just the end of life or the funeral or drawing our last breath or the failure of the body. Death is the power of negation before which we find ourselves helpless, that draws us into despair and that denies us the freedom and the energy and the will to care about the neighborhood. The snares of death are all around us, in our rhetoric, in our social systems, in our favorite ideologies, in our endless propaganda, and we are seduced by it much of the time.

2. We who gather around Jesus know about the rescue by the power of God. We do not know very well how to talk about it. Many of us are remote from the old phrases of substitutionary atonement and blood sacrifice and the mantra that "Christ paid it all." We prefer a gentler, less violent way to think and speak about God's rescue of those who are powerless in the snares of death.

So we prefer the account of the ancient disciples in Luke who sat at table with Jesus, who finally recognized him and were surprised to meet him in the bread of the table and who came to know that the essential nutrients of God's own life were being given to them. We only know from the old testimony that people who were around Jesus had their lives transformed. We only know now, because we see it among us. People who cluster around the church as God's body who engage in the disciplines and the singing and the eating and the mission of that body find our lives healed and forgiven and reconciled and unleashed afresh into the world. We know that even when we can only mumble about it.

And we know about the new life that arises from the rescue. That is why we pray, while we are still on our knees,

> Forgive us that we may delight in your will and walk in your way.

We stand up from our knees, having been given a new way in the world. And we sense it in our bodies:

- no longer fearful and anxious,
- no longer immobilized as the old world wants us to be,
- no longer paralyzed by the power of death that cannot hold us any longer.

We can be on our way with new life and new energy, and new noticing about the need in the world and the resources for healing, seeing now that old enemies are really needy neighbors, seeing that what looked like scarcity is enough when shared, enough to feed a crowd when there is gratitude. And we find that we are less greedy, less anxious, less coercive, less self-preoccupied, because we are able to rest our lives and our bodies down in the bottomless goodness of God. We come at the neighborhood with glad hearts and open hands and risk-taking lives, because the deep deathliness in our own lives has been overcome.

I am the one, today, who gets to invite you back into the drama again,

- to acknowledgement that the snares are real and powerful among us and we must pay attention;
- to point you again to the surprise of transformation,
- to witness to the gratitude that empowers.

It turns out, it's not just three points. It is the truth of our lives. It is no wonder that Peter, in the Epistle lesson, can write that this turn toward newness was "destined for us before the foundation of the world." And now it is on offer, again, today, for us. It turns out that the snares are powerless; they are overrun by waves of gratitude that has us on our way rejoicing. We come to the table again, and find the living presence and the gift of all that is required for faithful life in the world.

May 8, 2011
St. James Episcopal Church, New York, New York

27

Sorting Out Fantasy and Reality

PSALM 103
I JOHN 2:18–29
MARK 6:30–44

We have this wondrous story of Jesus transforming the wilderness into a place of nourishing plenty. Jesus radically disrupts how the world was thought to be. The wilderness, the "deserted place" in the story, was where there was no viable life support system. He thought he was going there to rest, but he was met by a big crowd of those who were drawn to him. They believed he would indeed disrupt their failed world, though they knew not how.

I.

Jesus does not disappoint them. He was moved with great compassion when he saw the hungry crowd. He had his stomach turned by their need. He engaged their hunger, because they lived in a false world without resources. His disciples accepted the barren wilderness without resources as a given; they wanted the crowd dispersed. They tried to protect Jesus from the need of the world. But Jesus scolded them and tells them to do the food for the crowd. But they are without resources. They say, "We do not have resources to do that," only puny supplies of bread and fish. They accepted the scarcity and force of the wilderness; the crowd may have expected food, but his disciples have no such hope. They have no such hope, even though they traveled with Jesus and had watched him work.

But Jesus jerks them to attention. He tells the crowd to sit. He disregards his weak-hearted disciples with their feeble notion of scarcity. He takes the

puny supply of bread and the puny catch of fish. And then, without fanfare, he
utters the four big verbs that are the center of the church's life:

> He took the bread and fish;
> He blessed the bread and fish;
> He broke the bread and fish;
> He gave the bread and fish.

You want that again? He took, he blessed, he broke, he gave. He enacted
a Eucharist right there in that deserted place for the hungry crowd without
resources. They all ate. They were all filled and satisfied . . . five thousand
men . . . plus women and children. And, we are told, they finished with a
surplus, with bread enough for all the tribes of Israel . . . twelve baskets! Fini!
Thanks be to God! The world is transformed; the wilderness has become a
place of abundance by the force and presence of Jesus in the midst of need.

II.

Well, the text is assigned for the day. And I am invited and paid to exposit it
for you. The story is a fantasy, the kind that the church enjoys about Jesus, the
kind of miracle that is given without explanation:

We try to explain it as best we can. They all pulled out their lunches, and
shared more than enough. But the text does not say that!

Or we say it is a retelling of the manna story of the Old Testament that is
itself only an older fantasy narrative.

Or it is a creation of the later church in order to anticipate the later sacrament of the Eucharist, as the Jesus Seminar might say.

In any case, the story is not credible, because we measure it by the story
that we know better. The one we know better is true; contrasted to that, this
one is a silly fantasy for nice romantic church folk. The story we know better,
the one we live out each day, is about scarcity. There really is not enough food
to go around. There really are starving people in Africa and in Philadelphia.
And because the story of scarcity is true, we hustle to get ahead, or to stay
even, to make sure we do not run out of money or bread or oil or security, to
make sure we and our grandchildren will have enough, to make sure the US
has enough power to protect our food and oil supplies. We work and work in
the rat-race to stay even, to make sure that our kids succeed.

And we limit and ration. We limit access because there is not enough. We
limit food and health care. We limit grace, cutting out those not qualified,
excluding those who are not like us. We live in anxiety on endless Orange

Alert, knowing that we must fend off others to protect ourselves. And I am invited and paid to tell you this fantasy that does not square with our society and our way in it, and the story we have come to believe about ourselves.

III.

Well . . . take a deep breath . . . and consider this: the reason we are here this morning together is to entertain the radical thought that the story of abundance enacted by Jesus is true. The story we tell about scarcity is a fantasy. It is not a true story. It is a story invented by those who have too much to justify getting more. It is a story accepted by those who have nothing in order to explain why they have nothing. That story is not true, because the world belongs to God and God is the creator of the abundant life.

So we meet to sort this out again. If we were not here together, we could adopt the story of our society and live out our lives in the anxious rat-race the world puts upon us. But here we listen to this other story. And when we hear it, we say, "Praise to you, Lord Christ." Praise to you, Lord Christ, for giving us a better story. Praise to you, Lord Christ, for a true story. Praise to you, Lord Christ, for a story of abundance with twelve baskets left over. Praise to you, Lord Christ, for your transformative verbs, "He took, he blessed, he broke, he gave."

The abundance that Jesus performs in this narrative is not a simple, safe church sacrament. It is the performance of a new narrative of the world, a narrative of well-being, satisfaction, abundance, and surplus. And when we place our hearts and our imagination and our faith in this story, the old narrative of scarcity turns out to be a fantasy.

In this dramatic act at the table, we see that the story of Jesus' feeding has deep implications for us in the church and, eventually, for us in the world. It invites us to bask in God's *shalom*. It invites us to act out that abundance, to perform abundance in the neighborhood with generosity and hospitality. It summons us to new policies, new money management, new relationships grounded in God's endless giving. It urges us to new policies that allow for sharing with all of the needy and the vulnerable who are in the scope of God's compassion.

So we do this sorting out. Some of us are so set in the scarcity story that we will take this as church fantasy. Some of us will be grabbed by the story of God's blessing, and tilt in fresh ways toward the world, toward the neighborhood. Some of us will be unsure and in wonderment, and will continue to sort out. But all of us are invited to be children and practitioners of this other story. The Gospel is not a fantasy. It is the true story of God's world. That is why we say with our will and our faith and our life, "Praise to you, Lord Christ." And then we act it out in ways that disrupt our society, even as he continues to disrupt our world of scarcity with his abundance.

April 29, 2012
St. Thomas Episcopal Church, Fort Washington, Pennsylvania

28

Interrupted . . . Again and Again

PSALM 148

JOHN 13:31–35

ACTS 11:1–18

REVELATION 21:1–6

The cat at our house is named Sammy. Sammy sits in the softest chair in the living room, sleeps in our bed from 3 a.m. to 5 a.m., sits close to the table when we eat, and in general administers our house. My brother and his wife are appalled by that, and by any contact with Sammy. Because, as they say, "Cats are dirty."

We are all like that. We learn, early and in ways we do not recognize, what is right and wrong, what is good and bad, what is clean and unclean, who is in and out, who we are and who they are. We learn all those distinctions and assume them and work from them. And then, over time, we keep unlearning them and revising them, and sometimes abandoning them.

I.

So it was with Peter, the lead guy in the early church. He had learned all the lessons of clean and unclean. He had learned them at home, inhaled them with his mother's milk. She had taught him about clean and unclean from the book of Leviticus, about shellfish and reptiles and other disgusting options. He had a keen sensibility about keeping things clean and in order and properly arranged. I imagine his desk was neat and his room was tidy as kid.

And then he was interrupted!

We are always being interrupted about what we have settled. We are variously interrupted

- by a new learning,
- by a fresh reading of a book,
- by a casual comment of a friend,
- by the observation of a teacher,
- by the insight of a therapist,
- by a dream . . . or by a nightmare.

We are interrupted when we thought we had it all settled; and then we unlearn and we relearn . . . again and again.

So Peter had a dream. He says,

In a trance I saw a vision. (Acts 11:5)

It was a vision, he says, of "something like a large sheet coming down from heaven." And on this sheet were,

four-footed animals, beasts of prey, reptiles, birds of the air.

It is all rather impressionistic, like a dream. That menagerie came, moreover, with a commanding voice. Peter does not know whose voice it is:

I . . . heard a voice saying to me, "Get up, Peter, kill and eat."

What a nightmare: an unidentified commanding voice summoning Peter to go against his mother and against the Book of Leviticus and against everything he knew to be true. He was to violate his code of disgust.

Peter answers the voice of disruption; he acknowledges that this interrupting voice is none other than the speech of God:

By no means, Lord; for nothing profane or unclean has ever entered my mouth.

I have been an obedient son of my mother. I have listened fully to the Book of Leviticus. I am pure and intend to keep myself that way. He refuses the commanding voice of God that presses him to new awareness.

But God will not quit. Now the voice from heaven:

What God has made clean, you must not call profane.

More than that: this happened three times, he says, three times a command to violate the deep code from his childhood. You mean I have to take it in a new way, so that the codes of Leviticus and of my mother are wrong? You mean God can redefine and relabel and make acceptable? You mean I have to give up my conviction about right and wrong, and good and bad, and clean and unclean, and us and them?

II.

Well. That is what Jesus does. Jesus interrupts again and again. But then, as always, the dream turns out to have meanings beyond the obvious. It turns out that the dream is not really about clean and unclean animals, even cats. Just as soon as the dream ended, Peter is visited by "three men from Caesarea," another unexpected interruption. They are Gentiles with whom Peter had had no dealings. They are people who do not keep Torah, who do not share established distinctions, and who are in fact "unclean" by every Torah regulation.

But the Spirit, intruding into all of our settlements and certitudes, tells Peter to go with these three men:

> Do not make a distinction between us and them.

The next paragraph of the story is about the work of the Holy Spirit, the great boundary crosser, the irresistible force of God's transformative presence, reaching out and baptizing those outside. And Peter draws the conclusion:

> God has given . . . to Gentiles [the unclean ones] the repentance that leads to life.

These Gentiles are invited into Gods' new life. God has made a way out of no way when they had no way to come to new life. God makes possible what I had crossed off as impossible.

So there is a nighttime trance and a daytime implementation of the dream. The trance and the daytime visitation together require the scuttling of old categories that had sorted everyone and everything into neat pigeonholes. Gods relocates everyone!

III.

That of course is what Jesus does. He challenges the Roman Empire and the Jewish law, the two forces that had sorted people out into acceptable and unacceptable. The Jewish distinctions are social and religious; the Roman distinctions are political and economic. But they all go so well together. We categorize people into socioreligious, political, economic good and bad. *The good* have privileges and influence and prosperity and entitlement—good schools, good jobs, good advancement into wealth and well-being. *The bad* are slotted into failure, poverty, food stamps, and despair. And we cannot tell whether those distinctions are finally political or economic or social or religious, because it all converges into slots of access or exclusion.

And then we are interrupted. Indeed, we live in a time of interruption:

- We thought we had the race thing settled with the "separate but equal," but then we were interrupted; they would not stay in "their place" and we had to decide again;
- We thought we had the gender thing properly arranged; but we were interrupted by women who refused to stay in the kitchen and then came the vote and women's ordination, and now combat, and we have to decide again;
- We were sure we had the gay thing settled: "hate the sin and love the sinner"; but we were interrupted when they refused to stay hidden and we had to decide again;
- Now we are interrupted about immigrants and are pondering what the distinction might be between citizens and undocumented workers;
- We know about "Christ alone" and we slotted Muslims, without really knowing any, as non-believers and we reckoned them all to be enemies. But then we were interrupted to discover that most Muslims are about the business of being human and are not to be confused with the small company of self-destructive nuts, and we have to decide again.

All of these fresh decisions are difficult, as difficult as Gentiles were for Peter, because in each case, the "other" is unlike us and unclean at best, unacceptable at worst. It is all so unnerving. It produces anxiety that in turn sometimes generates violence. It leads to an inordinate sense of self and preoccupation with ourselves and those like us of our own kind.

IV.

The decision of the early church to admit Gentiles was not an easy one. And Peter agreed to that decision with great reluctance. But it got done, because the church knew intuitively about the expansive love of God in Christ that reaches beyond tribe and slogan and fear and exclusion. It is done by the Spirit who keeps reaching, in the Book of Acts, out beyond settled categories. So we have on our hands a living Lord who comes in a trance and a vision and in many ways to shatter our settlements that are so convenient for us and so precious to us.

In the Gospel reading, Jesus gives a new commandment of love that reaches beyond our own kind, that we love one another. The reach of that gospel love is not contained in our preferred entitlements. The text in Acts says that when they realized it was the work of the Spirit that led to the inclusion of Gentiles, they praised God. The Psalm for today, Psalm 148, is an astonishing hymn of praise, with all of God's creatures joining together in one song, drawn together by their sheer nearness to God:

> Praise the LORD from the earth,
> You sea monsters and all deeps,
> fire and hail, snow and frost,
> stormy wind fulfilling his command!
> Mountains and all hills,
> fruit trees and all cedars!
> Wild animals and all cattle,
> creeping things and flying birds!
> Kings of the earth and all peoples,
> princes and all rulers of the earth!
> Young men and women all alike,
> old and young together!
>   (Ps. 148:7–12)

Who should we imagine in that one glorious doxology:

> Black and white, Jew and Gentile,
> Christian and Muslim, gay and straight,
> Citizen and undocumented worker,
> Rich and poor, haves and have-nots!

All are swept up in doxology that outruns our little systems of control and exclusion.

V.

My friend Gary Dorrien, who teaches at Union Seminary in New York, proposes that the deep chasm now in our society is between *the deserving haves* and *the undeserving have-nots*, the ones variously labeled in shrill polemic "moochers and takers," who want everything free for nothing. We live now in a society that emits resentment, anger, and sometimes rage toward those have-nots who are judged to be unclean, unacceptable, dispensable outsiders to our system of privilege and entitlement. The resentments are very loud and vigorous among us. But of course that self-congratulatory resentment, broad as it is in our society, is interrupted by this Jesus who breaks down every dividing wall between alienated peoples.

Because of this Jesus who interrupts, here we are, the church, that little body of the baptized, living with courage and freedom to cross those lines of resentment and exclusion to reach out with acts of love and initiatives of justice, imagining that such "unclean folk" are *included in his commandment* to love each other, *included as well in the doxology* that gathers all creatures around the throne of majesty and mercy. The commandment and the doxology violate our old codes, and put us in the presence of those who turn out, at the throne of grace, to be brothers and sisters alongside us.

Some of you are like me, finding such a mandate unnerving and anxiety producing. But it is the will of the Father, it is the act of the Spirit, it is the summons of the Son, it is the wave of God's future. Jesus came among us all, among us and the disqualified, the poor, the lame, the deaf, the lepers, publicans and sinners and tax-collectors, all the hopeless, and opened new life to them as to us. And we now, because of him, find ourselves acting in ways that we had not anticipated. Such an embrace, as the church has always done again and again, is the way to newness, "new heaven, new earth, new Jerusalem" and new life for us. All things new when the old codes are abandoned for a better God-given reality! Agreement in my family about whether Sammy the cat is "clean" or "unclean" is not very important. It is important that God, in Christ, is busy redefining us and those around us, breaking old codes and inviting us to new reality.

April 28, 2013
First Presbyterian Church, Pensacola, Florida

29

Love Wins!?

PSALM 98
ACTS 10:44–48
1 JOHN 5:1–6
JOHN 15:9–17

This short letter of 1 John from which we read is addressed to the little church in the Roman Empire. The Roman Empire, like every superpower including our own, was comprehensive, endlessly demanding, and impatient with anyone who did not sign on with loyalty and conviction. In the midst of that totalizing power of the empire is this little company of people who have signed on for another way in the world with Jesus. Consequently their life and their faith contradicted the claims of empire. Their life and faith, precisely because of the force of the empire, was always fragile and in jeopardy. Thus the letter written to the church is to remind and affirm to the church its special identity and its special purpose in the world. We continue to read this ancient letter to the church because it is as contemporary for us today. Now, like then, the church in our society is a fragile operation whose identity is in jeopardy and whose purpose is easy to forget as we are swallowed up by the empire. Thus the letter is to us, as it was to them. It offers to the church, now as then,

- a precious identity,
- a demanding summons,
- a radically different life, and
- an amazing promise.

I want to think with you about those four themes,

- precious identity,
- demanding summons;
- radically different life, and
- amazing promise.

I.

Our reading begins with a reminder of *identity and belonging*:

> Everyone who believes that Jesus is the Christ has been born of God
> and everyone who loves the parent loves the child. (1 John 5:1)

The opener likely refers to baptism for which the church uses all kinds of rich phrases, "bought with a price," "sealed as Christ's own forever," "that I belong to my faithful savior." Here the writer says, "Born of God," claiming a pedigree that connects earthly folks to the heavenly parent, welcomed into the family of God. And because of the connection to the heavenly parent, the baptized know Jesus, Son of God, as a brother, a partner, a companion for our life in the world. The sum of these phrases is to say that folks alongside Jesus are different folk who belong to a different family, a different identity, and a different loyalty. This is no generic religion. This is not faith that accommodates to every political claim, every economic possibility, and every pressure from the empire. There is always an awareness and a resolve to live a life that is congruent with the peculiar family to which we belong.

II.

That precious identity is followed in the letter by a *demanding summons*:

> By this we know that we love the children of God, when we love God
> and obey his commandments. For the love of God is this, that we
> obey his commandments. (vv. 2–3)

Serious parents have demanding expectations of their children and do not cater to their whims. So this heavenly father, this glorious mother god has clear expectations of the children who belong to this family. US religion, in a therapeutic mode, has made it easy to think that God's love is causal and careless. Not! This God of the gospel is always recruiting folk to an alternative purpose in the world. So Jesus, the Son, calls disciples, that is, people under discipline, pressed to reflective intentionality about life in the world. The substance of recruitment is terse: obey his commandments. This is not reference to the big catalogue of commandments that we have from Judaism, though there were Jewish Christians who took that entire inventory of commandments seriously. Jesus is more terse in his summons to obey. It is simply, "Follow me." Imitate me. Sometimes he added to that, "Sell all you have and give it to the poor and follow me." This summons to that young man was that

he should give up the life of the Roman Empire (or any empire) that is committed to power, control, and wealth, and be present in the world differently.
Notice that the summons to obey commandments is matched by "love God,"
and you know how that goes:

> You shall love the Lord your God with all your heart, all your mind,
> all your soul, and all your substance.

The church in the US has spent a lot of time and energy accommodating
conventional consumerism (with its strong military component), so that we
have become largely an echo of conventional society, both liberal and conservative. But here is a jolt of alert, that we have another life to live in the world.

III.

Then the summons is given specificity for the sake of *a radically different life*.
The wonderment is how to love God whom we cannot see. And of course the
conclusion of the gospel is that we love God whom we cannot see by loving
the neighbor whom we can see. That is what Jesus did and what we are to
do. He was out in the neighborhood. And as he went along, he defined the
neighborhood in radically inclusive ways: neighborliness is showing gracious
hospitality, mercy, and justice toward those in need. So love God and love
neighbor. This, in the empire, is no ordinary life!

The letter of John has a peculiar, distinctive notion of love that means
giving one's self away in deep engagement with others, especially the needy
and the disabled. The tradition in which we stand in the United Church of
Christ, moreover, insists and assumes that this notion of love concerns not
only spontaneous neighborly acts, but sustained, systemic efforts of program
and policy that have restorative impact.

When they asked him if he was the Messiah, he gave them no metaphysical
answer. But like any good teacher, he said, "What do you notice about me?"
Do you notice that,

> The blind see,
> The lame walk,
> The lepers are cleansed,
> The deaf hear,
> The dead are raised,
> The poor have their debts cancelled.

Love of neighbor as the way of loving God means to expend transformative
energy so that the neighborhood is transformed and enhanced in the interest
of everyone in the neighborhood.

That is what the people of Jesus, the ones born of God, do. They are not preoccupied with their own status in this world or in the next, but get their minds off themselves for the sake of the neighborhood.

It is a big cause for alarm that in our self-enhancing culture the church echoes that self-concern about its resources while reneging on its missional mandate. But of course this congregation has always known better. It knows, as the writer says, that the command for love that gives self away is not burdensome:

> His commandments are not burdensome. (v. 4)

This is the true joy of life; anyone who seriously invests in neighborliness as a way to love God will find joy that does not come from self-preoccupation.

IV.

Now you know all of this. What you may not know and what may surprise you is that the paragraph ends with an *amazing promise*:

> This is the victory that conquers the world, our faith. Who is it that conquers the world but the one who believes that Jesus is the Son of God? (vv. 4–5)

The sentence repeats the initial identity "born of God." But then stretches out a future that belongs to such folk. I was struck by the fact that in this quick sentence the writer employs the word "conquer" three times:

> Those born of God *conquer* the world;
> This is the victory that *conquers* the world;
> Jesus is the one who *conquers* the world.

The "world" here refers to the power arrangements of the Roman Empire. It refers to this managed world of power. It is the socioeconomic, political system designed to enhance the powerful at the expense of the vulnerable. It is the system-rooted *anxiety* that functions in *greed* that ends in *violence* that produces *poverty and alienation*. That arrangement goes on and on, to perpetuity. It will last and last and last, and nothing can be done about it, because it is so powerful and so comprehensive and so smart. That is the real world!

And then this evangelical gospel:

> Those born of God *conquer* the world.
> This is the victory that *conquers* the world.
> Jesus is the one who *conquers* the world.

As Rob Bell says it, Love wins!

But not just any love: self-giving love that has transformational capacity. This rhetoric for the church sounds a little like the faithful chanting, "USA, USA." Except it is now not force, and not worldly power and not money. This is not coercion or force or intimidation rooted in normal systems of power.

It is rather the transformative intention of God entrusted into our hands that brings the world into sync with the God who loves the world. We see this in Jesus, weak and vulnerable and foolish as he seemed to be. He had the touch! He had the word! He had the resolve! And when people were with him, all things were made new.

We are free to imagine that the death systems of violence, the greed systems of poverty, and the despairing system of exploitation have no staying power. They cannot be sustained in the face of self-giving, transformative love. They are "conquered!"

This little letter of John is an invitation to us to think, to reconsider, to recognize, and to affirm our peculiar status and role in the world. When it is faithful, the church is not impressed with the death systems of the world. Because we follow in the wake of the Friday guy who defeated the power of death. That is who we follow. Because we are disciples born of God. When we embrace that *identity*, that *summons*, that *vocation*, and that *promise*, we are our way rejoicing. We know that his rule has no end. We live as those whom God has birthed to new life!

May 13, 2012
First Congregational Church, UCC, Columbus, Ohio

30

At Midnight

A Way Out of Fear, Greed, and Abuse

PSALM 97
ACTS 16:16–34
REVELATION 22:12–14, 16–17, 20–21
JOHN 17:20–26

This story in the Book of Acts offers us a social crisis in which the faith of the church is on a collision course with established order, just what we would expect in the Easter season.

I.

The story contains all of the ingredients of a society that is frightened and anxious and greedy and at risk. These ingredients include:

A slave-girl who did fortune-telling. She imagined that she could predict the future because she believed it was all programmed and fated, so that there was no freedom about the future. You can imagine her as a sensation making the rounds of the talk shows, making all sorts of pronouncements about coming events. It says she made a lot of money; well, of course she did; she was interesting and she gave assurance to anxious people. Paul judged that she was demon-possessed.

There were her *"owners."* It turns out that she made a lot of money, but she made it for them. They used her, and she was glad to exhibit her gifts and let them get the cash. They are the money men; all you need to do is follow the money. Because the money men are often just pimps who exploit and use others to cash in. And they are, not surprisingly, upset when Paul frees her from the demon, so that she loses her gift, can no longer perform, and cannot make them any money. So the money men sue Paul. They "dragged [him] into the marketplace before the authorities."

149

There are the authorities, *the magistrates* who maintain civil order. They are committed to the existing social order and will rush to keep it the way it was. They are perhaps "activist judges" like our Supreme Court. So they listen to the charges brought against Paul for his preaching and action:

> These men are disturbing our city; they are Jews and are advocating customs that are not lawful for us as Romans to adopt or observe. (Acts 16:21)

We are not told about their verdict. The narrative rushes on to the sentence:

> [T]he magistrates had them stripped of their clothing and ordered them to be beaten with rods. After they had given them a severe flogging, they threw them into prison and ordered the jailer to keep them securely. Following these instructions, he put them in the innermost cell and fastened their feet in the stocks. (vv. 22–24)

This is close to torture; but torture is always available for frightened people who want to keep everything from changing. So the magistrates rule and act for the money men who did not want to lose their media star.

There is *the crowd*. They get only a half of a sentence in the narrative: "The crowd joined in attacking them" (v. 22). They are the street protesters who want to intimidate the court, and perhaps they did. The crowd is unwittingly allied with the money men in sustaining business as usual.

If you take all of these players—the fortune teller, the money men, the magistrates, and the crowd—all the drama flows toward that great symbol of the status quo, *the prison*. The prison is a safe place to put troublemakers. It is also a metaphor for keeping the lid on trouble, and for intimidating any who may think to question the status quo.

It strikes me that these five ingredients in the story—*the fortune-teller, the money men, the magistrates, the crowd, and the prison*—provide a map for a very fearful society.

II.

Then, in verse 25, the scene changes. All at once we have the camera moved to the jail where Paul and Silas have begun to serve their sentence, because they had challenged the settled, exploitative power arrangements of their society. The story does not say they were frightened about their imprisonment, or that they were angry. Rather they are "praying and singing hymns to God." They were engaged in a countercultural activity fired by their faith; they refused to give in to the social norms that had imprisoned them. They were operating in their uncommon freedom as followers of Jesus. And, says the text, the other prisoners were listening to them in rapt attentiveness, for their loud singing suggested to them a world outside the reach of settled society. We are able to see that the followers of Jesus in prison were something of a spectacle as they refused to knuckle under.

And then, abruptly, there was a quaking, a shaking of the jail that was an embodiment and symbol of that fearful society. It happened, we are told, at midnight. It happened in the dark, when no one could see and no one could explain, and the magistrates could not control things. At midnight something new broke loose in the world. The story does not speculate about the cause of the quake. It only reports that the foundation of the jail shook, the cell doors were blown open, the chains on their feet were broken loose; they were free to flee, to escape the shame of imprisonment. They had sung and prayed in freedom; and now they are free!

The jailer figured he would lose his prisoners and that he would be in big trouble with the magistrates; he would surely lose his job. But they did not run. They had not tried to escape. They stayed, even after the doors were open and the chains were loosed. They had stayed and they reassured the jailer, "We are all here . . . do not worry" (v. 28).

III.

So imagine the jailer. The action now focuses on him. The narrative has no more interest in the fortune teller or the money men or the magistrates or the crowd. He is the focus of the story and the wave of the future.

He is relieved that he will not lose his job. He is grateful that his prisoners did not flee. And he is mystified by their conduct. And so he asks Paul and Silas:

> Why are you still here?
> Why did you not run when you had a chance?
> Do you think your praying made a difference?
> Did you think your loud singing could overturn the court ruling?
> Do you think your freedom is real, even though you did not flee?
> Do you walk to a different drummer?
> How can I understand what you did and who you are?

Well, he did not in fact say any of that; what he said was, "What must I do to be saved?" Tell me the secret of your life that lets you be free and buoyant and confident and powerful and unafraid. The whole story turns on his question. Indeed, the whole future of the world (and of our economy) turns on his question and on their answer, "What do I have to do to be saved?" Already back in verse 17, the fortune teller had accused them, "These men proclaim to you a way of salvation," not about how to get to heaven, but how to be in sync with the rule of God in your daily life.

And so they answer the jailer:

> Believe on the Lord Jesus, and you will be saved, you and your household. (v. 31)

And the jailer responded:

> [H]e took them and washed their wounds; . . . he brought them up into the house and set food before them.

And then!
He and his entire family were baptized.
The story ends this way:

> He and his entire household rejoiced that he had become a believer in God. (vv. 33–34)

He signed on for another reading of reality, another way to live in the world:

> His life is no longer determined by talk-show *fortune tellers* who rob us of freedom;
> His life is no longer controlled by *the money men* who pimp us to their advantage by big time sports spectacles or by more electronic gadgets;
> His life does not depend on the frightened *magistrates* who try their best to keep the world from tilting toward justice and well-being, and who try to keep the old order going;
> His life is no longer shaped or intimidated by *the tea party crowd* of the right or of the left who unwittingly serve the money men.

He had got the news that Jesus has been raised in power, that Jesus is loose in the world, that the gospel offers an alternative way to live, apart from fear and from greed and from abuse and exploitation. He need no longer be a participant in the old world of death. At that moment, at midnight, he had seen with his own eyes that the people around Jesus acted differently, because their world is shaped by joy and boldness.

The story ends in hospitality. He feeds them; he cares for their wounds . . . like a Good Samaritan. He overcame the wounds inflicted by the abusive magistrates. And in the verses beyond our reading, the magistrates came and apologized to Paul and Silas and released them. The story invites us to think again about our commitments, our fears, and our hopes. It holds before us another way that is not defined by the foolishness of the world. Now it is defined by Easter news of life over death,

> of freedom over fear,
> of joy over intimidation,
> of buoyant generosity over anxiety.

The magistrates want to keep us on Orange Alert. But the Jesus people refuse. They sing and pray and feed and care and rejoice. What a strange bunch we are!

May 16, 2010
First United Methodist Church, Winter Park, Florida

PART THREE

Sermons for Pentecost and Ordinary Time

31

The Life-Giving Wind from Nazareth

(Pentecost)

PSALM 104:24–35
EZEKIEL 37:1–14
JOHN 20:19–23

Pentecost, fifty days after Easter, is the one day each year in which Presbyterians imagine that we are open to God's Spirit. We confess, after we say, "Father and Son" in the creed, "I believe in the Holy Spirit." And then we name the gifts of the Spirit:

> The church . . . holy and Catholic,
> The fellowship of the saints,
> The forgiveness of sins,
> The resurrection of the body,
> The life everlasting.

All gifts promised and given by the wind and force and mystery and goodness of God who infuses the world. We stay open to the gifts of the Spirit, as we are able, because it is the wind and the breath and the Spirit of God that makes life in the world possible. Without this life-giving force, we are hopeless and helpless, and the world will die.

For this Pentecost Sunday, we are given, along with the usual narrative texts, Psalm 104, a celebration of the good force of God's Spirit that infuses the world. For this Pentecost, my gift to you consists in three affirmations of our confidence in God's Spirit, affirmations that you can take for our own doxology.

I.

The Psalmist sings of the ominous sea and its busyness; the Psalmist sings that the ocean is habited by the evil sea monster that is a sign of disorder and upheaval in the world, not unlike a surging tsunami:

> Yonder is the sea, great and wide,
> creeping things innumerable are there,
> living things both small and great. There go the ships,
> and *Leviathan* that you formed to sport in it.
> (*Ps. 104:25–26, emphasis added*)

People in the Bible always viewed the ocean as a scary threat, as a symbol of chaos that makes life dangerous or unlivable. But, says this poem, the creator God has taken Leviathan, the great sea monster who represents all chaos, has tamed it, and made it a plaything, like a toy in a bathtub.

The word at Pentecost is that God's Spirit has ordered the world, so that you can trust and live in confidence and count on the proper functioning of the world. That work of taming chaos is done by the abiding Spirit of Jesus. It was Jesus, asleep in the boat on the sea, who woke up, looked the storm in its face, rebuked the waves, said, "Be Still!" Well, what he really said was, "Shut up!" The waves obeyed him and the world was made safe!

II.

In the next verses the Psalmist marvels at the gift of food that is generated by God's good creation:

> These all look to you
> to give them their food in due season;
> when you give to them, they gather it up; when you open your hand,
> they are filled with good things.
> (vv. 27–28)

Israel, in its faith, is aware that since Genesis 1 wherein God commanded the earth to "be fruitful," the creation is a gift that keeps on giving. It keeps on giving because it is infused with God's generative Spirit that makes provision for all creatures. "All" . . . all radishes and lions and minnows and Asians and Latinos and Africans and Europeans and porcupines . . . all show up at mealtime and all eat. There is enough food in the world God gives! We harvest. We share and the world is satisfied. That is what we acknowledge whenever we say table grace. We confess that we have food . . . through all the complexity of commercial processes . . . because God's Spirit is a force for food against the threat of famine and starvation.

The Spirit that authorizes fruitfulness in the world is the abiding Spirit of Jesus. It was Jesus who saw the hungry crowd. And, we are told, he took bread, he blessed it, he broke it and gave it to them . . . 5,000 people with twelve baskets of bread left over! And then he did it a second time for a second hungry crowd. He took loaves and fish. He blessed them, he broke the bread, he gave it to them. He fed 4,000 with seven baskets of surplus bread. And since then, we also are fed as we recite those good words, "He took, blessed, he broke, he gave." We are fed with *the bread of life* and *the bread of the world* that binds us to God's good earth.

III.

The Spirit that *overcomes chaos*, the Spirit that generates *ample bread* is the Spirit that sustains the life of the world. So the Psalmist says:

> When you hide your face, they are dismayed; when you take away their
>   breath, they die and return to their dust.
> When you send forth your spirit, they are created;
> and you renew the face of the ground.
>
> (vv. 29–30)

Everything depends upon God's life-giving breath. God is like a great iron lung, reliable, paced, regular, life-giving. When God gives God's Spirit, all creatures inhale and the earth throbs with well-being. And when God's breath is withdrawn, creation dies. This Psalm has a quite elementary, concrete notion of God's breath. The poem is aware that the first thing we do at birth is *inhale*. And the last thing we do is *exhale* and there is no more breathe in us. And between that first inhale and that last exhale, we rely on breath being given. It is given because we do not own it, cannot hold it, cannot commandeer it. We are dependent and choke or suffocate quickly if breath is not given. The news is that the world works because the breath-giving God is present among us every minute of all creation.

That breath that breathes the world to life is the breath of Jesus that pervades the world. We are told that when Jesus came among his disciples after Easter and they discovered that he was alive again, he came to them in their fearfulness and said, "Peace be with you" (John 20:19).

After he said this, he showed them his hands and his side. Then the disciples rejoiced when they saw the Lord. Jesus said to them again, "Peace be with you. As the Father has sent me, so I send you." When he had said this, *he breathed on them* and said to them, "Receive the Holy Spirit. If you forgive the sins of any, they are forgiven them; if you retain the sins of any, they are retained" (John 20:20–23).

Jesus came to the earliest church, breathed on them and empowered them to be forgivers of the sins of the world. Because without the work of the Spirit, without the power of forgiveness, the world will be devoured in anger, in violence, and in vengeance.

IV.

For your Pentecost, consider these three claims of Gospel faith:

- The world is whole because the Spirit acts against cosmic, seismic disorder to make it safe;
- The world is fed because the Spirit calls the earth to be generative and nourishing;
- The world is alive because God's reliable breath is given among us without fail.

All this we have seen in Jesus,

- Who said to the storm, "Be Still!"
- Who said to the earth, "Bring forth."
- Who breathed on his people to empower forgiveness.

The world is different because God's Spirit is indeed among us. All that remains is that we should bear fruit in our lives according to God's Spirit:

"By contrast, *the fruit of the Spirit* is love, joy, peace, patience, kindness, generosity, faithfulness, gentleness, and self-control. There is no law against such things" (Gal. 5:22–23, emphasis added).

All of that is permitted! People who are breathed on can live differently!

June 4, 2006
Fourth Presbyterian Church, Chicago

32

Safer Than You Think

(Pentecost)

PSALM 104:24–35

There are three things everyone in the church knows about Pentecost:

First, we know that Pentecost is about *the spirit* surging to make things new;
Second, we know that the surge of the spirit *creates the Church* according to the narrative of the Book of Acts;
Third, we know that *Calvinists* do not talk much about the spirit, because it makes us nervous to have things so out of control.

I.

But now there is good news! Because we have another text assigned for Pentecost, namely, Psalm 104. This long Psalm is a hymn of praise to the creator God for the wonder, beauty, and life-giving power of the creator God:

- The Psalm traces the structure of the universe as understood in pre-scientific terms . . . sky, earth, and water;
- The Psalm celebrates the gushy force of rivers and streams, and this in an arid climate;
- The Psalm marvels at the rhythms of nature, so that human beings work in the day and sleep at night, and lions sleep in the day and work at night, and the two need never encounter each other;
- The Psalm specifies the most elemental sustenance of life through bread, wine, and oil; these are the three gifts that bear sacramental markings in the life of the church.

The long inventory of creatureliness in this Psalm ends in a doxology of astonishment:

> O Lord, how manifold are your works!
> In wisdom you have made them all;
> the earth is full of your creatures.
>   (Ps. 104:24)

Now in this long hymn of praise, my gift to you is to consider three specific elements of the poem in the portion of the Psalm that we have just read.

II.

In verses 29–30, we come to the verses that have caused this Psalm to be designated for Pentecost:

> When you hide your face, they are dismayed;
> when you take away their *breath*, they die
> and return to their dust.
> When you send forth your *spirit*, they are created;
> and you renew the face of the ground.
>   (Ps. 104:29–30, emphasis added)

What interests us here is the double use of the same Hebrew term *ruah* that is rendered as "breath" in verse 29 and as "spirit" in verse 30. The two verses are related to each other antithetically. In verse 29, it is asserted negatively that when God is absent or silent, people die and can no longer inhale the breath that God gives. Everything depends upon that breath which is God's gift; when it is withheld we die. In verse 30, the same point is made positively. It is God's breath that makes the world work in Genesis 1:2; it is said that the wind of God swept over the chaos and made creation. But notice that the word "wind" is the same Hebrew word as in the Psalm. God's wind, God's breath, God's spirit swept the waters back and created a dry land possible. In Genesis 2:7, moreover, it is said,

> then the Lord God formed man from the dust of the ground, and breathed into his nostrils the breath of life; and the man became a living being.

Humankind is made out of clay or dust or earth, but when God blows breath on it, it comes to life. Now this double use of the word spirit in verses 29–30 in the Psalm and the creation texts in Genesis 1:2 and 2:7 altogether give us an expansive notion of Pentecost and the gift of God's spirit. It turns out that God's spirit, the third person of the Trinity, is not just a force and agent in the Church, but is in fact the life-force that infuses all creation and makes the world work for good.

So imagine in this great festival of Pentecost that God the creator is like a great iron lung that breathes in and out, in and out, day and night, summer and winter, from the beginning of creation until the end of time. It is the will of God and the gift of the creator that the world should have vitality.

From that, two points are worth observing. First, the breathing of God that keeps the world working is utterly reliable. The world will last in its viability. God wills the world to be in a healthy, functioning way and makes it so. The world is not under threat. And second, the world depends completely upon God's gift of life. The world cannot hold its own breath. It cannot exhale its breath until it has inhaled; it cannot generate the breath of life but can only receive it from God. The ambition of much modem philosophy and much modern science and much modern psychology is to show the world to be a great autonomous system. But this doxology knows better. Everything depends upon the God who gives artificial respiration to a world at every instant. The world lives because God is faithful.

III.

The second wondrous affirmation of the Psalm is found in verses 25, 26:

> Yonder is the sea, great and wide,
> creeping things innumerable are there,
> living things both small and great.

You may know that the Bible, for reasons partly practical and partly mythological, views the sea or the ocean as a threat. If you read about the thirty-foot waves that beat against the Queen Mary II on its first transatlantic crossing, you know that the ocean is wondrous and treacherous and dangerous and powerful. In that ancient world, they often refer to the ocean as the epitome of chaos, as that part of God's creation that was completely untamed and that placed all of ordered life in jeopardy. But here in these verses, the poet presents a serene, confident view of the ocean: "Yonder is the sea great and wide." Response here to the ocean is one of wonder but not of fear. Here the sea constitutes no threat to the creator. The sea, moreover, is filled with living creatures of all kinds, teeming with schools of fish and whales and sharks, etc., etc., etc. Of course faith knows that each creature is called by the creator God.

And then the punch line occurs in verse 26:

and Leviathan that you formed to sport in it.

The term "Leviathan" signals the evil sea monster, the symbol and embodiment of chaos that threatens to undue the order of creation, and to place in jeopardy the ordering of human society. "Leviathan" is a powerful and recurring reality in that ancient world. But here a very strange thing happens. The evil sea monster is now used by God to play. Chaos has been tamed and subdued so that God now toys with the raging waters that are no longer a threat to creation. Or as one Jewish scholar has said, chaos is now God's "rubber ducky."

As the verse on *God's breath* evidences God's reliability, so these verses on the chaotic waters assert that the world is safe in God's hands. Indeed the import of the Psalm for this spirit-defined day is that the world is safe, that we are much safer than we had imagined! So whatever we think the shape of chaos is . . .

- raging cancer in our bodies;
- wild Muslim terrorists;
- unbridled US military power
- or whatever . . .

It is no challenge to that settled rule of God.

IV.

The third theme I cite comes in the next verses, verses 27–28:

These all look to you to give them their food in due season;
when you give to them, they gather it up;
when you open your hand,
they are filled with good things.

Verse 26 on "Leviathan" has declared creation to be safe. This now is followed by an affirmation that the world as God's creation is an adequate food-producing system that will sate the hunger of every creature.

All the creatures turn to God for food, like little birds waiting for mother bird to bring food to the nest. God gives food and creatures, human and non-human, gather it up. God opens God's hands, and we are all filled. In that ancient world, they did not know all that we do about agricultural and scientific management of crops. But they understood the basics. They understood that for all human ingenuity to manage, the food supply still depends completely upon rain and sun and soil and seasons that are beyond human capacity.

These two verses are like a table prayer in childlike gratitude, giving thanks for food. But then it may be that our table prayers are our most genuine prayers, if we pay attention, for with mealtimes we are closest to the reality of faith, closest to the awareness that we are hungry and must be fed, closest to the recognition that we cannot in the end guarantee food apart from God's creative generosity, and closest to the gratitude that arrives when we see food as a regular, reliable, astonishing gift that is not to be taken for granted.

V.

These three vignettes in the Psalm are a good day's work on Pentecost:

- We depend completely on God's breath (wind) to cause the world to function and give us life;
- The powers of chaos have been tamed and therefore are no threat; therefore we are safe;
- The creator God is a reliable source of food that matches our creaturely hungers.

All three statements assert that the world is a matrix of life because it is infused with God's life-giving spirit.

So how to follow up and respond to these gospel assertions of reliable breath, safe from chaos, and grateful for food. We could hunker down in our privilege and property, behind our gates, turned in on ourselves. But the Psalm says otherwise. It concludes with a harsh note:

Let sinners be consumed from the earth,
and let the wicked be no more.
(v. 35a)

The "wicked" are those who squander God's gifts and who seek to possess and administer God's generosity. But it need not be so. If we are infused with gratitude for the good safe world in which we live, we are freed to look beyond ourselves, to move beyond ourselves, to be conduits for that safety and generosity that may pass from God through our lives to the lives of others and to the life of the world. The Psalm is an invitation to those who know that the truth of God is an antidote to the destructive pathologies that are all around us. Imagine God's glad, safe, grateful, generous creatures,

counter to violence,
alternative to greed,
emancipated from anxiety and hate and fear.

The human creature in this ordering of the world is especially entrusted to give access to others to this truth of creation. The Psalm ends with joy: "Bless, praise, rejoice." Gratitude is a launching pad for a different life of peace and justice and mercy and compassion and forgiveness. All of that is possible because the spirit continues to surge, making all things new . . . in the Church and beyond the Church into public practice and into public policy. It is very good news!

May 30, 2004
Wee Kirk Presbyterian Church in Linville, North Carolina

33

Choking the Word

GENESIS 25:19–34
PSALM 119:105–112
ROMANS 8:1–11
MATTHEW 13:1–9, 18–23

In our readings for the day, we get to watch while our ancestors make life-or-death choices. The implication is that we also can be in the process of making choices, just as they were. Or better, we are in fact making choices, even when we are unaware of what we are doing. The choice, lined out here in several versions, is to choose immediacy of what the world offers, or to choose an alternative life that is given by God for the long run. Our choices matter,

> whether short term or long term,
> whether selfish or communal,
> whether with dominant culture or in the alternative of Jesus,
> whether made in anxiety or in gratitude.

I.

The lead example for such decision making is the ancient negotiation between the twins, Esau and Jacob. Since their birth the twins in the book of Genesis have been in dispute and rivalry. Esau is the older. He seems the more sober and the more innocent, but because he is the elder, he has all the advantages and entitlements, just like almost any first-born child, especially first-born sons, even in our own modern world. His younger brother, Jacob, our ancestor in faith, is trickier, more clever, more daring, more ruthless, and more imaginative; and besides that, he has the conniving support of his mother, Rebekah.

Jacob caught his brother in a moment of acute vulnerability. Esau has been out hunting. He comes back from the hunt tired and very hungry. And Jacob is cooking up a storm, perhaps all part of his scheme. Tired Esau comes in and brother Jacob says to him, "How about a bowl of soup?" Esau says, "Smells good; I would like that." Jacob says, "What will you give me for a bowl of piping hot venison soup?" Esau answers, "I am very hungry. I will let you have whatever you want of mine." And Jacob, who could count real good, says, "I will take your birthright, your entitlements to land, name, and wealth as the first born." And Esau in his hunger says, "It's a deal!"

The tradition does not blame Jacob for his shrewd manipulation of his older brother. The tradition blames Esau for his being stupidly propelled by his hunger and his readiness to satisfy his appetite, and his willingness to give up long-term advantage for the sake of immediate satiation. We might say, he is a consumer and he wants it all now, right now! And from this birthright transaction, the tradition reflects on a choice between immediate stuff and long-term benefit that is of much more value. And the text suggests that this is still the big issue in our world, long-term well-being or short-term satiation.

II.

The verses of Psalm 119 that we read get at the same issue, but only want to accentuate the positive. In ancient Israel the core birthright is the Torah, and our Psalm celebrates Torah teaching.

> I hold my life in my hand continually,
> but I do not forget your law . . .
> I incline my heart to perform your statutes
> forever, to the end.
> (vv. 109, 112)

The Torah is not just a flat set of commandments, though it includes the commandments. It is, rather, the entire teaching tradition of interpretive lore and memory about what it means to belong to the covenant community, to belong to the community of God, and to be under the disciplines of that belonging. The Psalm attests that reading, studying, pondering, and keeping Torah is the source of life. The negative counterpart is only implied here. It is that life outside the Torah, life outside the disciplines of this community, life apart from the God of the covenant, life lived on one's own terms, is foolish and destructive and can come to no good end. Thus the move from the Genesis story of Esau and Jacob to the Psalm of Torah presents Esau as a foolish man, outside the Torah, out for quick satiation. The summons of the poetry is that those among the people of God's covenant live by a different reference point that is outside of self and beyond immediate and private satiation.

III.

The same issue shows up differently in the parable of Jesus. This is the complicated parable of the sower and the seed. The seed is the gospel and Jesus, as God's sower, is the one who offers the seed of the gospel. But the primary concern of the parable is not the sower or the seed, but the soil, the capacity of the soil to receive the seed, a readiness to hear and respond and host the truth of the gospel, so that it will grow the good grain of a different life in the world. Jesus' story is mainly about bad soil that does not well receive the seed of the gospel, rocky soil, soil covered with briers and thorns, dry soil where nothing can grow.

The punch line in the parable, according to Matthew (who always wants to instruct us) concerns brier-occupied soil where nothing good can grow:

> "As for what was sown among the thorns, this is the one who hears the word, but the cares of the world and lure of wealth choke the word, and it yields nothing." (Matt. 13:22)

Thorns are a metaphor for lack of receptivity. But then Jesus steps outside the metaphors of the parable and becomes more direct about what he means. There are three phrases piled up here that explain:

> "The cares of the world."

Surely he means social expectation and social requirements of doing well in a demanding culture. What would you list as the cares of the world that press in upon us with endless demand? Perhaps the right car, the right job, the right house or neighborhood, the right clothes, the right cell phone, the right schools for the kids, the right tennis lesson and the right soccer team, the right portfolio, the right war, the right everything to demonstrate one's self and one's worth in a society where we want to be noticed or affirmed or validated, or at least not left behind. Those seem to me the cares imposed by consumer advertising. We care a lot about all of that, and it is a care of the world that makes us unreceptive to the Torah/gospel teaching about the neighborhood.

The second phrase in his teaching of the parable about thorns is even harder:

"The lure of wealth."

Greed is the big assumption that we ought to have more and that more is better, and we will be better with more. We do not all have to be Albert Pujols to demand thirty million a year for ten years. We can be much more modest and still be propelled to get ahead and have more at the expense of the neighborhood. What happens in a society of greed is that the poor disappear from the screen, and we use euphemisms like "reform" to fool ourselves into thinking that we can have a safe, working society with the lower part simply "left behind." This is the real "left behind" not in the "final rapture" of God's judgment, but in the day-to-day work of writing a tax credit policy that concerns loans and debt, so that the squeeze is on. Jesus calls it a "lure," a seduction because it feeds the yearning for more, so that the more we have, the more we may fret about not having enough, and the more cynical we become about the neighborhood and the legitimate public cost of a sustainable social infrastructure. Thus the lure of greed is causing among us the disappearance of a sense of the common good that is at the heart of a gospel ethic.

Thus Jesus parses these two phrases, "the cares of the world" that I identify with social requirement and social expectation, and "the lure of wealth" that I take as systemic greed that leads to policies and practices that are anti-neighborly.

But it is the third phrase in Jesus' statement that interests us. Jesus says that such cares of the world and such lure of wealth will "choke the word." The reference is to briers in the field where the farmer plants seed for a crop. Briers, like kudzu, will choke everything and nothing can grow. Or as Jesus puts it, "It yields nothing." The good seed cannot sprout, flourish or produce, and the outcome is crop failure, crop failure of gospel expectation.

The cares of the world (social expectation) and the lure of wealth (greed) function like briers, bringing us to a life without the word of God. The word of God that we are without is a promise of sustaining companionship. The word of God that we are without is a summons, a commandment to shape our lives in a neighborly direction. The word of God that we are without is a generative force of hope that calls us to new possibility.

> A *promise* of companionship is choked off so we are alone;
> A *summons* to the neighborhood is choked off so that we have only an isolated self;
> A *commandment* of God is choked off so that we are on our own hook and must make it up as we go along.

After such a heavy word, Jesus reverses field at the end of his teaching. The good soil, the ones who hear and understand, the ones who are not exhausted by social expectation and not frazzled by greed, are blessed with abundance (v. 23). This is not a "prosperity gospel." This is rather an offer of another kind of abundance, of being in sync with our creator, of coming down simply where we ought to be. Thus the choice in the parable is briers or abundance. It is not a both/and!

IV.

The rhetoric is different in Paul's epistle, but the argument is the same. Paul writes of those whose minds are "set on the flesh." That phrase in Paul does not mean "sex" or even other "material things." It means rather a life lived in a self-centered way which is, says Paul, a way of death. The alternative is a life in which the spirit dwells in us. That does not mean something mystical or pious, but a life received from God's generosity and lived back to God in gratitude. This life with the God of promise, summons, and command leads to abundance and well-being, whereas a life lived apart from or against God's purposes is a life of destructiveness without healing force or possibility.

There is always choosing:

- soup or birthright;
- briers or abundance;
- flesh or spirit.

These are always the issues that God puts in front of us. That choice is now, I judge, an acute one among us. It is a chance to join the rat-race of rich commodities, fast pace, greedy self, that leads to policies of greed and military violence and oppressive markets in which the quality of shared humanness is cheapened and trivialized. The people who gather around Jesus are people who know, to the contrary, that our life belongs with the neighbors. Thus the Torah of our Psalm reading is about the weak and marginal who have standing and value before God.

It is this either/or that matters now. The church is a body of people who are to be intentional about the purpose of our life. We live in a world where the word of God is choked, and we arrive at a time when we cannot breathe any more. The briers will have come, and we will be as stupid as Esau, because we are hungry for immediate satiation. We can choose otherwise, toward a neighborly future, the one that brings common abundance and well-being.

July 10, 2011
First Congregational Church UCC, Hendersonville, North Carolina

34

Follow in Freedom

I KINGS 19:15–16, 19–21
PSALM 77:1–2, 11–20
GALATIANS 5:1, 13–25
LUKE 9:1–62

The church consists in people who sense and smell and taste . . . and live . . . freedom. Paul states it right out:

> For freedom Christ has set us free. (Gal. 5:1)

I want to think with you about how that God-given freedom feels among us.

I.

There is no doubt that the God of the Gospel has broken the tired old world open, and created space for freedom. In the narrative of Elijah, the break is dramatic at Mount Carmel when YHWH, the God of Israel, is shown to be Lord of lords and God of gods. In the Jesus narrative, by the time we reach our text in Luke 9 Jesus has already healed and cast out demons, has calmed the chaotic waters, and has made clear that a new path in the world is now open. Wherever this God has stirred, there will be no business as usual.

And then characteristically, God's agents (Elijah, Jesus) recruit folk to walk with them into the new space of freedom. The recruitment is abrupt and urgent. Elijah does not even say anything. He just throws his coat over Elisha and you can see that he just got a big coat to wear and big shoes to fill. And Jesus, intermittently through these chapters in Luke, is recruiting and summoning workers to go with him on the dangerous road of God-given freedom that defies old practices that offer no healing or transformative capacity. Thus the setup is a *dramatic opening of new possibility* and *an invitation to embrace the new possibility* with a differently lived life.

It is God who breaks the world open; it is human agents who sign on for the new freedom.

II.

The repeated response from these pitiful human recruits to God-given freedom is pretty consistent. Folk who are called are *held back* and cannot immediately sign on. They . . . and we . . . are held back by many things.

In the Elisha narrative, given the new coat to wear and the new shoes to fill, he says, "Let me kiss my father and my mother, and then I will follow you" (1 Kgs. 19:20). Elijah is terse and impatient with him: "Go back again; for what have I done to you?" I think he means, "If you don't have time for me, I surely do not have time for you. This is too urgent."

In the Jesus narrative, the first recruit says, "I am ready." But Jesus cautions him by saying, "You need to know what you are signing on for. We are going to be deeply at risk":

> "Foxes have holes, and birds of the air have nests; but the Son of Man has nowhere to lay his head." (Luke 9:58)

We are going to be exposed and vulnerable every day of the journey.

The second recruit says, "First let me go and bury my father." I guess this is an echo of the family thing with Elisha: "Let me kiss my father and my mother."

The third recruit says, "First let me say farewell at home."

Jesus is singular: "Follow me, follow me, follow me." And he ends the paragraph by saying:

> "No one who puts a hand to the plow and looks back is fit for the kingdom of God." (v. 62)

And even the Psalmist in Psalm 77 cannot quite yield, because he is completely preoccupied with himself:

> I cry . . . hear me . . . my trouble . . . I seek . . . my hand . . . my soul.

It's all about him! And in verses 3–10, the part of the Psalm that the lectionary will not let us sing, the Psalm is saturated with first person pronouns, the happiest pronoun in the world!

We can see in all three cases . . . Elisha, the disciples of Jesus, the psalmist: the ones recruited for God's new freedom are held back . . . as are we. They are held back by old loves, by old loyalties, by old commitments, by old fears, by old selves mesmerized by old worlds. It is the truth of our lives: we are called to follow, held back in more ways than we have suspected. So we sing:

> [T]he hopes that lead us onward,
> The fears that hold us back,
> Our will to dare great things for God,
> The courage that we lack.

At best we walk up to God's new freedom, tentatively, cautiously, reluctantly; it is the story of our lives.

III.

But we have to keep reading. Because being *held back* is not the last truth of our lives. The last truth of their lives . . . and perhaps ours as well . . . is that the invitation to follow is overwhelming and persistent. We find ourselves yielding to God's freedom in ways that we ourselves could hardly imagine:

Thus Elisha, after his pause for old loyalties, takes on a new vocation. He receives a double portion of the spirit (2 Kgs 2:9). The first thing he does is to divide the waters, not unlike Moses (2:14). He heals the sick; he raises the dead; he feeds the desperate widow; he turns war to peace. He fully occupies the new freedom given him by God, and finds himself propelled to a profound newness that is transformative for those around him.

The disciples of Jesus, the ones called who made all sorts of excuses, finally, in the next chapter of Luke, are dispatched in new obedience. They were sent by Jesus and, we are told, they returned from their mission with joy. They said,

> "Lord, in your name, even the demons submit to us!" (Luke 10:17)

They were ecstatic, because they had discovered that in their service to Jesus they had the inexplicable capacity to overcome the disorder of the world and enact healing. Jesus answers them: "Good enough." But more than that, he says:

> "Rejoice that your names are written in heaven." (Luke 10:20)

Be glad because the angels in heaven have recorded you as worthy of note. They no longer held back, and they had transformative power.

And even the Psalmist, after too much narcissism, makes a big leap, turning attention from self to God. Now the Psalmist is able to remember what had been forgotten in self-preoccupation:

> I will call to mind the deeds of the LORD;
> I will remember your wonders of old.
> I will meditate on all your work,
> And muse on your mighty deeds . . .
> You are the God who works wonders;
> you have displayed your might among the peoples.
> With your strong arm you redeemed your people,
> the descendants of Jacob and Joseph.
> (Ps. 77:11–12, 14–15)

What she remembers is the Exodus. What she remembers is emancipation. What she remembers is being turned loose from the old *holdbacks* to new life and joy and transformative power.

What a company!

> Elisha set free to raise the dead;
> The disciples set free to cast out demons;
> The Psalmist set free, emancipated from Pharaoh in contemporary form.

Paul characterizes the new liberty. He always has a list ready. Here is the stuff to avoid: fornication, licentiousness, enmity, strife, jealousy, anger, dissension, envy, drunkenness, and "things like these." He lists the stuff that will damage the neighborhood. The new obedience is to act to enhance the neighborhood and to bring joy and well-being to the neighbor.

IV.

So imagine, as you come to the table, that you are on the same journey as these disciples, as Elisha, as the Psalmist. Ponder the ways in which you are *held back* because you want to bury your father or kiss your mother. Consider that you are invited to follow out beyond "held back." If you find it helpful, take two steps toward the table and one step back, in order to dramatize the way we are all in the grip of what is passé, and yet being led into newness in spite of ourselves. Come to this edge of newness from the God who gives freedom. Taste the wine, chew the bread, smell the freedom.

Imagine this diocese not held back, but following, following in freedom, following in transformative power. Smell it, and inhale it . . . never to be the same again.

June 27, 2010
Sermon preached for the Diocese of Southern Ohio at Kenyon College

35

The "Long Game" in the Short Run

PSALM 30

GALATIANS 6:1–16

LUKE 10:1–11, 16–20

The day after the dreadful bombing at the Boston Marathon, your well-beloved pastor wrote a column in our daily newspaper. Some of you will remember it. He walked us through the violence and reflected on the need for Christians to hold to their confession in practical, concrete ways. What caught my eye in his writing was this:

> Hope plays the long-game, and is not dependent on winning every skirmish in the battle. It reminds us that we are part of a whole that will continue long after our work is done. (Joe Phelps, "Light in the Darkness," *Courier Journal*, April 16, 2013)

That is, hope is not defeated by the many concrete instances of diminishment, dismay, and discouragement. Hope rooted in God has a very long reach and great staying power out beyond the troubles of the day. The readings for today gave me the theme of hope. I want to think with you about the long game and the short run, about *the goals* of Christian hope and *the practices* of Gospel hope.

I.

The goal of our hope is the conviction that God's will for the well-being, peace, and justice of the world is intense and durable, and will come to fruition. We pray that God's Kingdom will come on earth as it is in heaven. We dare to pray that because we do not doubt that it will be the case, because God is relentless and tenacious about that outcome. The readings for today give us three wondrous phrases that bespeak that divine relentlessness.

The Gospel reading gives us the phrase, "The kingdom of God." Jesus sends his disciples out and he said to them, "When you come into a village of needy folk, say to them, 'The kingdom of God has come near'" (Luke 10:9) and then three verses later, he says this to his disciples: "You know this: the kingdom of God has come near" (v. 11). You know that! The rule of God's *shalom* is about to break in among us. This is the same phrasing that Jesus used in his initial declaration of the Gospel (Mark 1:14–15). God is about to bring well-being into the world that will displace the kingdom of Rome and every other exploitative power. He does not mean it will occur in some dramatic rapture that we get in too many current films. He means that it comes in his very person, in his very body, in his very ministry and in the ministry of his disciples. This good governance is displacing the governance of defeat and despair that is sponsored by Rome and by every other combine of ruthless power and oppressive money. We can trace the emergence of that new governance, that new kingdom in the life of Jesus. It is happening and it will happen. We do not doubt that.

A second phrase is at the end of the Gospel narrative. Jesus says to his jubilant disciples who are so impressed with themselves: "Rejoice that your names are written in heaven" (v. 20). The phrase is a metaphor for saying that God notices and remembers those who serve the new rule of God. God is not a score-keeping God, not making a list and checking it twice. Rather in this intimate figure God has a roster of *best friends* who share God's passion; God in the very long run cherishes now and forever those who perform God's good *shalom*. What counts is not the accomplishment of that *shalom*; what counts is the relatedness that arises from our embrace of the coming rule of God.

The third phrase is in the Epistle reading. Paul writes that our religious differentiations are not significant. In dismissing the distinction between circumcision and uncircumcision, Paul says, "Don't sweat the small stuff." What counts, he asserts, is that the "new creation is everything" (Gal. 6:15). In this poetic idiom the Bible imagines that all that is old and weary and violent and failed will be outflanked by the regime of God's goodness and compassion. The old world will end. It will not end in a great fire or in a rapture of judgment. It will end because it will be overrun by the new creation of God that fully embodies God's will for our world.

That deep conviction of faith was nicely voiced in the film, *The Best Exotic Marigold Hotel* by the young, quite inept manager of the hotel. He said in the film more than once:

In the end all will be well.
And if it is not well, it is not the end.

Well, clearly it is not well among us, not well with violence and greed and
anxiety and alienation. So this is not the end. But the end of all that is old and
failed is coming. We wait; we wait with confidence. We play the long game
because of who God is. The long game is marked by:

The kingdom of God has drawn near;
Our names are written in heaven;
The new creation is everything.

That is the long game we play in faith! We rely on this poetic metaphorical
language for the reality of the Gospel that lies outside all of our explanatory
capacity. We say it in wonder, because it is more than we can explain. But we
do not doubt the claim!

II.

But of course the long game of hope has within it *short-term mandates*. The
long-term indicative brings with it short-term imperatives. What do we do
when we lose skirmishes all along the way, skirmishes with bombs and brokenness and hurt and violation and alienation and disappointment and all
the rest? How shall we live now in light of that great hope? Here are three
notions I received from these readings:

1. Short term work now, in light of the long game of hope, includes *honest,
critical alertness* to the ways in which things are out of sync. It is easy enough
to accept less than that, to give assent to a world that does not work, to accept
anxiety and fear as a normal state, to compromise the *shalom* of God and lower
expectations. We are always in danger, as were the disciples, of being narcoti-
cized by the force of the present tense.

Psalm 30 is a great script for such honest, critical attentiveness. The Psalmist tells how he was doing so well, as stable and sure as a mountain. In a flash,
he was dismayed. He does not tell us what happened. But it was not good. It
could have been a bad diagnosis, or a pink slip at work, or a bombing, or news
of torture done by our government, or a dozen other violations of the good
order of God's world. It could have been that God was, for now, found to be
unreliable and absent, and life without God fell apart for him.

The Psalmist will not let it go at that. He does not accept such dismay as
normal. He says in a loud voice, "That is not right! I expect better than that! I

insist on better than this!" He calls God out! He pushes God to consider the cost of such dismay even for God:

> What profit is there in my death,
> if I go down to the Pit?
> Will the dust praise you?
> Will it tell of your faithfulness?
>   (Ps. 30:9)

He presses God to see that the dismay is expensive for all parties. And then he issues imperatives to God: "Hear, be gracious, help me!"

People like us who live in this text are not intended to be quiet, complacent people. We belong to a tradition that notices, that exposes, that insists, that tells the truth about failed reality, failed reality in the neighborhood and in the larger world. Such "calling out" is an act of hope. Right in the midst of the skirmish, we make insistent claim for better.

2. A second short-term reality of our faith is that hopers are people who *act in transformative, specific, concrete ways.* Hope is a ground for action, not for passive waiting. So Jesus sends his disciples out. He has assured them that the kingdom of God has drawn near. But then comes the imperative to travel light:

> Carry no purse, no bag, no sandals. (Luke 10:4)

Among receptive people rest your peace there. That is, be an agent and presence of God's *shalom*, for such a presence has transformative force. And then this: Cure the sick.

The followers of Jesus are a great force for good health care policy. That surely means the sustenance of a viable infrastructure of health. But more immediately the mandate assumes that right in their own bodies, their presence, and their work, the disciples have healing juices and capacities entrusted to them by God.

This healing mandate reverses the common processes of life and death. It is ordinary and easy enough to imagine that diseases would be contagious, that pathologies would expand, and that epidemics would catch us all. But the Gospel reverses that and affirms that God's power for life will trump the force of death. So Jesus, along with his disciples, enters the zones of death—the diseased, the dysfunctional, and the lepers—and there makes new. In the long run, all will be well. In the short run, the power of well-being is entrusted to the company of Jesus.

Thus it is testified that Jesus had the force of life. He sent word to John:

The blind receive their sight, the lame walk, the lepers are cleansed, the deaf hear, the dead are raised, the poor have good news brought to them. (Luke 7:22)

And here the disciples report on the outcomes of their work, missional work. They say to him:

"Lord, in your name even the demons submit to us!" (10:17)

This stuff really works! And Jesus assures them:

I have given you authority to tread on snakes and scorpions, and over all the power of the enemy; and nothing will hurt you. (v. 19)

This is not a mandate to handle snakes! It is rather to say that the power for life given to the disciples will be authority to make life possible where death seems to have the last word. The demons want to negate life, want hate to win, want fear to prevail. And the healers refuse that, and get on with life-giving engagement.

3. The third practice for the short run of hope is offered in the epistle. Paul writes to the church:

So then, whenever we have an opportunity, let us *work for the good of all*, and especially for those of the family of faith. (Gal. 6:10, emphasis added)

It is, he says, soon harvest time, a biblical phrase for divine reckoning when we will come rejoicing, bringing in the sheaves. Paul's mandate to the church is in three parts:

"Do not grow weary in doing what is right." We call that "compassion fatigue," worn out from caring so much. A friend at my church asked in seriousness, "How long must we care for the poor?" Well, until there are no more poor.

Paul says, "Work for the good of all." That is now termed "the common good." We live in a society of privatization in which we want to extend well-being only to our kind, only to the well-off, only to the responsible and the productive. Against that, the Gospel insists on the good of all, those unlike us, those not well-off, those who do not act responsibly and who do no production of anything. Paul knows that if we do not invest our lives in the public good, our own smaller life will be unlivable.

And then Paul qualifies further, act especially for the good of the family of faith. Care for the church. Care for church people. Care for the church by prayer, by engagement, by generosity . . . where it is persecuted, where it is seduced, where it is compromised. Be good members of the whole body.

III.

The truth is that God has destined the world for well-being. As Dr. King said:

> The long arc of history is bent toward *justice;*
> The long arc of history is bent toward *peace;*
> The long arc of history is bent toward *inclusiveness.*

The skirmishes we lose make it seem otherwise:

> The bombing makes it seem like we are bent toward *violence.*
> The failure of the infrastructure makes it seem like we are bent toward *injustice.*
> The collage of fear and hate makes it seem like we are bent toward *exclusiveness.*

Not! Not true! We know otherwise:

> We know that the Kingdom of God has drawn near.
> We know that our names are written in heaven.
> We know that the new creation is everything.

So we invest in our little patch of work where God has put us, bearing witness right in the midst of the skirmishes, part of the whole that will continue after our own work is done. We will let the Psalmist have the last word:

> Weeping may linger for the night,
> but joy comes with the morning.
> (Ps. 30:5)

July 7, 2013
Highland Baptist Church, Louisville, Kentucky

36

Maintenance, then News!

GENESIS 37:1–6, 12–28
PSALM 85:8–13
MATTHEW 14:22–33

Maintenance of the status quo takes a lot of energy. And we do it for lots of reasons. We do it because we rather like the way things are and do not want them to change. We do it because we despair of the possibility that it could be better than it is. We do it because we are made anxious by uncertainty and change. So we maintain. We maintain our position in the world as the only economic-military superpower. We maintain our leverage in the church for our particular convictions. We maintain the level of our portfolio because its erosion worries us. We maintain our role in the family and our position among the siblings in the family. We do all of that because of satisfaction, despair, or anxiety. We maintain by resistance to those who would change things. We maintain by writing careful memos that confirm and assume the status quo. We maintain by keeping our anxiety on Orange Alert and thus occupying our full attention.

But we are here this morning, like every time that we are here together, to ponder the news from God, the Gospel news that breaks open every status quo and invites us to new God-given gift, demand, and risk. In our readings today, the news that works on our status quo maintenance comes as *dream*, as *poem*, and as *narrative act*.

I.

The Joseph story is told among his many older brothers who had leverage and power arranged in the family the way that they wanted it. Joseph was a

183

younger brother; we would call him a "late surprise" in the family on whom his father Jacob doted. Joseph, in his naiveté, shared his dream of preeminence with his older brothers who of course resented him in powerful ways.

His dream of preeminence, it turns out in what follows, led to Joseph being elevated to prime minister of Egypt so that he could provide food to save his brothers from the famine that was severe. It turns out, moreover, that what he and the narrator came to understand is that all of this was God's intention from the beginning. It was a very big dream that was to be lived out to the advantage of the entire family. But of course none of them knew that at the time. So the brothers resented him.

As a little kid, his father sent him out to check on his brothers who were at work in the field. He did not work like they did. He was too young, but he was their monitor on behalf of their father. And when he appeared in the field where they were hot and tired, they said to each other, "Let's kill the dreamer." Let's nullify the kid who thinks he will upset the order and pattern of privilege in the family. Who needs a new kid to upset everything! So the brothers are dream-killers in the interest of the status quo. As it eventuated they did not kill Joseph, but sold him into slavery. The narrative is a perfect episode in killing dreams (and dreamers) in order to maintain status quo.

And of course, we can never read this story without thinking of Martin Luther King Jr. and his dream speech. He had a dream; it was a dream of freedom and justice that pulsed with our deepest faith and our deepest patriotism. But the dream had to be killed by the killing of the dreamer. Such violent maintenance . . . as we see now in some Arab states . . . is the way maintenance of status quo works. Except, of course, when the dream comes from God, as it did with Joseph and with Martin Luther King Jr., you cannot kill the dream. They can kill the dreamer, but the dream persists and will have its say.

II.

Our second reading is from Psalm 85. It is a large, sweeping poem of the way in which the goodness of heaven reaches down into the earth:

> Steadfast love and faithfulness will meet;
> righteousness and peace will kiss each other.
> Faithfulness will spring up from the ground,
> and righteousness will look down from the sky.
> (vv. 10–11)

The poem names the big terms of covenant: steadfast love, faithfulness, righteousness, and peace, and imagines a meeting, a convergence of earthly faithfulness and heavenly righteousness, when all things will turn out whole and healthy and healing and transformative. The phrases are elusive; but they are what we pray for when we say, "Thy kingdom come on earth as it is in heaven." We pray for "your power arrangements" that are altogether good and healing, let your power arrangements be established on the earth:

> Let steadfast love overrun alienation;
> Let faithfulness overrun mistrust and betrayal;
> Let righteousness overrun exploitation;
> Let peace overrun hostility.

Let your will be done on earth as it is in heaven. The language is almost erotic, let them "kiss each other," in embrace and genuine affection.

Some of you will remember Isak Dinesen's story *Babette's Feast*, in which this wondrous French cook, Babette, comes and serves a feast of extravagance to sober people in Scandinavia. One of the guests at the dinner table is General Loewenhielm who reflects in a wistful way about his life. He makes a little speech and he says, "Mercy and truth, my friends, have met together . . . righteousness and bliss shall kiss one other." It is a quote from our Psalm. He becomes, for Dinesen, the speaker of theological truth. He asserts:

> "Grace, my friends, demands nothing from us but that we shall await it with confidence and acknowledge it in gratitude. Grace, brothers, makes no conditions and singles out none of us in particular; grace takes us all to its bosom and proclaims general amnesty. See! that which we have chosen is given us, and that which we have refused is, also at the same time, granted us."

And then he adds:

> "Ay, that which we have rejected is poured upon us abundantly. For mercy and truth have met together, and righteousness and bliss have kissed one another!" (pp. 40–41).

And then the general says:

> "I shall be with you every day that is left to me. Every evening I shall sit down, if not in the flesh, which means nothing, in spirit, which is all, to dine with you, just like tonight. For tonight I have learned, dear sister, that in this world anything is possible."

And Martine, one of the host sisters, answers the general:

> "Yes, it is so, dear brother. . . . In this world anything is possible."

The entire exchange is grounded in our Psalm. It is all poetry. It is all an act of forward-looking expectation for newness that God will give.

I thought about Babette and our Psalm, and I wondered, how do we maintainers of the status quo resist such poetic possibility? And the answer is, we resist by memo. We resist by flat, one-dimensional thinking and settled certitude, from the left or from the right. And playful possibility as a gift from God is thereby nullified, because we are satisfied or we are in despair or we are propelled by anxiety. In the poetry of the Psalm, there is no self-satisfaction, no despair, no anxiety, only trust in God's good power. And in Babette's tale, there is no self-satisfaction, no despair, no anxiety, only generous self-yielding to this transformative convergence of heaven and earth.

III.

In the gospel reading, Matthew tells of the disciples in a storm at sea. The disciples are in a boat, terrified by the fear of chaos that is about to undo then. They are deeply afraid. But then, in their fear, they see Jesus! He is walking on the sea. He has mastered the chaos and tamed the storm. He says to them, "Take heart, it is I; do not fear." He invites them beyond their panic by the power of his presence. Not only has he mastered the storm. He invites the disciples to walk across the storm, freed for him in safety and well-being. Their leader, Peter, will try it first. He gets out of the boat willingly. But then looks away from Jesus and to the storm. He begins to sink. He cries out in his fear and Jesus rescues him; but he also reprimands him, "You of little faith, why did you doubt?"

The gospel gives us a one-time dramatic exhibit of the power of the gospel and the transformative presence of Jesus. This is not a generic tale. It is not a universal truth. This is a one-time happening of chaos being governed by Jesus, and the disciples being overwhelmed, not by the storm, but by their fear.

So how do we maintainers resist the force of Jesus' presence? Well, we always knew the storm was so powerful. We always knew that the wind blows wild and will overwhelm us. We always cling to our anxiety. He says, "It need not be so," but doubt resists the transformative presence of Jesus by clinging to our long-established anxiety. Peter had long lived on Orange Alert and he is not inclined to give it up now. He cannot believe that Jesus is more powerful than the surging sea, so he looks away from Jesus and focuses on the chaos of the storm. It is the way he thought it was. He did not calculate that Jesus' presence had changed anything. He had not learned anything; and he had not trusted.

IV.

These three texts converge in powerful ways concerning maintenance and news:

> The narrative of the brothers shows the way in which violent resistance keeps things as they are, but the dream has its own say.
>
> The poem imagines a new world, and lets us see that a memo of certitude can refuse the poem;
>
> The gospel story shows chaos tamed, but well-established anxiety wins for Peter.

So I thought of these three textual witnesses to maintenance and news:

> The maintenance of *violence* and the news of a *dream;*
>
> The maintenance of a *memo* and the news of a *poem;*
>
> The maintenance of *anxiety* and the news of a *presence.*

The news concerns a *dream,* a *poem,* and a *presence.* The world is pretty much stuck with and committed to maintenance through *violence,* through *memos,* through *anxiety.*

And then it occurred to me. That is what the church is about. We meet regularly to *renounce our violence,* to *abandon our memos,* and to *relinquish our anxiety.* We meet regularly in order to *reengage the dream,* in order to *retrieve the poetry,* in order to *re-trust the presence.* That is what fills the church with enormous missional energy and generosity and joy. Sometimes the church falls back into old practices of violence, into old habits of memos, into old embraces of anxiety. But that is not our true character or our best way in the world. The gospel news announces that the old ways of maintenance in the world are a kiss of death. Better that faithfulness and peace should kiss each other. That is the kiss of life!

August 7, 2011
Capitol Hill Presbyterian Church, Washington D.C.

37

Our Antiphon Interrupted

2 KINGS 4:42–44
PSALM 145:10–19
EPHESIANS 3:14–21
JOHN 6:1–21

Maybe you are like me, with a strange antiphon going in your life with voices responding to each other:

- In Psalm 145:15 it says, "The eyes of all look to you."
  but the voice of fear says there is not enough oil and we had better send the fleet somewhere.
- Verse 16 says, "You satisfy the desire of all living things,"
  but the voice of fear says there is not enough food for everyone, so don't worry about the "food desert" without Kroger in some parts of the city.
- Verse 17 says, "The Lord is kind in all his doings,"
  but the voice of fear says, there is not enough health care and we should practice triage on the poor.
- Verse 19 says, "He fulfills the desire of all who fear him,"
  but the voice of fear says, there is not enough education to go around, so we have a new kind of "separate but equal."
- Verse19 says, "He hears their cries and saves them,"
  but the voice of fear says there is not enough support for all, so no immigrants.
- Verse 13 says, "He is gracious in all his deeds,"
  but the voice of fear says there is not enough truth, and surely Islam does not have any.
- Verse 20 says, "The Lord watches over all who fear him,"
  but the voice of fear says there is not enough grace to share it with gays.

This is an antiphon that lives deep in our society and I suspect deep in our hearts, at least in mine. It is a common antiphon that is shared by liberals and conservatives. We all love the Psalm (even if you think I may have over-read it), but we find these fears of "not enough" always speaking to us.

The Psalm is a meditation on the word "all." I counted eleven uses and the word "every" in verse 16 is also "all," so twelve times "all." The Psalm is about the overflow of God's generosity that floods creation with the force of life, given to every creature without limit. God the creator, every day, overwhelms God's creatures with all that is needed for an abundant life, no lack, no shortage, no deficit.

But our world is in the grasp of deep anxiety and I practice that anxiety . . . not enough, so I work and calculate and count . . . just another effort, just another phone message, just another competition, fear of falling behind, fearful of lacking, fearful of not getting it right, fear of someone else getting what should be mine. And I find my life sitting somewhere between the overflow of life force from God and the mantra of "not yet enough."

II.

And then, right in the middle of this antiphon that goes on and on in our much hurry and rush and in our sleepless nights of worry, right in the middle of that, comes this text from John 6.

He comes on a hungry crowd . . . again, as last Sunday in Mark.

He says to Philip (who is a stand-in for the church): "Where are we to buy bread for these people to eat?" (v. 5)

But John tells us that it is a trick question that Jesus puts to Philip. He wanted to see whether Philip understood. He hopes that Philip by now would understand that Jesus is to enact God's gift of abundance in the world. Where Jesus comes, life overflows with well-being. But Philip—the church—does not get it. Philip is thinking in old-world categories of there not being enough. He says to Jesus in disbelief, "It would take six months of my salary to feed this big crowd" (v. 7). We cannot afford it. We just can't spend it that way on people who want a free lunch. Jesus already knows about his own capacity for abundance; he knows the source of bread for the world. He knows there will be more than enough! But his church still is trapped in scarcity.

Thank goodness this exchange with Philip is interrupted, because it is not going anywhere. Andrew steps in to the conversation and says, "We have found some bread" (v. 9). Good news, because the crisis is averted! Then he said, "It's not much; but at least we have some starter seed for the big meal that will be needed." But then, after that, Andrew sounds just like Philip: "But what is that among so many?" It is not enough! Philip and Andrew and the church are still calculating about bread in the old frightened way, because they are still in the grip of the voice of scarcity. They are caught in the anti-phon that they cannot escape. They know about Jesus and his goodness; but they could still hear the mantras of scarcity ringing in their ears.

Jesus, however, is not held back by his disciples who do not yet get it. He takes the narrative in a quite fresh direction that we would not have anticipated.

> Tell the crowd to sit down; please come to the table . . . 5,000 of them!
> Jesus takes the loaves;
> Jesus gives thanks (the word is *eucharisto*; Eucharist. Imagine a meal called "Thanks"!)
> He distributed the bread, as much as they wanted!

And then, immediately, when they were all satisfied ("he satisfies the desire of every living thing"), he tells his disciples to gather up the surplus (v. 12). He did not need to look to see about that. He did not say, "Did you have enough?" He knew there was more than enough. Loaves abound! More than enough! Twelve baskets full!

III.

But notice. John does not explain. He does not even express curiosity about the abundance of bread. He does not, with Bishop Spong, think it could not have happened. He does not, like a good liberal, think they all pulled out their lunches and shared, as though they were running a black market in bread. No, what John tells us is that this is a new reality right before our eyes. Jesus enacts a new world. What he does is an exhibit of his capacity and authority as the center of the new world in which all things work together for good to those who sign on.

When the ushers came forward with the surplus bread they had collected after everyone had eaten, there were twelve baskets full! Who would have believed it? Well, nobody would have believed it who lives in the old world of scarcity, not Philip and not Andrew. In that old world of scarcity there is not enough, and we must cringe and save and protect and not share and not let anyone get a free lunch . . . because we might run out.

Except we see the surplus! We see something new that invalidates our old world. No wonder they said, "This is indeed the prophet who is to come into the world" (v. 14). This is the one for whom we have been waiting, when we did not even know for whom we waited. This is the fulfillment of all the old, best promises. This is fulfillment beyond all our hopes and wishes. The old world no longer can hold us or our fearful imagination. And by the end of the Gospel reading, he said to them, "Be not afraid" (v. 20). Because the world works in a new way!

IV.

I imagine you and I will continue to be haunted by the antiphon, the contradiction between the notion of scarcity and the wonder of much bread in abundance. But we also know this. That antiphon has been interrupted by none other than Jesus. We are the people who have witnessed and know about the abundance of bread among us, for the world. That is what makes the church such an odd bunch. The church is a pump station for abundance that overflows. We do not need to explain. We do not need to dispute economic theories. We do not need to measure grace according to our anxieties. The truth of Jesus is this: all of our fears that lead us to parsimony have been overwhelmed by the goodness of God. He said, "Be not afraid"; and they said. "This is the guy!"

July 29, 2012
St. Timothy Episcopal Church, Cincinnati, Ohio

38

Prayer

A Two-Sided Deal

HOSEA 1:2–10
PSALM 85
COLOSSIANS 2:6–15
LUKE 11:1–13

Some of you may have listened to the Gospel reading enough to notice that it included Luke's short version of the Lord's Prayer.

I.

Did you also notice, as I did this time, that the prayer, in this brief form, voices to God a series of imperatives. We call them "petitions," but they are imperatives that might have the force of command:

> *Give* us this day our daily bread;
> *Forgive* us our sins;
> *Do not bring* us to trial;

And some versions add a fourth imperative:

> *Rescue* us from the evil one.

Jesus instructs his followers to pray such imperatives that recognize both *need* and the *source of help*. The imperatives seek from God what we cannot do for ourselves:

> We cannot, on our own, supply bread, but depend on the creator.
> We cannot, on our own, forgive our sins, but turn to the redeemer;

192

We cannot, on our own, avoid trial before the authorities, but count on
   God as our litigant.
We cannot, on our own, rescue ourselves from evil, but rely on deliverance
   from God.

The prayer acknowledges the limit of our capacity to save ourselves. Thus
the imperatives are voiced with some urgency.

II.

In order to underscore the point, Jesus, good rabbi that he is, adds a narrative
for illumination. He tells of going to a friend at midnight in need of three
loaves of bread, not having enough bread of one's own. The bread in this
story is no doubt the same daily bread for which we have just been instructed
to pray. But it is midnight, and the friend is asleep; he does not want to be
disturbed:

> Do not bother me; the door has already been locked, and my children
> are with me in bed; I cannot get up and give you anything. (Luke 11:7)

The request fails. But says Jesus, "Pound on the door of your friend harder."
If you do that long enough, the friend will get up at midnight, inconvenient
as it is, and give you the bread you need. But, says the rabbi, the bread given
at midnight will not be because of friendship; it will be given because of your
"*persistence*." That is the word in the text. That is the only time the term is
used in the New Testament. It can be translated "impudent" or "shameless."
Knock on the door of a friend at midnight impudently, with a shameless voicing of urgent need.
   The best recent example I know of such impudence happened at the State
House in Nashville. A legislator, Stacey Campfield, had filed a bill in the leg-
islature providing that if the grades of a child from a poor family went down,
less state money would be given to that family in need as a part of welfare
support. Financial support would be linked to grade performance! But Aamira
Fetuga, age 8, would not accept such a proposal. She followed Campfield
around the State House all day, continually talking to him and telling him
how cruel his bill was. He tried to dismiss her as a "prop," but she was relentless all day long. She was persistent; she was impudent in his eyes. But then,
after a long day when the cameras would give Campfield no relief, he relented
and withdrew his bill. Aamira is a model of persistent petition that bordered
on shamelessness.

Later on in Luke, Jesus will tell another story about prayer, about the "importunate widow" who nagged a judge until he was exhausted with her nagging and gave her justice (Luke 18:1–8). And Jesus says, "Pray like that and you will not lose heart."

That urgency in the parable points to God. It is God who is the friend with bread. It is God who is the friend who sleeps at night who does not want to be inconvenienced. God is the one who will, late in a night of urgency, be move to act. Prayer will disturb God's snooze.

And then Jesus adds an interpretation to further explicate God:

> *Ask* and it will be given, but only if we ask;
> *Knock* and it will be opened, but only if we knock;
> *Seek* and you will find, but only if we seek.

The accent is on active intervention that refuses to accept the status quo. And the one who responds to our asking, knocking, and seeking?

Jesus tells another quick parable. God (with gender specificity) is like a father only more so. Or we extrapolate, God is like a mother . . . only more so. Even a failed father will respond to a child, Jesus imagines. No father will give a child who needs a fish a snake. No mother will give a child a scorpion who needs an egg. Parents who are selfish and preoccupied will do better than that to respond to the urgent need of a child.

And then . . . deep breath: How much more! How much more our heavenly father! How much more this mother God who responds even at midnight. Matthew, in remembering this teaching of Jesus, has Jesus say, "How much more will your heavenly father give good things to those who ask him" (Matt. 7:11 CEB). But Luke ups the ante: "How much more will the heavenly father give the Holy Spirit to those who ask him." That is the gift from God that trumps all gifts from God. God will give the Holy Spirit, the force of life, the urge of vitality from God's own life that we cannot conjure for ourselves. No doubt Luke has his eye on the Book of Acts that he will write wherein the church is energized by the Spirit to daring testimony and obedience in the face of the Roman Empire. God will give life-force to be free for Easter truth.

III.

This text is about prayer. It exposits the strange transaction between God and us that has no parallel anywhere else. It is more than a teaching about prayer. It is a comment about the defining engagement of our lives that disturbs God and evokes God's generosity.

It turns out that *human persons* are agents of need, urgently requiring what we cannot secure for ourselves. To be a creature of need is a countercultural claim in a society that imagines self-sufficiency, a culture that can conjure a drug or a cosmetic or an exercise program or a technology to master everything. Because what Jesus knows is that there are not enough resources among us for our self-sufficiency. Finally we are creatures dependent upon the graciousness of God.

But we are not, on the other hand, passive recipients of God's gifts. Jesus invites us to assertiveness in the presence of God, to speak imperatives, to demand, to require, to inconvenience God, to make our need into God's preoccupation. No wonder Karl Barth can say, "Prayer is simply asking" . . . asking in need, asking in boldness, asking until gifts are given so that our life together may flourish.

But this text also *re-characterizes God*; this God is not like a helicopter parent who hovers over us to cater to our every urge and whim. This is a God who has a life to live, who sleeps in weariness, who does not want to be interrupted. This is a God who must receive bold wake-up calls. But this is also not the God of progressives who cringe at the thought of an "interventionist God" who violates our treasured reasonableness wherein we can get along if we have enough resolve and are smarter and stay at it.

Finally we arrive, in this testimony, at a *deep honesty* on our part about need and boldness and at *deep amazement* concerning generosity on God's part. Such honesty and amazement require some doing. Such a transaction is more than a little sobering for us in a rational world that prizes control and does not want serious engagement with holiness that refuses our mastery. In the end, Jesus summons us to be like eight-year-old Aamira, shameless and impudent, and then receiving God's own spirit, which is the gift of new life out beyond ourselves.

July 28, 2013
The Church of the Holy Spirit, Orleans, Massachusetts

39

What Did You Have in Mind?

EZEKIEL 18:1–4, 25–32
PHILIPPIANS 2:1–13
MATTHEW 21:23–32

"What did you have in mind? That is the easy form of inquiry. The more scolding form is this, "What could you have been thinking?" Either way, the probe is to see what you think, what you imagine, what you entertain, what you ponder in your unguarded, uncensored moments. In these moments together, we consider our minds, making up our minds, changing our minds, and refusing to change our minds.

I.

The epistle reading from Philippians 2 is one of the great hallmarks of evangelical faith, often thought to be a hymn in which the church becomes lyrical about Christ. It says of Jesus that he was exalted as God's own regent; he emptied himself in obedience on the cross, and was raised in Easter glory. He gave himself up as an act of obedient faith.

And then Paul writes to his beloved church, "Have the same mind in you that was in Jesus Christ." Think like him! His mind, his intention, his self-understanding was to give himself up in glad faith for the purposes of God in the world. And you, think like him!

Paul writes to his friends about how to think and imagine and act and live in the church . . . do it the way Christ did. He said, "Do not look to your own interests; look to the interests of others." And let your mind be filled with compassion, sympathy, love, and humility, without selfish ambition or conceit. He reminds his listeners that the people gathered around Jesus live in the world differently, fully committed to God's love, fully confident in God's love, and so not needing to use energy for winning, or controlling, or having our own way.

And when we do that, we find ourselves filled with joy, a surprising abundance, and gladness. So the question lingers for us, "What did you have in mind?" and the church answers, What we have in mind is the interest of others toward whom we reach with compassion and sympathy.

II.

But take the harder form of the query, "What could you have been thinking?" The Bible knows that the people of God are not always thinking noble, generous thoughts and having regard for the interests of others. The Bible assumes that the faithful always have in mind the righteousness of God, the will of God for well-being of the world. That is what the agenda is.

But the ancient prophet, Ezekiel, knows that other stuff enters our minds, and so he scolds, "What could you have been thinking?" Our verses from Ezekiel leave out all of the particulars that we are not supposed to read or know about. In the verses left out of our reading we learn what was more likely on the minds of the faithful, more than they would admit. Three things:

- shrewd, exploitative economic maneuvering to take advantage of the poor;
- abusive sexual relations that dishonor others;
- and idolatry, the treatment of some things with absoluteness even when they are not really that important and do not deserve to be worshipped.

That, says the prophet, is a recipe for wickedness, for unrighteousness, and it is quite a list of the topics that dominate much of our thinking! The economic dimension of such ignoble thinking is put there for theological liberals who worry that the economic stuff matters the most. And sexual misconduct is put there for theological conservatives who worry most about sex. And idolatry is put there for all of us who get our priorities confused and distorted. And that, says the prophet, is what is typically on our minds:

- how to get ahead with money;
- how to have our way with sex;
- how to absolutize what we treasure the most.

But then, if that is what is on your mind, says God through the prophet:

> Repent and turn from all your transgressions . . . cast away from you
> all the transgressions . . . and get yourselves a new heart and a new
> spirit! (Ezek. 18:30b–31)

In other words, change your mind. Get something else on your mind. Get the
purpose of God for your life on our mind. And then God says,

> Why will you die? . . . For I have no pleasure in the death of any-
> one. . . . Turn, then, and live. (vv. 31b–32)

Thus Paul invites to a new mind in Christ. Ezekiel exposes the old mind of
death. Paul and Ezekiel together invite us to change our minds, to get in sync
with the true stuff of our life with God.

III.

And then this story about Jesus. He argues with the authorities, the chief
priests and the elders. They are the ones who recognize him as a threat to
their power arrangements, so they engage him and try to trick him so that
they can deter him and get him off the street where he causes too much trouble for them.

But because he is very clever in his argument, the exchange ends in a stale-
mate. They cannot "get" him. Their trickery did not fool him, so the debate
winds down. There is a pause. And then Jesus takes the initiative and tells
them a story. Jesus is always quick with a story that subverts all of our conventional thinking.

He tells a story of two sons in a family.

One of the sons refused to go to work as his father required of him; but
after he refused, he changed his mind and obeyed his father. Get it; he
changed his mind!

The other son said to his father that he would go to work; but he did not go.

The contrast between the two sons is symmetrical. One said "no" and did
"yes." The other said "yes" and did "no." And Jesus said to his adversaries,
"Which one obeyed?" But they know and are quick to answer. They got it and
said the one who said "no" but went anyway.

And then Jesus, master teacher that he is, moves the story to a didactic
point. The two sons in the story are stand-ins for the people in front of Jesus.
The obedient son represents in the story (this might surprise us!) the tax collectors, the prostitutes and other riff-raff who lack control of their lives and so
are open to the leading of Jesus. But they are just a foil in the story for the second group, namely, the good powerful people who keep to social convention

and manage everything well and keep control. In the story they are the ones who say "yes" and do "no." They are the ones who settle for a thin righteousness of social convention and conformity to the ordinary, but never get around to the radical alternative of Jesus. They finally do not believe in or accept Jesus and prefer to continue their life uninterrupted by him. But the losers, the tax collectors and prostitutes, embrace his alternative life, because they were not hooked on convention and power. That is, they emptied themselves, while the leading people were so full of themselves that they could not turn or trust. Jesus delivers the punch line by saying, surely to shock, that they were the ones who would enter the kingdom of God first, because they were open to his possibility and could stand alongside of him.

And then comes the point to rebuke the power people:

> Even when you were shown the new way of righteousness in the world, you did not change your minds and believe him. (Matt. 21:32)

John taught you the new righteousness, but you would not embrace it. Jesus invited you to another way that looked to the interest of others, but you could not accept it.

> In Philippians there is a bid to get a new mind in Christ;
> In Ezekiel there is an offer of a new heart and a new spirit;
> In the story of Jesus, there is an exposé of hard hearts that dare not change to receive the good news of Jesus.

So, what's on your mind?
So, what were you thinking of?
So, you did not change your mind!

IV.

It is not easy to change our minds, especially toward Jesus. I have been reading the autobiography of Robert Lifton entitled *Witness to an Extreme Century*. Lifton is a Jewish psychiatrist at Yale who has spent his long life studying social extremity, the suffering at Hiroshima, the nuclear threat in the US, the savagery of Auschwitz, the abandonment in Viet Nam. He finds a common pattern in all of these extremities that he calls "totalism," the embrace of an idea, an ideology, a conviction that is totally comprehensive of all reality that explains everything, and excludes everything and everyone that does not fit. Such totality that tilts toward totalitarianism is often linked to religious passion and is ready to enact violence to sustain itself. Thus Lifton comes to see that the force of totalism produces unbearable menace, all understood as being morally justifiable. And my point from Lifton is that people caught in a totalism cannot change their minds.

> Paul exposes the force of those who look only to their own interests;
> Ezekiel identifies the totalism of wickedness that majors in economic and sexual exploitation, legitimated by ideology;
> Jesus confronts the entitled people of his society who are enmeshed in a totalism of their own thin righteousness who could not receive the newness that God is giving.

All these texts invite the question:

> In a soft form: What did you have in mind?
> In a harsh form: What could you have been thinking?

And the news that I get to announce to you is this: In the Gospel we are invited to a new mind, a new heart, a new spirit, a new engagement with the world, a fresh sense of our role in it.

Jesus, and the God who dispatches Jesus, moves against every totalism, of the right and of the left, of morality, of technology, of economics, of sexuality, of communism, of capitalism, of militarism. Totalism is the refuge of those who find the world too dangerous, who must create little packages of certitude and control. And Jesus came otherwise. He came among tax collectors and invited them out of their greed. He came among prostitutes and invited them out of their despair. He came among elders and invited them out of their power. He came among chief priests and invited them out of their certitude. He himself understood the power of giving one's self away. And he invited others to be of the same mind, ready to let go.

At the end he declares:

> You did not change your mind.

So, what did you have in mind?
So, what could you have been thinking?
Or what will you have on your mind now that is fresh and life-giving, and beyond the ordinary?

September 25, 2011
University Congregational Church, Wichita, Kansas

40

Don't Bet against the Neighborhood

JEREMIAH 32:1–15
1 TIMOTHY 6:6–19
LUKE 16:19–31

If you have been tracking it through the summer, you know we have had a steady diet of prophetic texts from ancient Israel. If you have been listening carefully, you are likely pretty weary of these prophetic texts. And no doubt the original listeners in ancient Jerusalem got pretty tired of the prophets as well. Because they kept up a relentless, shrill poetry of warning and castigation. They kept saying that if you don't get in sync with God, you are going to get in big trouble. If you don't practice justice in the neighborhood, you are going to be sorry. If you don't honor your covenant with God, all of your power and wealth and smarts will not save you.

They were worn out from the message, as we might be. Except for one thing. As it turned out, the prophets were right. Big trouble did come. Jerusalem was sorry, in the end. They were not saved. All at once they lost their king. They lost their temple. They lost their political identity. The economy collapsed. Real estate values sank to new lows. A world of confidence and security had ended for them. Sound familiar? They had everything bad happen to them except an oil spill. And that was only because they did not have any oil. So the prophets were right!

I.

But what do you do after you are right? Jeremiah did not gloat or even say, "I told you so." He got silent. And he waited. Because after you are right and after the big trouble comes because you have been out of sync with God, you have to say something new, something different, something unexpected. And so, in the wake of the big trouble that came, there is opened a whole new vista of prophetic poetry.

In our text, Jeremiah is under house arrest by the king in Jerusalem because he has said these unwelcome words. And while he was there, he waited; and then, he says, a new word came to him. It is an unexpected word, a quite specific word. He is instructed by the word of the Lord to go buy the family farm back in his home village of Anathoth. The word is terse, but he says, "I knew it was the word of the Lord."

It was such an odd command from God, so specific and concrete. It was a hard assignment. He had to keep the family farm in the family because it was their shared inheritance. Somebody had to do it, and he was next in line. You know about the old family farm. It is filled with memories, some good, some not so good. But it is run down, unproductive, a tax burden, a real inconvenience for a city guy, at best a fixer-upper, and a mortgage imposition. But he is commanded to pay for it, just when the economy had tanked.

II.

We are told that he obeyed the command. He obeyed in detail. He paid seventeen shekels of silver for the property, about thirty-four tons of barley, a lot of money for a peasant farm. He got the deed; he sealed it; he weighed the money; he had a contract with terms and conditions. And he filed the deed in the presence of witnesses. He was very careful to complete the full process, and the Bible gives us every detail on the purchase. It must have been important that they report all of that to us!

- He was careful because it was his family obligation;
- He was careful because he kept the inheritance for his uncle;
- He was careful because this was a part of the promised land.

So here is this purchase of land just as the armies marched and the bombs exploded and the rockets gave off their red glare, and the world seemed totally out of control; he bought the property!

III.

Now I know you do not care about this ancient property transaction. Except for this. As he finished the process Jeremiah got another word from out beyond. The word of the Lord came to him:

Houses and fields and vineyards shall again be bought in this land. (Jer. 32:15)

The first word was, "Buy the property." The second word is that the land—this property and all of the land—will have a flourishing future, because God will see to it that the whole land will prosper, with new habitation and new agriculture, houses and fields and vineyards and well-being and safety and *shalom*. The promise is against present circumstance. The land was poor and it did not look like much; but it is a land over which God has made a pledge for a new, wondrous future.

This little land transaction in the book of Jeremiah becomes the pivot of all of biblical faith. The economy had sunk to zero. The prophet was compelled, just at that low point, to live in wonder and hope and expectation that God will work a newness that is inexplicable and beyond anything that we can ask or imagine. The little land purchase becomes a wedge for a new world of well-being that God will give. But he had to invest!

IV.

What I got out of this story that is so specific and concrete about Jeremiah's life is that God commanded him to deal, in hope, with the stuff that was right in front of him. He was led to see that specific investment would open new futures where God would work a newness. He learned not to bet against his family farm that at the moment was worth almost nothing. I am led in three directions about the way in which such specific investment opens to God's future. He is commanded to bet on the farm against all the data that is available to him:

1. Do not bet against the body of Jesus. On Friday we were ready to give up on the body of Jesus that had been sold for thirty pieces of silver. His body was worthless and hopeless, as worthless and as hopeless as Jeremiah's property. But God took his body and raised him up to new life. And his body of new life that we receive at this table is the bread that feeds the world. Every time we come to the table, we bet on Jesus' body.

2. In the gospel reading there is a map of the world economy. There is a rich man who ate like a banquet every day in his party clothes. And there is Lazarus, the poor man with bad medical care. There is the rich man and the poor man, the haves and the have-nots. Ordinarily we would bet on the rich man against the poor man. But, says the story, do not bet against Lazarus. Do not bet against the poor who embarrass and inconvenience us. Because the poor are carriers of God's future . . . just like that old farm back in the

village. We watch and we see how Lazarus ends up in well-being with father Abraham.

3. And us? Well, if you keep it local and specific, I get this: do not bet against the neighborhood. Do not bet against this seething world of the homeless and the unemployed and Muslims and "losers" and others unlike us. We would rather not deal with all of these. We would rather live in a safe, guarded place to keep our children uninvolved, so that we would not need to notice. But the narrative says, bet on Lazarus. Bet, as we do in this church, on the future of the world of which we are a part.

So I thought about the temptations that I face that you also may face:

- I would rather bet against the body of Jesus and find an easier way to be in the world, because Jesus always calls us out.
- I would rather bet against the poor and wish we had a better, less needy company all around us.
- I would rather bet against the neighborhood, just like Jeremiah would have preferred to bet against his family farm.
    But let this ring in your ears,
    When you bet on the family farm;
    When you bet on the body of Jesus;
    When you bet on the poor loved by God;
    When you bet on the neighborhood as a place of newness,
    The words keep sounding:
        Houses and fields and vineyards will flourish here.
    We do not know how; but we bet on it . . . every time we come to the table!

September 29, 2010

St. Timothy Episcopal Church, Anderson Township, Cincinnati, Ohio

41

The "Yet" of Endurance

PSALM 66:1–12
JEREMIAH 29:1–4, 7
2 TIMOTHY 2:8–15
LUKE 17:11–19

Two affirmations are given in the lectionary texts for today. First, people of faith look reality in the face, deny nothing, and endure. Second, they do so by a tenacious confidence in the amazing rule of God that defies the facts on the ground. People of faith, we among them, have a deep capacity to watch for the extraordinary from God and so to endure ordinary with boldness and confidence and freedom.

I.

I am led to this awareness by focusing on the Psalm for the day, Psalm 66. (Since we have this weekend been studying the Psalms, this seems the right place to begin). The Psalm acknowledges trouble from God, the kind we know about currently:

> For you, O God, have tested us;
> you have tried us as silver is tried.
> You have brought us into the net;
> you laid burdens on our backs;
> you let people ride over our heads;
> we went through fire and through water.
> (vv. 10–12)

I thought the notion of "through fire and through water" makes a good connect to our wars and our oil spill, and all the troubles that come with them.

But before the Psalmist gets to such candor, he celebrates what he has witnessed and what he now remembers:

> How awesome are your deeds!. . .
> He is awesome in his deeds among mortals.
> He turned the sea into dry land;
> they passed through the river on foot . . .
> [He] has kept us among the living.
>   (vv. 3, 5–6, 9)

The pattern for life is set in the Psalm:
First, remember the extraordinary goodness of God.
Second, tell the truth about the present.
And then, third, in verse 12, "Yet!"
Nevertheless!
Notwithstanding!
"Yet you have brought us into a spacious place." You have made us safe. For that reason (in the verses we did not read), I will remember to give thanks. I will be seen in public as one of your people. And the conclusion is:

> He has not rejected my prayer
> Or removed his steadfast love from me.
>   (v. 20)

We end up facing the real troubles, confident of God's good, faithful, steadfast love for us.

II.

This is an extraordinary act of resolve and defiance. It is not, however, unusual in biblical faith. Because biblical faith is not soft, sweet romanticism. It is hard, tough truth-telling, but truth-telling in the context of God's good love. This is a different story from the one the world tells. The world tells us either that it is all right and you do not need to worry . . . or that it is a jungle out there. But people who cluster around Jesus refuse either easy romanticism or angry cynicism. The wonder of faith is to trust in the midst of the truth.

It is the same in the text from Jeremiah. The people of God are deported away from their homeland. The cheap preachers are saying that it will all return to normal in two years. But Jeremiah tells another truth. No, no return to normal, any time soon. Get used to strangeness. Get used to being an outsider. Get used to having a new home in a place that feels threatening to you.

Indeed, pray for the Babylonians whom you fear, for when God gives *shalom*, God will give it to you with them, all of us together. The letter from Jeremiah is a summons to have faith amid the real world, to make a difference by being an agent of God's *shalom*, even there.

It is the same when Paul tells his life story to his friend, Timothy. Paul tells of his hardship, of being chained like a criminal because the empire feared his Gospel news. But Paul did not give in. Indeed he writes four times of the defiant "yet" of his endurance:

> If we have died with him, we will also live with him;
> If we endure, we will also reign with him;
> If we deny him, he will also deny us;
> If we are faithless, he remains faithful . . . for he cannot deny himself.
> (2 Tim. 2:11–13)

As a result, Paul says to the church, "Quit quarreling. Quit quibbling fine points and get on with the task of ministry." Because no matter how tough it is, God is reliable and will give you life.

Thus we have three witnesses:

- The Psalmist with "yet."
- Jeremiah with the work of *shalom*.
- Paul assures that God will not deny God's own purpose.

III.

The ground for such confidence, as we have seen in the Psalm, is that we remember the wondrous gifts of God that run beyond all our worldly possibilities. The Psalm is nearly generic about God's awesome deeds. But the narratives are more particular. They concern leprosy. We have to remember that in the prescientific days of old, leprosy was a deep threat to society; they could not control it when it reached epidemic proportions. So their strategy was to quarantine people who had it, to isolate them and exclude them from social life. The way they did that was to declare them "unclean" and impure and a danger to normal life. To have leprosy was to be banished; we practice some of the same banishments for some of the same reasons, of gays, immigrants, Muslims, those who are unlike us and who threaten our way of life . . . sometimes Blacks, sometimes women, anybody who is not a good-looking white male! Keep the world of power and control as it is!

So the story goes in the Book of Kings. There is a Syrian general, Naaman by name, who has leprosy. He risks, like General McChrystal, losing his spectacular command. He gets word of healing that is available in Israel, among those who are his perennial enemy. He goes there because he is desperate. He comes with an impressive entourage, as would an important general. But Elisha, the quixotic "man of God," is not impressed. He simply says to the general, "Go wash seven times in the Jordan River and you will be clean." After some resistance, the general does so. We are told that his flesh was restored, as sweet and tender as the flesh of a young baby boy. It is a wonder! It is the power of God that reaches into unacceptable places among unacceptable people, and makes all things new. No wonder the Psalmist could say:

> How awesome are your deeds;
> He has kept us among the living!

The story of Jesus is not different. There are ten lepers on the road. They are dangerous threats to society, unclean, impure, excluded, banished. They cry out to Jesus. He stops to speak with them. He risks exposure. He moves close to their danger. He says, "Go and show yourselves to the priest." As they went, we are told, they were healed. Jesus' word healed them; he did not flinch at their danger. No wonder the Psalmist could say:

> How awesome are your deeds;
> He kept us among the living!

IV.

So here is the word for us today. The world is filled with danger. The world is filled with threat and danger. There is so much to fear, so much we do not understand, so much that is beyond our control. And the church gathers, this odd people with a strange vocation. As Paul says, we are a people "approved as those who have no need to be ashamed." It is not news that the world is a troubled place. But it is news that amidst such a troubled world, there are those who linger over the miracles whereby God has broken the world open to well-being, for lepers and for all those who are excluded.

> For that reason the Psalmist says,
>   Yet you have brought us to a spacious place.
> For that reason, Jeremiah can say to the deported:
>   Yet, even here, in time to come God will make this a place of *shalom*.
> For that reason, the Syrian general, as he was healed, can say,
>   Yet God has brought me to a new healing.
> For that reason, the one leper who came back in gratitude can say,
>   Yet the healing of God came to me, even though I am a Samaritan.

For that reason, Paul could write,
    Yet the word of God is not chained.

So dear people of God, as we look the world in the face, consider the bold, defiant "yet" of faith that is grounded in God's extraordinary capacity for life. We have signed on with this news. It is the ground of our hope and of our joy. It is the ground of our ministry. The place where God has put us is indeed spacious enough, enough for joy and freedom and obedience. Even now, yet!

October 10, 2010
Edgewood United Church of Christ, East Lansing, Michigan

42

The Scroll That Would
Not Be Shredded

2 KINGS 22:3–13
JEREMIAH 36:4–8, 14–26
MATTHEW 23:1–12

Every social organization, if it prospers and lasts a long time, is prone to complacency and self-indulgence and illusion about its true character and future.
And when a social organization gets distorted in such a way, there is need to
re-form and re-formulate and re-shape according to its true character. And if
that social organization happens to be the church that is formed according to
God's good news, the self-indulgence is much more serious and the need for
re-form and re-formulation and re-shaping according to its true character is
all the more urgent. That is why we speak of re-form of the church that we
call re-formation. It is an urgent need to recover the church from its toxic
self-indulgence and complacency.

I.

On this Re-formation Sunday when we remember the dramatic work of
Martin Luther who called the church in his time to be re-formed according to its true character, I want to tell you the story of the most dramatic
re-form in the Old Testament. It was in the seventh century BCE, about
620, during the reign of King Josiah, about twenty kings after King David
and King Solomon in Jerusalem. Josiah's grandfather, Manasseh, had been
king for a very long time, a king, we are told, much given to self-indulgence
and carelessness about covenantal responsibility. In the wake of his grandfather, King Josiah wanted to clean things up. So he decided to renovate the
temple in Jerusalem so that it would look spiffy and compelling. And while

the workmen were renovating, they found what we always find around the
edges of the church building, stashed in a closet somewhere . . . some old
Bibles, if you are Episcopalian, some old prayer books, some old worship
bulletins, some angel wings left from the last Christmas pageant, some old
church music. And among all of that stuff that no one had authority to throw
away, they found an old scroll. They showed it to the priest, Hilkiah, and the
priest gave it to Shaphan, an advisor to the king. Shaphan read it and was
astonished by what he read. He took it and read it to the king. And the king
was astonished by what he heard. More than astonished, Josiah was frightened and filled with dread at what the scroll said. Because the scroll said that
when you violate God's covenant and God's will, you may have big disaster
from God, external threat and internal collapse. Most people think that the
scroll they found was the Book of Deuteronomy that is filled with ominous
prospects for the kind of self-indulgent complacency that Jerusalem featured
under the rule of grandfather Manasseh.

The surprise of the story is that King Josiah took the scroll seriously, so
seriously that he tore his clothes in repentance. More than that, he instituted
a policy of re-forming Israel as God's covenant people. He recovered the old
practice of Passover and we are told in the book of Jeremiah, that he introduced new policies to care for the poor and the needy (Jer. 22:15–16). He
responded to the scroll, took it seriously as a word from God, and imagined
from the scroll a new way of being God's people in the world. That is the
drama of Josiah's reform in which Israel had a fresh chance to be God's faithful people.

II.

But let me tell you a second story in the same time frame of Josiah. There is no
doubt that the prophet Jeremiah was, as a young man, nurtured in the scroll of
Deuteronomy and from it he had his vocation as a prophet. We are told that
he also made a scroll, one that became the book of Jeremiah. He dictated the
scroll to his secretary, Baruch. Like many bosses, Jeremiah asked his secretary
to do the hard work. He told Baruch that it was too dangerous for him to go
public with the scroll, and he asked Baruch to go read it in public. Baruch
did so; he read the whole scroll in the public square in front of the Jerusalem
temple. When he read it, it of course came to the attention of the authorities
who are always on the look out for any inflammatory, subversive scroll. The
authorities invited him to read it to them in the royal cabinet room. When he
read it, they asked him where he had gotten it. He told them that Jeremiah
had dictated it to him. The cabinet officers had sympathy with the scroll, for

it reminded Israel of its covenantal mandate from God and it warned Israel of dire outcomes for neglect of that covenant. The officials sensed that the scroll was important; but it was also very dangerous, because it criticized the present king, the son of Josiah.

They took the scroll to the king. One of the cabinet officers read it to the king. And in one of the most dramatic scenes in the Bible, as they read the scroll, the king very ostentatiously took out his penknife and cut the scroll and threw its pieces into the fireplace to burn them. This is the earliest example we have of shredding documents. The king acted with contempt and imagined that when he got rid of the scroll he could get rid of the summons and the warning that had been voiced by Jeremiah. More than that, he organized a state posse to hunt down Jeremiah and Baruch, the scroll-makers, who were seen as enemies of the regime. But, we are told, after the scroll was shredded, Jeremiah dictated a second version of the scroll to Baruch and added more to it, because you cannot get rid of the scroll. The scroll keeps reemerging with its serious voice of truth, unwelcome as it may be.

III.

In our readings we have these two narratives, one in the book of Kings and one in the book of Jeremiah, closely related to each other. We have two scrolls, apparently the book of Deuteronomy and the book of Jeremiah that are connected to each other. And we have two kings, the father Josiah and the son Jehoiakim. What interests us most is that we have two responses to the voice of the scroll. On the one hand, King Josiah responds seriously; he tears his clothes and institutes reform. On the other hand, his son King Jehoiakim reacts to the scroll in contempt, tears up the scroll and tries to eliminate it. It turns out that these two scrolls refuse to be shredded. They have staying power and cannot be eliminated by contempt or by burning or slicing and dicing or ignoring. The reason these scrolls will not be shredded is that they are truth-telling scrolls about the will of God for the people of God. They insist upon being taken seriously through new resolve and new obedience and new well-being.

IV.

It does not take much imagination to transpose this crisis of the scroll to the urgency of Martin Luther. He lived in a church in Europe that he saw to be distorted and complacent and self-indulgent. And as he was studying the

Bible, that scroll that refuses to be shredded, he had the profound insight that gave impetus for his bold challenge to his church. He saw that the church in his time was deformed and so he forcefully called that the church be re-formed according to the word of God. His take on the deformation in his time was that we could not earn God's love but that God's love is free to all those who trust and obey. And so the connections is scroll . . . re-form, Bible . . . Re-formation, gospel . . . new resolve of obedience to the gospel.

V.

All of this is not ancient history, not about old King Josiah and his scroll, not about old Martin Luther and the Bible. It is rather about the church in our time being deformed and now being re-formed according to the good news of the Gospel. There is no doubt that in our time, as in the time of Josiah and in the time of Martin Luther, the people of God have come to a distorted shape in the world. Most people thinking about this today would judge that the church among us is distorted because it too much accommodates to and lives in collusion with the dominant values of our Western world, the values of power and entitlement and anxiety that lead, most often, to exclusion along the lines of class or race or gender or ethnicity or whatever, an exclusiveness because we believe ourselves to be the especially chosen and entitled of God. That need for exclusion and entitlement, moreover, takes on the anxiety of our society that is fearful for its life and a church that in many places is preoccupied with its survival and well-being. Indeed, in our Gospel reading, Jesus warns about those who are too much preoccupied with themselves and their location in the social pyramid and which seat they have at the table. When we inhale the anxiety of the world around us, we no longer breathe in the love of God that leaves us free and unencumbered and unafraid.

Thus in our time, as olden times, the crisis of de-form and re-form is upon us. And I imagine that the deformation we are now called to recognize is that gospel truth entrusted to the church is not congruent with but too comfortable with the common assumptions of Western democratic capitalism, with our consumer greed and our military anxiety, and with our attempt to secure ourselves and our dominant place in the world. Thus the hope of the word of God for the church is that the church be freed from its anxiety and its self-preoccupation to give itself away for the good news of God and of God's good love for the world:

- The good news of hospitality that refuses the fearful exclusions that seduce us into seeing those unlike us as a threat.

- The good news of generosity that refuses the greedy parsimony of a society that is on the make for more.
- The good news of forgiveness in a world that endlessly keeps score and
  makes the losers pay and pay and pay.
- The good news of justice for the vulnerable in a society that is increasingly hostile toward the vulnerable.

Thus the word to Josiah was so that Jerusalem would not be on the make
for its own security, but as Josiah tried to do, open itself to the truthful claims
of the poor and the needy.

So the impetus for Martin Luther was that the church would not be mesmerized by its security and wealth and influence, but would give itself away
according to the goodness of God.

So the impetus for the church in our time is to be a people so fully settled
in God's goodness and love that it can give itself away for the sake of the
neighborhood.

Not long ago I got asked a tricky question that every preacher dreads. The
question was: Is Jesus allied with capitalism or with socialism? Of course the
one who asked the question assumed that I would answer "socialism," so that
we could have an argument. But I answered: "Neither; Jesus is not allied with
socialism or with capitalism; Jesus is allied with the neighbor." Especially with
the vulnerable neighbor, especially with the neighbor who is of no conse-
quence in the world, especially with the neighbor who has more needs than
resources, especially with the vulnerable neighbor who needs housing, health
care, and education.

That it seems to me is the crisis question for the church in a society that
is hostile to the neighbor, for it is written, "If you cannot love your sister or
your brother whom you see, you cannot love God." If you do not love your
neighbor whom you see, you cannot love God. The gospel does not imagine that the world is an armed camp. The gospel does not imagine that the
world is a market place of competition. The gospel does not take the world
to be a rat-race in which we may become winning rats. Rather the gospel
takes the world as a neighborhood. Jesus is the good neighbor because he is
the one who shows mercy. And we are the ones, after him, who believe that
the neighborhood can be re-covered and re-formed and re-stored. The issue
of neighborliness is everywhere among us, because the greed system of our
society does not want neighborliness. Neighborliness makes the greed system
nervous. The greed system organizes posses to stop courageous people in the
neighborhood. It does what it can to stop the reading and singing of neighborliness. So here, I believe, is the word of re-form that is faithful for us. Our
life in faith is grounded in the old scroll about the God of love poured out

for all the neighbors. That word cannot be shredded. It has staying power because it tells the truth that our society can hardly bear. And it cannot be shredded! It cannot!

October 30, 2011
Covenant Presbyterian Church, Cleveland, Ohio

43

The Living God

More Than "Tastes Great . . . Less Filling"

PSALM 146
HEBREWS 9:11–14
MARK 12:28–34

When I looked at the texts designated for this Sunday, I was reminded that the church is not unlike the familiar beer commercial of "tastes great . . . less filling." As you likely know, in the beer ad, each party of the beer-drinking crowd has determined a point of view about the product and shouts it out loudly and with great resolve, to try to prevail in identifying the attractiveness of the product. It is possible to see the church in conflict shouting its slogans to try to win against other slogans and other perspectives on the product, in this case, the truth of the gospel and the faith of the church.

I.

On the one hand a conservative construal of the gospel . . . we might call it "tastes great" . . . interprets the gospel in terms of blood atonement and consequent purity; this perspective operates from a priestly metaphor that has to do with the offer of sacrifices. The metaphor is not often identified in terms of animal sacrifice and the priestly assumptions are not much probed; but these affirmations yield a kind of certainty whereby we can say, "Christ died for my sins," "I am saved by the blood," "Christ paid it all." There is a truth in this that we richly value, even if it emits a somewhat static notion of God's love for the world. The truth is that in the death of Christ, God is shown to be utterly self-giving for the world in love: "God so loved the world . . ."

The epistle reading in Hebrews expresses this notion of the gospel:

216

[H]e entered once for all into the Holy Place, not with the blood of goats and calves, but with his own blood, thus obtaining eternal redemption. For if the blood of goats and bulls, with the sprinkling of the ashes of a heifer, sanctified those who have been defiled so that their flesh is purified, how much more will the blood of Christ, who through the eternal Spirit offered himself without blemish to God, purify our conscience. (Heb. 9:12–14)

The statement appeals to the ancient rituals from the book of Leviticus; it makes the argument that the self-giving of Christ's life is more valuable and more efficacious than any animal sacrifice of a goat or a cow. The rhetoric is metaphorical, but the claim is serious. Christ's self-giving counts for everything, well beyond all ancient animal sacrifices. What it counts for is to permit contaminated people to commune with God. The imagery takes a quite palpable, material view of sin that renders one unclean and defiled and banished from the presence of God. We confess that in Christ God holds nothing back of God's self for our sake. The outcome of self-giving for those who receive this act by the New High Priest is a purified conscience; we are no longer outsiders but are now safe in God's love. This is an act that changes our status before God.

II.

On the other hand, a liberal or progressive view of the gospel . . . we might term "less filling" . . . will find comfort and support in the Psalm we read this morning. Progressives believe that our faith is all about transformative justice in the world. The Psalm celebrates such justice and affirms that God is on the side of such racial justice:

[The LORD] executes justice for the oppressed;
. . . gives food to the hungry.
The LORD sets the prisoners free;
the LORD opens the eyes of the blind.
The LORD lifts up those who are bowed down;
the LORD loves the righteous.
The LORD watches over the strangers;
he upholds the orphan and the widow.
(Ps. 146:7–9)

The Psalm exhibits God as the one who is transforming the political economy of society. Progressives, moreover, gladly take on God's work as their own, tending to believe that "God has no hands but our hands," and the way God does this transformative work is to get our own hands involved in issues of power, money, health care, housing, prison reform, and all of that list. It does not bother progressives that we slide from God to our own assignment. The outcome is a dynamic process of social change that results in changing social relationships, all as a part of God's work and will.

III.

I do not think I overstate the tension:

> Conservatives . . . Progressives;
> Static . . . transformative;
> Hebrews 9 . . . Psalm 146, lessons for the day;
> Tastes great . . . less filling;
> Blood atonement . . . social transformation;
> Holiness . . . justice.

We shout slogans at each other and have no doubt that we are right, while being impatient with the other chanters and doubting their motives. I like to think that if the "tastes great" and "less filling" groups had been in the crowd the day of the gospel story, the taste great people would have said that the great commandment is to love God, for sometimes the purity people do not notice the neighbor. And the less filling progressives would have said that the first commandment is to love neighbor, for very often the less filling people do not truck much with God who wants to be loved by us.

Except that Jesus did not parse the question in either direction. They asked him about a first commandment and he said, "You get two. You never get just one." You never love God without the neighbor; you never love the neighbor without God. Both commandments are a summons to move beyond our preferred posture to a bigger vision to see at the same time *the God who gives self away* in love and *the neighbor who waits for emancipation and justice*. He said: You get two!

IV.

So I puzzled at the text, Hebrews 9, that talks of the blood of Christ that is offered, like a sacrificial animal, without blemish . . . and Psalm 146 that has God in solidarity with all the social rejects, orphans, widows, immigrants, prisoners, oppressed, and hungry. And then I noticed. In Hebrews 9, the last phrase is, "purified our consciences from dead works to worship *the living God*" (v. 14). The priestly metaphor offers a drama of the high priest and all of us entering into the holy of holies, into the presence of the living God. And in the Psalm God is contrasted with princes and mortals who are no help, but God is lively as help and hope so powerful, so engaged, that it is this God and no other who is creator of heaven and earth, who is the giver of justice and food, who is faithful. The Psalm contrasts the God who makes new with all other would-be sources of newness who in fact have no life and cannot give life. The Psalm affirms that:

> Princes: (government, banks, wealth, power), and
> Mortals: (self-sufficiency, self assertion),

finally cannot produce life or well-being or peace or justice in the world. None of these agents can make us safe or make us happy, only God!

So I imagined that conservatives (who prefer priestly metaphors) and progressives (who crave social transformation) are like taste great and less filling, finally have more in common than they have that separates them. What they have in common is that we are children and subjects of *a living God*, that we are disciples of *a life-giving Christ*, that we are carriers of a *life-giving spirit*. The Bible, from beginning to end, is a witness to *the life-giving power of this God*:

- It is this God who brought life into heaven and earth, and daily sustains the world;
- It is this God who presides over the food chain and gives food in due season and satisfies the desire of every living thing;
- It is this God who came bodied in Jesus of Nazareth of whom it is said, everywhere he went the blind see, the lame walk, lepers are cleansed, the dead are raised, the poor rejoice;
- It is this God who blows the winds of justice and freedom in the world and here and there breaks the brutality of hate and violence.

Finally, in our telling of the tale, *the living God* emerged from *the power of death* on Easter day, broke free of the grip of despair, broke all the power of denial and loss and silence, exposed the fraudulent posturing of pride, self-sufficiency, and exploitative leveraging, and called us into Easter existence. Now such an Easter voicing of evangelical reality does indeed give comfort to progressives who cherish the new justice of God in the world. But the letter to the Hebrews asserts that the self-giving of God can purify our conscience of dead works. It takes a purity of heart and conscience, a willing of one thing, and a singularity of obedience to be in sync with the self-giving God who makes all things new.

So I have a word of summons to speak to you today. It is this: if you are using your energy to become a powerful agent of control, give it up for a gift from the living God. If you think that by hustling, by more knowledge or money, by more expenditure of energy you can make yourself safe or happy, give it up for the self-giving of the living God. Receive the gift of God who is worshiped in truth. The gift is given by the God who is without blemish who lives and gives life.

But I also have a word of invitation to speak to you today. Be on the receiving end. Be on the other end of the gift of life from the living God. It is counterintuitive in our society to receive. Indeed it may be un-American to notice that the free gifts of God and the well-being of healing, transformative possibility are all around us. They come to us because this God is always doing what the world judges to be impossible:

> It is impossible that the orphan and widow will be cared for;
> It is impossible that food will be given to the hungry;
> It is impossible that justice will be given to the oppressed.
> You can continue the list.

When we live by what is possible by us, we either end in despair or we end in a demanding ethic that can never let us rest. When and if we fall back into the arms of the Easter God, we find ourselves with freedom that the world cannot give, with safety that the world cannot assure, with happiness that outruns our hopes. When we turn toward the living God, we know for sure that here are no analogues, no parallels, no competition, and no alternative to this God. That is why we cling to the Psalm and to the epistle, to transformative possibilities and to the self-giving of God.

I do not believe that in the beer ads the competitive slogans were ever resolved. But I do know that in God's church that conservatives who champion the first commandment of love of the self-giving God and progressives who keep before us the command to love neighbor do come together into God's good presence. We come together before the living God. That Easter God puts the whole world into a new form out beyond us. Because the Easter God is for us and with us, we can be creatures of life, creatures who receive life and creatures who transform life. This is the news. If you know about deathly shadows of hopelessness in your life, imagine the whole company of the church in praise of the God of life. Imagine, Easter is a surge of the living God, every day, for this is the God who holds nothing back of God's own self from us.

November 8, 2009
First Presbyterian Church, Ithaca, New York

44

Sheep—Preoccupied Shepherds

EZEKIEL 34:1–6, 11–16, 20–24
JOHN 21:15–19

For a very long and well-established time, there has been a marvelous congruity between the values of our faith and the values of our society. More than anywhere else since Calvin's Geneva, we Presbyterian types in America have been able to affirm a convergence between faith and public practice, and we could do so in good conscience. We could trust that the relationship between American values and Christian affirmations was a comfortable one. Now that congruity and that convergence are coming apart. It does not take any great insight and it does not matter whether one is liberal or conservative to see that there is a growing tension, an alarming misfit between the dominant values of our nation and the confession we make as Christians.

I take the two Pastoral Letters of the Roman Catholic Bishops in the U.S. as among the most important religious acts of our day. I take them also as serious signs of the unraveling of the fabric of religion and politics in our society. On the two great issues of our time, peace and economic justice, the Bishops have articulated the incongruity and have invited Christians to think about that problem. Of course the letters are not universally agreed to or accepted. But that they have been written, and that they have evoked such a response, is a measure of the growing problem for us who are faithful Christians and loyal Americans.

Now what I have in mind in this sermon is very modest and I want to set your mind at ease. This is not a sermon that is liberal or conservative. It is not a sermon that is especially critical or especially supportive of national policy. I have in mind a different aim. It is that we admit together that we American Christians are in a crisis precisely because there is a new incongruity and a

221

new lack of convergence between our faith and our public values and practice. That crisis requires us to rethink, to think as we have not thought before, to care, to hope, to repent in quite new ways.

You see, the alternative to facing the crisis is that we should dig into our favorite position, perhaps shout at each other, perhaps join up with our favorite posture and then later discover that we have not been thinking about obedience to Jesus but we have been thinking only about our vested interest, and we have been doing our thinking only through our fears. There is need now for reflective people to think what the new incongruity means. The impetus for Christian involvement in public life is still present, but it is clear on all sides that we cannot any longer claim to be a Christian nation. I suspect if we can once face that reality, then we will be freed to think in new ways and as Christians to take a more decisive part in the discussion, but we cannot until we finish with our illusion.

I consider the text from Ezekiel 34 not to persuade you, but to slip it into your imagination. It is a marvelous text and you may find in it some more material through which to think about this incongruity. Ezekiel had watched the failure and destruction of his beloved Jerusalem and he reflects on how it has happened. He concludes that it happened because of bad government. So at the outset we notice the strange manner of discourse. On the one hand, the discourse is all one long speech of decree by the God of Israel who speaks in strong first-person assertions, "I, I, I." Yahweh, the God of Israel, is here at the most sovereign speech available. It is the voice of this awesome dreadful God that now sounds in the conversation about government. And when that voice sounds, we have a very different conversation about government.

The other fact is that it begins, "Ho, shepherds." Shepherds means kings. I thought if Ezekiel were a southerner he might begin, "Hey, kings." But what is astonishing is that Yahweh addresses the kings. Yahweh has a right to speak. The kings must listen. They do not get to answer back. Usually kings do all the talking, but not in Ezekiel, not with Yahweh. Now the kings must listen to the one who has a right to speak. That already is crucial in this season of Fourth of July. Kings and governments and public systems of value are addressed by God in a sovereign way and are subject to that voice. This dreadful voice of Yahweh says there are things that the kings who brought the civil destruction must listen to.

1. The first point is this: *Governments which are self-serving and which practice greed and a failure of compassion are in big trouble from God.* That is a basic premise of the Bible that goes clear back to the Exodus. The kings condemned were likely not wicked people. Rather they had fashioned a system of value that was self-serving, that benefited established interests and from which the

issues of justice and compassion had disappeared. So the prophet feeds back to the kings what they had done:

> You eat the fat. You clothe yourself with the wool. You slaughter the fatlings, but you do not feed the sheep. The weak you have not strengthened, the sick you have not healed, the crippled you have not bound up, the strayed you have not brought back, the lost you have not sought. You have ruled with harshness. (Ezek. 34:3–4)

The indictment is that those with power and influence have used their place to advance their own interest and have neglected the public values of compassion and care. I do not think Ezekiel means these are wicked individuals. I think he means that the flow of power and the arrangements of access and value have been arranged so that the issue of the marginal, the weak and the needful has simply disappeared. And the kings did not notice.

Now if we listen to this text, it may become a hint or a mirror of what is wrong among us. What is suggested is that public power is misdirected, because its goals have been forgotten. It is the relation between sheep and shepherd that is forgotten. It is the relation between the governors and the governed, the relation between power and need, which depends on the issue of justice and the power of compassion. In that time and this time, there is evidence that the shepherds have forgotten the sheep entrusted to them.

2. Then in this decree from the throne, *Yahweh speaks out an alternative.* Yahweh is going to rule directly so that we get a picture of what public practice should look like. This God is not much interested in religious matters but this God is fully engaged in the matter of public power: "I, I myself will intervene." It sounds like a decision of Presbytery to declare a pastoral vacancy and govern the parish directly. That is what happens to rulers and governments who forget their work. Yahweh declares the throne vacant and rules directly without such human agents. This is what such a proper rule would look like:

> I will seek out my sheep.
> I will rescue them.
> I will bring them back.
> I will feed them.
> I will be shepherd of my sheep.
> I will seek the lost.
> I will bring back the stranger.
> I will bind up the crippled.
> I will strengthen the weak.

And then this conclusive word is spoken: "I will feed them in justice." The text insists that the final issue of government is justice, which must not disappear from public life. Of course we need to be clear on what this means. The Bible has a clear and odd notion of justice. It does not mean that one gets what one deserves. Rather it means that one gets what one needs in order to live, no matter how marginal or weak one is. The governance God proposes in the public sphere is precisely such a practice of justice toward the weak, marginal, poor.

I suggest that this decree from the throne gives us very much to think about, for the rights of the marginal are difficult among us. And we abuse the poor in so many ways, direct and indirect, as when we redeploy our material wealth into more and more arms that clearly secure nothing. It is not a matter of being hawk or dove any more than it is of being capitalist or socialist. It is rather a matter of deciding if the ways of this shepherd God apply to public life. It is an issue if biblical faith provides us a clue about how to order our nation, if our faith is true, even if we have forgotten the text, or if these texts are now irrelevant because we do not believe the decree of this God. This is an enormous promise found in the mouth of God that this new kind of governance is intended by God, is promised by God and will surely come. And we are the people who hold to this sovereignty, who are baptized to trust in it, and who notice when and where this promise is resisted or violated in the name of greed and fear.

3. Now this decree may not seem very realistic. It sounds like a heavenly rule on earth and that does not seem to touch public reality very directly. Can you imagine that in Judah and Israel one gets rid of ruler and turns things over directly to God? Well, the text knows this is a problem. So in verses 23–24, implementation is suggested:

> I will set up over them one shepherd, my servant
> David, and he shall feed them: he shall feed them
> and be their shepherd. And I, the LORD will be
> their God and my servant David shall be prince among
> them. I, the LORD, have spoken.

The specificity of governance is placed in the hands of David and the line of David. Ezekiel makes a quite concrete proposal about government and social structure in the midst of the exile. God does not rule directly out of the sky. God rules through structures and agents and institutions and there will come another David, a real David, a new dynasty, a new order, which will become like all the Davids were supposed to be, agents of justice, righteousness, peace, dignity, humaneness.

Now Ezekiel does not claim that the real shepherd has come, but to us Christians we have discerned in Jesus of Nazareth that the real shepherd has come, the new government is at work, a new kingdom of justice, righteousness, peace and dignity has begun. There was a debate about this new David. Some, including John the Baptist, were unclear so they sent a messenger, "Are you the real David?" And Jesus sent word back, "Go tell John that justice has begun, that righteousness is underway, that peace is on the move: the blind see, the lame walk, lepers are cleansed, the dead are raised, the poor have their debts cancelled." Many were offended by this new public practice and they sought to kill Jesus because they did not want such a public order. They liked it the other way when public life was based on greed and fear.

Now I suggest that in this Sunday of Patriotism, we are left with these three questions:

1. Is it time that public order that is into greed and self-serving and lacks compassion is in big trouble with God?
2. Is it time that our God invites us to an alternative public order that is marked by compassion and justice?
3. Is it true that in Jesus of Nazareth new public order has begun to happen in ways that unsettle all that has been routine?

I do not urge you to my precise conclusion. I only propose that those questions come out of the text, that they are our questions, that we have Fourth of July questions of a very different kind because we take the Bible seriously.

The rulers of this age want to reduce the claims of Jesus to spiritual matters, which are private, but the Bible will not let that happen. The rulers of this age want our thinking to be shaped by our fears . . . fear of communism, fear of egalitarianism, fear of the collapse of the free market system, fear of the erosion of our morality. But this decree from the throne, out of God's very mouth, is not grounded in fear, but in the truth of God's powerful gospel. We are now driven to ask about the truth of the gospel as it relates to public life. Our fears have carried us as far as they can carry us in terms of selfish economic policy and in terms of the mad pursuit of armed security. Our fear will take us to no better place.

Now we are having to decide if God's sovereignty is true. God's sovereignty is of a very special kind. It concerns compassion, attentiveness, passion, care, justice. The old quarrels of liberal and conservative are now irrelevant. We are at a new place in public life in America where we must decide about reality, about human community, about the gospel. It is a small step from saying, "Ho, shepherds," "Hey, kings," to the question put to Peter and to the whole church: "Do you love me?" The question pounds at Peter and at us. It asks, "Are you serious? Will you obey?" Then it becomes more specific: "Feed my sheep." The metaphor has not changed. It is still sheep tending. Facing Jesus is the story of our lives. It gets translated into feeding the sheep, bringing back the strayed, binding the crippled, strengthening the weak, feeding in justice. The real question of patriotism is, "Do you love me?" The answer sends us to public issues as the place where Jesus will be obeyed, not in private acts, but in matters of policy. The kingdom coming is not a private party. It is a new public way in the world.

Eden Theological Seminary, Saint Louis, Missouri
July 7, 1985

45

The New Math of Fidelity

JOB 19:23–27
PSALM 17:1–9
2 THESSALONIANS 2:12–15, 13–17
LUKE 20:27–38

They asked him a trick question. They appeared to probe his wisdom, but in fact they were trying to catch him out.

I.

"They" are the Sadducees, the religious elite who served the big steeple churches, perhaps the Dean of the Cathedral and a tenured theological professor or two. They are the opinion-makers who had things arranged the way they wanted them to be. They recognized that Jesus, in his subversive way, was a threat to their power arrangements. As a result they tried to trick him, to expose him as a dangerous fraud, to exhibit his hostility to the status quo, and so to eliminate him.

They asked him a question about the next age, a zone of immense speculation. They knew about marriage between one man and one woman, about their being together in this age and in the age to come. But what, they asked, about a woman who had married seven brothers in succession? How could seven be one in heaven? How could one accommodate seven? How could we do that math for the next age? They tried to trick him and expose him as a false teacher. Their reasoning was simple, to extend present practices into future possibilities, assuming that it would all be the same. They imagined that their math would let them be the big players in the next age as they are in the present age.

II.

But Jesus sees what they are trying to do with their trick questions. So he bamboozles them with answers that do not answer their trick question at all. He gives three cagey answers:

First, he says, your calculus about the new age does not work, because in that age people do not marry as they do in this age. Your calculus for the present simply does not work for God's future. Your big mistake is to assume that the future will be like the present that you control. But you will not control the future with your careful self-serving reasoning. Your calculus of seven and one and one and seven is irrelevant.

Second, he says that the resurrection of the dead is an explosive event in God's life that blows away all of our meticulous assumptions and our capacity to control. Resurrection is not just life after death or revivification of the dead; it is the coming of the new rule of God that breaks open all of our patterns of control. As support for his teaching of this radical newness he appeals to Moses whom God, at the burning bush, sent into the world to work new freedom according to God's purposes.

Third, he asserts that the God of Abraham, Isaac, and Jacob is the God of the living and not of the dead. We do not spend our time worrying about the dead, but focus on the living and being alive in God's world. That is our proper vocation.

All of these responses are enigmatic enough to put the Sadducees on notice:

- Your calculus does not work for God's future.
- The resurrection is not a stabilizing assertion; it is rather a summons to new possibility out beyond all of our management.
- The summons is to engage in new life and not to worry about the dead who can be left with God.

Jesus changes the subject on the Sadducees. He must have taken their breath away. They get very quiet. They say, "Good answer." What else could they say? And then Luke says, "They no longer dared to ask him another question." They did not ask, because they had been had, and they knew it. Jesus had declared their irrelevance for the future. He asserted that God's future was coming at them in a way they cannot control or factor out as business as usual. The sweep of God's power for life is too large and too deep and too compelling to be comprehended in their explanatory categories. This story rings true because we are discovering the same, that God's sweep of new life is beyond our categories.

III.

It is no wonder that we read verses from Psalm 17 to go with this Gospel narrative. The speaker of the Psalm—it could be any of us—is under considerable pressure. Just as Jesus in our narrative is under assault from his adversaries who want to eliminate him, so the speaker of the Psalm is under assault from his adversaries whom he identifies as the "wicked," "deadly enemies":

> Guard me . . . from the wicked who despoil me,
> my deadly enemies who surround me.
>   (vv. 8–9)

He urges God to intervene on his behalf:

> Hear a just cause, O Lord;
> attend to my cry;
> give ear to my prayer from lips free of deceit.
> From you let my vindication come;
> let your eyes see the right.
>   (vv. 1–2)

He states his own innocence to God as a ground for his petition:

> If you try my heart, if you visit me by night,
> if you test me, you will find no wickedness in me;
> my mouth does not transgress . . .
> I have avoided the ways of the violent.
>   (vv. 3–5)

> My steps have held fast to your paths;
> My feet have not slipped.

And so he petitions God:

> Guard me as the apple of the eye;
> Hide me in the shadow of your wings.
>   (v. 8)

He wants to be cherished by God. His big petition is this:

> Wondrously show me your steadfast love.

The speaker wants God's own wondrous covenantal loyalty to sustain him in his risk from those who are out to get him. He trusts his future to God in the midst of the threat, just as Jesus does.

IV.

It does not require much imagination to see that the Psalm can be read in the midst of the Gospel reading. The Sadducees are indeed adversaries, the enemy, the wicked named in the Gospel. What they want to do is keep the world the way it is. Jesus is the petitioner who is at risk before them. He will be the apple of God's eye, for God will protect and guard him in the shadow of God's own wings. Jesus finally falls back on God's steadfast love in this age and in the age to come, because that steadfast love outlasts all of our old calculus, all of our old explanations, and all of our efforts at control that become irrelevant, all of our desperate attempts to keep the world the way it was. The Psalm shows the way in which the faithful, at wits ends, fall back on the fidelity of God.

V.

It does not take much to transfer this Gospel confrontation and this Psalm-prayer to our own time and place. The truth is that we are all now at a risk point. We know that the old categories do not work, but we cannot see the new categories in which there will be no more business as usual. We know that the old categories in which the church dwells do not work anymore. The old categories of the economy, or the neighborhood, or our schools, or health care delivery do not work. We are like these old Sadducees; we would like to imagine that the future will be like the past, that the new age will be like the old age that we have for so long been able to sustain. We would like to maintain the old math of "seven and one" and "one and seven."

But Jesus knows better. Jesus knows that the future is not cast in our old categories. The future is not handed over to our mastery. The future is in the hands of the narrative-breaking God who makes all things new out beyond our mastery and our control. He says to his adversaries, you cannot manage the future in the old ways, because God's newness is a big, inscrutable leap beyond us. And that is what we face, even as the Sadducees faced the coming of the new age that they could not manage.

What then? What then of our old patterns of control? What then of our old categories of explanation? What then if our old math fails? Well, it is the new math of fidelity. So we pray with the Psalmist:

Wondrously show me your steadfast love.

We are invited to be the apple of God's eye. We receive from God sustenance for God's future. We are invited to walk out of our old certitudes into the new wave of God's faithfulness.

When we come to the table, it turns out to be a place where old certitudes do not govern. We find that we are not fed by bread that we bake in ovens that we own, but by *bread broken*. We are nourished not by great gulps of control and certitude, but by *the cup of steadfast love* that is given us. It is no wonder that they did not ask him any more questions. We do not ask, as they did not ask, because our questions are always about control and certitude and management. For now we need not ask. We need only to be dazzled and grateful, open to God's fidelity that is quite unlike the world past that we have mastered. It is God's future; we will be safe there, because his steadfast love is bottomless. We are free enough, as the apple of God's eye, to get on with the new life to which we have been called, a life beyond fear and control, to give as we have received.

November 10, 2013
Christ Church Cathedral, Nashville, Tennessee

46

Vision That Trumps Violence

HABAKKUK 1:1–4; 2:1–5
PSALM 119:137–144
LUKE 19:1–10

Sometimes it seems like Scripture was written yesterday, in our context, and directly addressed to us. So it is with this poetry from the prophet Habakkuk. He lived in the decades just before the destruction of Jerusalem when everything was falling apart.

I.

This is how he describes his context:

> O LORD, how long shall I cry for help,
> And you will not listen?
> Or cry to you *"Violence"* and you will not save?
> Why do you make me see wrong-doing
> and look at trouble?
> Destruction and *violence* are before me;
> strife and contention arise.
> So the law becomes slack and justice never prevails.
> The wicked surround the righteous—
> therefore judgment comes forth perverted.
> (Hab. 1:1–4, emphasis added)

The language piles up: violence, wrong-doing, trouble, destruction, strife, contention ... justice never prevails. It was a society in which people were devoured by anxiety, institutions were failing, people took matters into their

232

own hands, and turned against their neighbors. The poet uses the term "violence" twice to characterize a failed neighborly infrastructure.

That could be our poem. We could use the same words for our world that is in free fall. The level of rage, the ton of anxiety, the deep fear, the thirst for vengeance is all right there. So we want to have more guns, we want to kill all the terrorists with drones, and we have violence even close at home, toward women, in our families. That hidden violence close to home matches the overt violence in the street and that perpetrated by the government on our behalf. It happens when the viability of a society collapses, now as then.

II.

So what to do? Hunker down, put the wagons in a circle, build up the arsenal, privatize and withdraw from the public, private schools, private security systems, private health plans, private civic services, not to share, not to risk, not to be exposed.

But Habakkuk offers an alternative to such action propelled by anxiety:

> I will stand at my watchpost,
> and station myself on the rampart;
> I will keep watch to see what he will say to me,
> and what he will answer concerning my complaint.
> Then the LORD answered me and said:
> Write the *vision*, and make it plain on tablets,
> so that a runner may read it.
> For there is still a vision for the appointed time;
> it speaks of the end, and does not lie.
> If it seems to tarry, wait for it;
> it will surely come, it will not delay.
> (Hab. 2:1–3, emphasis added)

There is still a vision! It is the business of the prophet to offer a vision, to imagine a scenario of a coming future that is willed by God. It is the urging of the prophet that this vision, grounded in faith, is enough to override and defeat violence. Imagine, *vision versus violence,* and vision wins! It is a daring calculation, because in our anxiety we are mostly not available for such a vision.

But biblical faith is always in the business of vision, believing that a coming future from God will prevail over the deathliness of the present. So the church's business is to watch for the vision, to wait for the vision, and to receive it. In faith we know about the vision that embodies God's own purpose for the world. Since the Exodus event we have had this vision of emancipation from every form of enslavement and exploitation. Since the poetry of the ancient prophets we have had a vision of disarmament, of beating "swords into plowshares and spears into pruning hooks." Since the giving of the Torah we have had a vision of mercy and generosity toward the vulnerable, toward "widows and orphans and immigrants." Since the prophecy of Jeremiah we have had a vision of a new covenant with God and a readiness for obedience to Torah. Since the oddness of Ezekiel, we have had a vision of a new temple when God would dwell in our midst. Since Isaiah we have had a vision of the holy city, a new Jerusalem that came last night while I lay sleeping.

And then comes Jesus; he performed the vision:

> [T]he blind receive their sight, the lame walk, the lepers are cleansed, the deaf hear, the dead are raised, the poor have good news brought to them. (Luke 7:22)

All of that in our own time comes to expression with Martin Luther King Jr., "I Have a Dream." Dreams . . . visions . . . it is all the same. King dreamed a neighborhood, a welcome practice of justice and mercy that included blacks and whites, women and men, gay and straight, Christian and Muslim, citizen and immigrant, in a world where God has got us all in his hands.

It is always a contest between *violence and vision*. In the eyes of a frightened world, violence will always veto vision, because in our anxiety we cannot look beyond the present moment. But faith, in the Bible and in our midst, is a refusal to succumb, to give in to, or to participate in such anxiety. Faith is confidence that the vision will prevail.

Habakkuk details those who refuse the vision. He targets:

> wealth that is treacherous,
> arrogance that cannot endure (2:5).

The attraction of self-sufficiency is great; we thought we could make it on our own, or we thought we had to make it on our own. But the future is not to be found in our self-sufficiency. The future is with the God who counters our violence and invites to vision.

III.

The word is "watch and wait." But then, in context of "the proud," Habakkuk says, "The righteous live by their faithfulness." The righteous are the ones who can move past themselves. They are the ones who trust rather than fear, who receive the vision and risk against violence; they do so in faith!

So it seems to me that those who live in faith do two things. First, they envision. Our work is to fill out the vision:

- To imagine a new economy not based on greed but on local generosity.
- To imagine a new international world not based on US domination, but on a peaceable network of nations.
- To imagine a new church not based on sectarian certitude, but on the largeness of the gospel.
- To imagine a new neighborhood not based on fear and control, but ready for welcome and solidarity.
- To imagine a new politics not based on money, but on citizen participation that trusts the citizens.

Such imagining is an act of courage and defiance of violence.

But the task is not simply to envision. Second, the task of those grounded in faith is to act, to embody the vision as a wondrous alternative to fear, anxiety, greed, and violence that are all around us. The church is an odd lot of ordinary people who do not give in. You may know the story of the little French village of Le Chambon that, under pastoral guidance, hid Jews in their homes during the war. Later, after the war, a journalist interviewed people from the village and asked why they had run such great risks. They offered no particular explanation. They just shrugged their shoulders and said, "Well, that is what we do. It seemed right because that is who we are." That is how it is in our baptism. Such visioning action is in our baptismal DNA. We do it because we are called out of anxiety, summoned beyond violence, to obey hope.

IV.

We can see all of this played out in the story of Zacchaeus.

Zacchaeus knew all about violence. He was a revenue man for the Roman Empire. The purpose of that empire, like every empire, whether Babylon among the Jews, Rome in the time of Jesus, or the US empire in the Philippines . . . is to coercively extract wealth for the sake of the center. Zacchaeus served such a regime, so that he was an agent of the violence of the empire.

But Jesus offers Zacchaeus a vision of himself that contradicted his current practice of extortion. He addressed him in a tree where he had climbed:

> "Zacchaeus hurry and come down; for I must stay at your house today." (Luke 19:5)

And then he says to him:

> Today salvation has come to this house, because he too is a son of
> Abraham. For the Son of Man came to seek out and to save the lost.
> (vv. 9–10)

Imagine that! Zacchaeus thought he was simply a servant of Rome. And Jesus
says to him, No, you are not. I will tell you who you really are. You are a son
of Abraham. You are a child of God's promise. You are a carrier of God's
open possibility for time to come. You need not operate in fear or be propelled by greed. Your body is loaded with the force of the spirit, and you can
be different.

That same vision is uttered in the gospel for us. It gives us a new identity.
Watch for it. Wait for it. Receive it.

And Zacchaeus responded to the invitation of faith:

> [H]alf of my possessions, Lord, I will give to the poor; and if I
> have defrauded anyone of anything, I will pay back four times as
> much. (v. 8)

And then he came down from the tree to eat with Jesus. He was no longer
a spectator who watched Jesus from his tree; now he became a participant in
the new world that Jesus was initiating. He acted in faith by coming to eat
with Jesus. We may imagine, but do not know, that he no longer had to be an
extortionist. Everything had changed for him by the invitation to generosity.

> Zacchaeus traces the poem of Habakkuk exactly:
> He knew about violence and participated in it;
> He is caught up in a vision of himself as a son of Abraham, a new identity;
> He responds in faith to perform the vision in his life.

V.

I finish with verses from Psalm 119 that might be on the lips of Zacchaeus:

> I am small and despised,
> yet I do not forget your precepts.
> Your righteousness is an everlasting righteousness,
> and your Torah is the truth.
> Trouble and anguish have come upon me,
> but your commandments are my delight.
> Your decrees are righteous forever;
> give me understanding that I may live.
>   (vv. 141–144)

Those words on the lips of Zacchaeus might arrive on our lips. Each of us is not more than "small and despised." But the embrace of the vision is a huge act. So we do not forget the Torah to which we are called in obedience. We have work to do. It is a defiance of violence. It is the bet of our baptism . . . an alternative way in the world!

November 3, 2013
Highland Baptist Church, Louisville, Kentucky

47

Enacting God's Power for Life

ISAIAH 65:17–25

PSALM 98

2 THESSALONIANS 3:6–13

LUKE 21:5–19

The church has always known that God's Easter power for life is loose in the world. The church has always trusted in God's capacity to bring life out of death, well-being out of trouble, and joy out of tribulation. But the church has not always known how to respond to these gifts from God, or how to live differently because of the power of new life that is among us. As a result, the Bible is filled with counsel, advice, and urging about how to be church. Since these are the lectionary readings for the day and since the church is now seeking its way in a very different world, the counsel of these texts seems to me useful and suggestive. I dare to go there, even though you are all strangers to me, because I believe that the issues are the same everywhere among us in the church. The summons is how the church—people like us—can give daily evidence that we are different people because of Easter truth. So here is the counsel I read in these texts.

I.

First, *everybody has to contribute*. The early church to which Paul writes was in a very tough place, and it could not afford to have members who were not helping out. Maybe you caught in the epistle reading the well-known verdict of Paul:

Anyone unwilling to work should not eat. (2 Thess. 3:10)

That text has of course been used against all manner of welfare programs to make work a condition of aid, because nobody should get a free lunch. But that is not what Paul is writing about. Rather the words are addressed to the church, insisting that there should not be any idle members, but everyone needs to be at the witness of the church.

The temptation is always present in the church to drop in and drop out and not commit. Indeed, the new popular mantra, "I am spiritual but not religious," is often a drop-out formula for those who want no task, no discipline, no summons, and no accountability with others. But the church is not a venue for such self-preoccupation. The church rather is a body of folk who believe that in Jesus a new world has begun, a new world of generosity and forgiveness and hospitality and justice. Church folk are those who by their lives and their actions and their money and their time and their energy and their speech give evidence of the new world. This means to slant one's life toward the newness of Jesus that he acted out before our very eyes. It is clear that the old world of greed and fear and threat has failed. There is no joy or security to be found in that way of life. But it is not clear to many that there is an alternative. The church witnesses to that alternative enacted by Jesus, the gathering of our life around practices that contradict that old world and declare it is no longer our habitat. Everyone in the church has a calling to that, even though we live it out in many different ways. And the world, in its bewilderment, is watching to see if the case can be made, concretely, that a new world of neighborliness has begun. Everyone in the church is called to be a contributor to that new world of neighborliness.

II.

Second practice of discipleship: *Watch your mouth!* The Bible knows, of course, that the human tongue, human speech, is a huge instrument for destructive action or up-building. So watch, says Paul, what you talk about, how you say it, with whom you speak.

Negatively, Paul says, some of you are busybodies. Some of you have nothing to do except to comment endlessly on how bad things are, how they used to be better, how we think it should be different, or not be different, how disappointed, how angry, how anxious. Or the speech of liberals who dismiss conservatives, or the speech of conservatives who readily excommunicate liberals. And of course, we have many models in our society of those who chatter, even called the "chattering class," those who can say anything in public and never have to take any responsibility for what they say. Paul believes that folk who are like that just do not have enough to do, that is, are not taking seriously the task of contributing to the well-being of the whole body.

But of course, positively, there is a better use for your mouth. In this really hard Gospel reading in Luke, Jesus warns his followers that crunch time is coming with wars and rumors of wars and earthquakes and plagues and famine. He mentions everything except the oil spill; if he had known that, he would have included it in his inventory of disasters. He names all the things that make for social unrest and social dispute. And when such big troubles come, the status quo will be both nervous and vigilant. And, says Jesus, if you witness to the new world that is coming from God, they will arrest you and persecute you and haul you into court and interrogate you. Christians are people who tell the truth they know about the new rule of God that challenges all of our old practices and about the implications of that new rule of God for all kinds of policy questions from health care to immigration policy and all of those tough issues.

And then Jesus says to his friends:

> This will give you an opportunity to testify. So make up your minds not to prepare your defense in advance; for I will give you words and a wisdom that none of your opponents will be able to withstand or contradict. (Luke 21:13–15)

Do not try to have a prepared speech, because you will have to respond ad hoc with the truth you know in Jesus. The English has it, "I will give you words." But the Greek is, "I will give you mouth." You will know what to say, because the guidance of Jesus is powerful and immediate in a church that stays on mission. Now I know that not many of us will stand in court. But we do, by our lives and in many ways, have a chance to evidence the truth of the new world that challenges all of our old worlds.

So I thought that the negative warning of Paul and the affirmation of Jesus on speech make a nice combination:

> Negatively: do not be a chattering busybody;
> Positively: let your truth-telling be guided by Jesus' own purpose in the world.

What a time for truth-telling! As we all know, the world is baffled and confused. It does not know where to turn, because there is so much deception and seduction and manipulation out there. But the mouth that Jesus gives tells the truth that may be simple and direct and clear. When faithful, the mouth of the church has always been on the side of justice and mercy and compassion and against fear and greed and brutality. What a way to think of a local church (this one!) as a place where the truth of Jesus is offered. And says Jesus to his disciples; if you have courage for truth-telling, you will surely get into trouble.

> But not a hair of your head will perish. By your endurance you will gain your souls. (vv. 18–19)

III.

So first, *contribute*. Second, *watch our mouth* and use it for up-building God's future. Now third, *Live in hope*. Live in the sure conviction that God's promise of *shalom* for the world can be resisted and can be delayed, but it cannot be defeated. The Old Testament reading for today is the wondrous poem in Isaiah 65 that is the capstone to the wondrous book of Isaiah. It is a vision of the coming world of God that anticipates Martin Luther King Jr. and "I Have a Dream."

> I have a dream of a new heaven;
> I have a dream of a new earth;
> I have a dream of a new Jerusalem.

And the poet proceeds to line out the new world that is to be given by God. It is not a vision of heaven with gold streets and angels and harps. It is a vision of a new earth, a new policy to end infant mortality, a new economy to end foreclosures, a new reconciled environment. I am not making this up:

New economy:

> They shall build houses and inhabit them;
> they shall plant vineyards and eat their fruit.
> They shall not build and another inhabit;
> they shall not plant and another eat. (vv. 21–22)

New health care:

> No more shall there be in it
> an infant that lives but a few days,
> or an old person who does not live out a lifetime. (v. 20)

A new environment:

> The wolf and the lamb shall feed together,
> the lion shall eat straw like the ox;
> but the serpent—its food shall be dust. (v. 25)

It is promised! It will come because God will give it, and will not stop until all is well.

IV.

So imagine a local congregation—in Thessalonica or here—gathering around these texts, imitating the folk around Jesus, to take a deep breath, take heart, and live in joy. Each of these counsels is deeply countercultural:

- Contribute: this means to invest in the neighborhood, and not be preoccupied with #1.
- Watch your mouth: that means stopping destructive talk and witnessing to the truth of Jesus that has been entrusted to us.
- Live in hope . . . refuse the despair of the status quo that keeps us on Orange Alert for what we may lose.

It is a truth long known in the church that lives lived in this way are filled with joy and well-being, not turned in on ourselves, but turned toward the neighborhood.

Yesterday some of us spent time on the issue of hunger. There is a large hunger for bread in the world; there is a huge hunger for the power of life in the world. The truth is that it is always this faithful minority who knows that when we hunger and thirst for God's justice, we will be filled . . . filled with joy and well-being and security, a new life that has transformative power of an Easter kind.

November 14, 2010
Mount Washington Presbyterian Church, Cincinnati, Ohio

48

On Being Designated Truth Carriers

(Reign of Christ)

JEREMIAH 22:1–6
PSALM 46
COLOSSIANS 1:11–20
LUKE 23:33–42

It is unnerving to discover that what has been true for a long time is no longer true, and indeed, never was.

I.

I had the thought that a basic reason we are on edge, anxious, quarrelsome, and driven is that we are watching old truths turn out to be untruths, and it feels like free-fall.

> It turned out not to be true in Iraq that scud missiles would prevail.
> It turned out not to be true in Israel that one could be Jewish enough to make a secure nation.
> It turned out not to be true in South Africa that having enough dogs can keep people down.

But we can come closer home:

> It has turned out not to be true that science is an adequate way to articulate our humanness, important as science is.
> It has turned out not to be true that high finance shaped like a pyramid will make us prosperous, because it does not trickle down.
> It has turned out not to be true that a strong military can make us safe, because our massive military effort manufactures enemies, and it is intractably porous in its protection.

243

It is not different in our religious practices:

> It turns out that the new atheism is not true, because it leaves us alone before a mystery that we cannot decode.
> It turns out that so-called evangelicalism is not true, because it lusts for certitude that is not on offer.
> It turns out that progressives had no truth when they declared that "God has no hands but our hands."

Well, that may not be our list of untruths. But you get the idea. We have trusted the claims we preferred, propelled by our various ideological convictions. But these declarations of truth turn out to be out of sync with the reality of our life in the world.

II.

Because of this tsunami of failed truths, the field is clearer than we had imagined. There is a waiting and watching. And Paul plunges into that open field of truth-become-untruth in Colossians 1, the epistle reading for next Sunday, the twenty-fifth after Pentecost, our celebration of "Christ the King." Paul attests to a different truth. It concerns the new self clothed in compassion, kindness, humility, meekness, and patience, forgiveness, and above all, love (Col. 3:12–14). The language of being "re-clothed" is here the rhetoric of baptism, a change of clothes, a change of identity, and a change of self through the waters of baptism. Paul knows the old failed truth of distinctions of hostility between Greek/Jew, circumcised/uncircumcised, barbarian/Scythian, slave/free, all that is passé (3:11). Paul knows that the long truth of the world as God's creation is that self-giving love to the other for the sake of the common good is reliable truth that deeply contradicts the failed truths of scientism, high finance, militarism and the several religious vagaries of autonomy, certitude, and can-do liberalism. It is the truth of our life in God's world. It is the truth that holds up against all the softer truths that run from wisdom through surveillance to might and wealth. It is the truth for which we all yearn; and when we have courage and freedom, we readily engage in self-giving love to the other for the sake of the common good. Every time this truth beats the seductions of greed, anxiety, and our ready idolatries.

III.

Like us, Paul knows that because of Jesus:

> Jesus is the one who is profoundly self-giving;
> Jesus is the one who makes hospitable room for the other;
> Jesus is the one who focuses on the common good.

In Paul's horizon (and ours), Jesus is the quintessential embodiment of the long truth of God's world, the long gospel truth that contradicts the seductions of our culture. Paul musters all the lyrical flow of rhetoric that he can imagine. He voices Jesus,

> As the first born of creation,
> All things have been created through him and for him.
> He is before all things;
> All things hold together in him;
> He is the head of the body, the church;
> He is the beginning, the first born of the dead,
> He is in first place in everything. (Col. 1:15–18)

This is not creedal reasoning. This is not linear argument. This is a lyrical eruption, because Paul is swept off his feet when he thinks from all the failed truths that are displaced to the truth of the God who gives God's self away in love. This surely is an anticipation of what became creedal, "God from God, light from light, true God from true God, begotten not made." It can only be sung!

After he recites what will become high Christology, Paul reverses field to speak about the suffering humanity of Jesus. He is the one who makes peace through the blood of his cross (v. 20). There is an old myth and old magic about "the blood." But here he means the giving of one's life, the offer of self to overcome hostility and be reconciled. It takes a reach across to reconcile. It takes a leap of self-risk. You may know that some progressives are deeply offended by talk of "blood atonement and sacrifice." But I read recently, a new thought for me, that any act of forgiveness requires a sacrifice of the self for the other. Every act of reconciliation requires a risk of self-regard for the sake of the other. And it has been done! It is a new truth now that reverberates in the world when much else has turned out not to be true. The road to peace is the offer of the self; and he has done it!

IV.

I am amazed how Paul's Christology turns to ecclesiology. He turns regularly from Jesus and winds up talking about the church.

So in Romans Paul goes on at length about the good news, and then he urges the church, "I beseech you by the mercies of God, . . . be transformed" (12:1–2).

So in 1 Corinthians 1, he writes of the foolish wisdom of the cross and the weak strength of the cross. And then he says, "Consider your . . . call" (1:26).

So in 1 Corinthians 15, he testifies about the resurrection of Jesus and then he says, "Therefore . . . be steadfast" (15:58)

So here all around the high claims made for Jesus, it is the church that occupies Paul. In verse 11, at the beginning of our reading, he says, "May *you* be made strong." In verse 21, in the next verse after our reading, he says, "And *you* who were once estranged." He writes of Christ, but before and after it is *"You, you, you, you* church, *you* pastors, *you* elders, *you."* You have the mind of Christ who emptied himself in obedience.

In Paul's lyric, the church stands very close to the truth of reconciling love, very close indeed! But we have devised our own truths about the church that do not require so much:

- We made a truth out of much doctrine, that we might have certitude to impose on others;
- We made a truth out of certain sweet piety and imagined it would legitimate control;
- We made a truth out of a particular morality and kicked it upstairs to be absolute.
- We made a truth out of liturgy and used our energy getting it right;
- We fenced the table and ordination, and imagined the others did not belong, first Blacks and then women, and now gays.
- We generated programs and substituted busyness for the costly work of reconciliation.

All of that has turned out to be flimsy, and we are left with the self-giving God who brings peace for the world that passes all human understanding. At his pastoral best, Paul recited the marks of "You."

It occurred to me that you pastors and elders are the "designated hitters" of the gospel task. It seems funny to me that in the American League we have a "designated hitter," because I thought every player was designated to hit. And so in the church, every baptized member is "designated" for gospel obedience. In the lineup of odd saints, however, you really are "the designated." And here are the marks of that designation:

May you *be strong* with all the strength that comes from his glorious power (v. 11). This is not worldly strength. This is strength that the world judges to be weak. We are called to a different strength that contradicts the strength of a can-do society, one that breaks the power of death by self-giving.

May you *endure everything with patience* (v. 11). I don't know how you pastors do it. There is a lot to endure with patience . . . pettiness, deception, slander, resistance, quarrelsomeness . . . because this is for the long haul. It is not the next budget or the next youth trip or the next anything. It is rather for the sake of the kingdom that comes through and beyond such endurance.

May you *joyfully give thanks* to the Father (v. 12). Gratitude is a hallmark of those whom Paul has in purview. It seems clear to me that we cannot be fully grateful when we are excessively fatigued or anxious. Thus there is implied here, I suggest, enough self-care to be in a posture of gratitude, thankful for the goodness of God right through the vexations of the day. Gratitude matters enormously, because it reminds us that we are not self-starters; we start from a gift. Such gratitude is a sure antidote to despair, which then can have no authority over us.

In which we have *forgiveness* (v. 23). What a great gift to be forgiven! I think sometimes that we in the "forgiveness business" do not ponder enough that it is for us first, it is for us in our failure, in our excessive zeal, in our self-indulgence, in our self-importance, in all of the affronts that beset us in this calling—without shifting from *the hope promised by the gospel.* We do not shift our hope and divert it to the next happening, the next capital drive among us, the next session of Bible school, the next turn of the GA. These self-invented matters will not last. What will surely last is the good news of the self-giving God.

The task to which we are assigned is to be carriers of the truth that brings peace. It is a truth that is oddly and distinctly embedded in Jesus of Nazareth. It is a truth for which the world waits, but waits in confused bewilderment amid many false truths. It is entrusted to us. It is a truth that marks our bodies and our body together . . . strong, patient, thankful, forgiven hope that does not shift. We will not do better than the lyrical admonition of Paul:

> Above all, clothe yourselves with love, which binds everything together in perfect harmony. And let the peace of Christ rule in your hearts, to which indeed you were called in the one body. And be thankful. Let the word of Christ dwell in you richly; teach and admonish one another in all wisdom; and with gratitude in your hearts sing psalms, hymns, and spiritual songs to God. And whatever you do, in word or deed, do everything in the name of the Lord Jesus, giving thanks to God the Father through him. (Col. 3:14–17)

November 19, 2013
Presbytery of Milwaukee

PART FOUR

Sermons for Other Occasions

49

A Second Sighting

(Graduation)

2 KINGS 6:8–23
LUKE 10:21–24

What a day!

Some of you have been brilliant in your studies . . . and your parents are very proud;

Some of you have done all right . . . and your parents are glad;

Some of you have just gotten by . . . and your parents are relieved.

But by sundown, none of those gradations will matter, because you will all be, uniformly, "women and men of Colgate," all the same, all honored, all completed, all certified. And all of you will be quickly into the next thing . . . perhaps making money, or a trip to Europe, or moving back home until a better offer comes, or on to graduate school. You are now equipped to do those quintessential things of *knowing how* and *moving ahead* and *being entitled*.

But for a moment, we make a deep, traditional pause in this glorious day. For this moment, we have this ancient ceremony of baccalaureate. We pause to entertain a religious thought—when we think about the inscrutable holiness of God that is all around us today. A holiness that assures us, and questions us, and summons us. I have no claim to make about something wise to say, nor about something clever to say. But I ask you to think for this moment of God's holiness that saturates this day and this event.

The story I cite, Jewish based—inviting Christians and inviting Muslims who hold to the same text—is in a long symmetrical recital of power figures, the kings of Israel and the kings of Judah. They are indistinguishable in the recital . . . each had a mother, each began to rule at a certain age, each lived in his capital city, each did good or did bad, each died, each slept with his fathers. They are replaceable parts, all a part of the royal continuity, all committed to

251

power, all children of the dynasty, all given royal perks, all held accountable
. . . the tale repeated endlessly, like so many episodes of *Cheers* or *Seinfeld*, in
which the *same plot is endlessly reenacted*. The beat goes on, they manage . . .
just barely, everything ordered and routine, everything predictable.

But then an *interruption*. A strange interruption, by a storyteller who has
little respect for royal time lines or regularity or controllable patterns. The
interruption is a story of an odd legendary figure who squeezes into the Bible,
who illicitly occupies space in the royal time line, and who turns out to be
much more interesting than the routines of royalty. Your education in this
wonderful place of excellence, privilege and passion is a nurture so that your
life may be, in time to come, *interrupted*, a pattern of routine and regularity
and control, control by power, by money, by technology, shrewdness . . . but
then a story that does not fit and will not accommodate, that draws us out and
holds us, reminding us that there is something deep and hidden and fierce
and demanding about our existence that is not managed by the thinness of
our ordered life. The ultimate mark of education . . . you educated people . . .
is to host and attend to the *density and fierceness* in the midst of our privilege,
interruption as assurance, *interruption* as invitation, *interruption* as summons
and insistence, to notice it and to pay attention.

Listen to this interruption of the symmetry of the royal time line. Lend an
ear for a narrative that shattered when first told and that shatters each time
it is told.

The king of Syria was at war with Israel. Nothing new there; likely it was
about the Golan Heights. The Syrian king made aggressive military plans
against Israel. . . . Nothing new there. It is what every state does. The problem is that there is a security leak in the Syrian military; everything that is
military plan or stratagem is a leak, and immediately the Israelite government
knows. Nothing really new there, except a leak in security is an occasion for
wonderment; it produces a story that breaks the predictable pattern of state
conduct. The king of Syria is furious at the leak, as heads of government tend
to be. He conducts an investigation and taps phone lines. Except that his advi-
sors tell him, "It is not a leak, sir. It is Elisha, the prophet in Israel." There
is this Elisha, this man of wonder and oddness who does not live in ordinary
categories. He violates the rationality of the state. He intrudes into the time
line. He makes normal military operations impossible. Because he knows and
reports everything to the king of Israel. He knows in extra ways that we do
not understand.

The king is quick and decisive. He sends a great army of horses and chariots
to apprehend this dangerous security leak. The entire army rides up to the
house of Elisha. Much clattering and shouting and macho conduct. This is
a big maneuver to apprehend one eccentric character who is a threat to the

status quo. The prophet is a modest man. He lives alone, except for his servant boy who shines his shoes. The boy hears the military clatter and looks out the window and sees the great army assembled. He says in anxiety, "Alas, master, what shall we do?" That is not really what he said . . . a lot is lost in translation. What he said was, "Oh my God!" He still thinks in conventional categories of traditional power. He is frightened because of his common assumptions about reality. He has a lot to learn that he will now learn very quickly.

The prophet is unflappable as the royal army surrounds his house. He is rooted in faith beyond royal routines that do not upset him at all. He knows a lot the boy does not yet suspect. He says to the boy, "Do not fear," the supreme trump card of serious faith. Then he says:

There are more with us than there are with them. The boy begins to count, "one, two . . ." He recognizes that this is the new math, strange math indeed that is beyond him. Then the prophet prays, that is, he goes to the larger world beyond the horizon of the conventional:

O LORD, please open his eyes that he may see. (2 Kgs. 6:17)

The boy has not yet seen *the real world*. He is too young, too traditional, too fearful. But now he sees for the first time:

The mountain was full of horses and chariots of fire! The immediate environment was saturated with *allies of well-being* that he had not seen before, because he had permitted the military ideology of his environment to determine the categories and limits of his perception. But now he looks a second time, and sees differently, authorized by the assurance to step out of conventional discernment. The world is peopled with agents of well-being, so the story goes, because it is a world governed by the God of well-being who has not yet turned the world over to military control, to technological management, or to ideological flatness. The boy now sees, authorized by this strangeness with *a second sight*, refusing now to accept the world given him by conventional technology, ideology, or military habits.

Strange indeed! But there is more. The prophet prays again. The Syrians are struck blind through the prayer, made helpless in the hands of the prophet who leads them blind and helpless into the capital city of Samaria. This tough army, in its traditional posture of aggressiveness, is made helpless and hopeless by this collusion of "man of God" and God. When the Syrians arrive in the city, the prophet prays them back to sight. They see where they are and they are even more frightened. They are frightened as prisoners of war in the capital city of the enemy. Then the king of Israel appears . . . who only now enters the story as a latecomer who has done nothing. The Israelite king acts like any conventional state leader. He asks of the prophet:

Can I kill them? Can I kill them?

That is what one does with enemies, what Israel would do to Syria or Syria would do to Israel. But the prophet says, "No, you cannot kill them. They are not your prisoners. They are mine. And I am not a killer."

The king wonders about an alternative: what to do with enemies but to kill them? The boy wonders about an alternative. So do we, if we are paying closer attention. And then we are told:

> He prepared for them a great feast; after they ate and drank, he sent them on their way, and they went to their master. And the Syrians no longer came raiding into the land of Israel. (v. 23)

He prepared a great feast. He fed the enemies of his people in a generous, celebrative context. And they went away and did not come raiding anymore. He broke the vicious cycle of threat. He turned enemies . . . at least provisionally . . . to friends. The narrative ends in a miracle, a miraculous transformation of human power. It is, however, a doable miracle. It is one done by human will and human agency and human generosity. It does not wait on an act of God. And then the story is completed. The war is ended.

That story is a long way from us. That innocent boy is a long way from you sophisticated graduates. That wild Elisha is a good distance removed from most of us tenured academics. In fact the story does not have anything to do with us.

Except that it is *thick* with meaning *below the surface*. And baccalaureate is that moment in this splendid day when we pause before the *thickness* of our life, to be reminded that we must not trust the thinness of success and self-sufficiency and autonomy and technology all too much, because there is more.

The story is a bid to you and to us that you allow such stories to break the enchantments of your privilege and power. Stories like this one are always an odd *interruption* into the life we had planned out. They always come from unexpected, unauthorized sources . . . the surprise of a child, the gesture of a poor person, the utterance of a loser, the verdict of a poet. We are taken up short and our easy grip of control is broken. We permit humanness to surge in odd ways, in ways that are driven by holiness.

Almost all of these kinds of stories and gestures and utterances have common themes:

They invite a *second seeing*, like the boy who was made suddenly aware of resources for life all around, resources given by God. But he had not been able to notice them until he had been prayed for.

The plot of the narrative concerns *an inversion of power*, wherein the weak ones prevail and the strong ones are reduced to hoping and begging;

The story explicates the way in which *vicious cycles are broken*, cycles of death and brutality and indifference and cynicism, just when we thought the cycles could never be broken, and neighborliness is made an option;

The action *permits new possibilities* in the world long thought to be impossible, practical, concrete, on the ground . . . miracles done by human agents, making a different life possible.

I bid you attend to such *a second seeing*, women and men of Colgate, because without the capacity to see a second time, to see *allies of life* all around the environment, you are only half educated. Our society awaits your second look, a newness given fresh by God's holiness. Our dominant technological explanation of life wants to nullify all of this business of a second sight, and so to leave us in control on our own terms. Our control, however, cannot stop the gift of second sight by which we live. Our humanness depends upon it. We are like the little boy, bumfuzzled and then blessed with new sight. It is a gift!

May 18, 1997
Baccalaureate Sermon, Colgate University, New York

50

Four Moves to Newness

(Church Anniversary)

MARK 6:30–34
MARK 8:1–10, 14–21
I CORINTHIANS 11:23–27

I of course do not know what you have been doing at First Church for two hundred and seventy-five years. But I can guess, because I know a little about churches:

- You have been singing and praying;
- You have been caring and loving;
- You have been eating together, at least as often as you can get down to the basement; and
- You have been quarreling now and then with each other.

I.

Here is one more thing you have no doubt been doing with regularity—if not with frequency—because you are the church. You have been celebrating Holy Communion, which is "the innermost sanctuary of the whole Christian worship." We do not understand the Eucharist well, but it is the decisive mark of the church:

- Sometimes people celebrate communion only four times a year, the way they have done it in my home church;
- Sometimes congregations do it every week, as almost every theologian thinks that we should;
- Sometimes we compromise between the two and celebrate it once a month.

But we do it. We do it because it is a habit. We do it out of conviction, because it is a sign of God's forgiving mercy, it is a sign of God's abundance in creation, it is a sign of our dependence on God's goodness, it is a sign of joy and thanksgiving about the truth of the gospel. I read to you the "words of institution" from Paul in 1 Corinthians 11:

> On the night . . . he was betrayed, [he] took a loaf of bread, and when he had given thanks, he broke it and said . . . (v. 23)

I read the gospel story of Jesus about the five loaves and two fish:

> Taking the five loaves and the two fish, he looked up to heaven, and blessed and broke the loaves, and gave them to his disciples. (Mark 6:41)

And in Mark 8, in a second feeding wonder:

> [H]e took the seven loaves, and after giving thanks he broke them and gave them to his disciples. (v. 6)

Both times in Mark he finished the meal served by Jesus with surplus bread, twelve baskets full and then seven baskets full.

II.

Now I want you to notice one particular thing about these Mark narratives that they have in common with Paul's paragraph. In every case it says, he *took* the bread, he *blessed* it/or gave thanks for it, he *broke* it, and he *gave* it to his disciples. *He took/he blessed/he broke/he gave!* Jesus has been doing that forever in the church and you at First Church have been doing it for two hundred seventy-five years, doing it more than you think about, doing more than you could understand. My word to you—about the church today, about First Church in its long past and about First Church in its future yet to be given—is this. Those four verbs constitute the pattern of faithful church life. When we do these four verbs, in worship and in daily life, we draw close to the mystery of God and close to the truth of Jesus Christ. So consider:

1. *Jesus took the bread.* He took five loaves and two fish. He took what the people had with them. He took the produce of their work and the worth of their life and, as you know, in more self-consciously liturgical churches the bread and wine are brought by the people to the altar. Jesus takes, he does not ask, he takes what we have, because he acts as Lord. He is the one who has

claim on the bread and the wine. This verb "take" is a confession among us in the church, that Jesus claims our lives, our property, and our future, and we yield them to him in gladness, at our best not withholding or keeping back anything for ourselves.

2. The second act of Jesus is that *he blesses the bread and the wine.* He claims them for a sacramental act, recognizing that they are infused with wondrous gospel significance when he acts upon them. By his word and by his gesture, Jesus permeates the bread of ordinary life with the plus of God's mercy and the generosity. That is why the people leave the table fed and nourished, standing tall and braced for faith in the world, aware that Jesus transposes the ordinariness of our lives into a miraculous center of power and energy and courage. The alternative text says he *gives thanks* to God for the bread, acknowledging that what we have and what we bring is in fact a gift of God's goodness, because "all that we have is thine alone."

3. The third act is that *Jesus breaks the bread.* When we use a loaf of real bread for communion, we twist and turn to pull it apart. If we use a wafer, we can hear it snap. Either way, when the bread is pressed into Jesus' service, it is broken and becomes something that it was not before. It is claimed for Jesus' purpose, broken beyond its own will and character, summoned out of its autonomous purpose and recruited for a new purpose. And of course every Christian knows that the brokenness of the bread bespeaks the crucifixion of Jesus when his body is broken as a carrier of God's love and God's purpose in the world. Acted upon by Jesus, the bread is not what it was.

4. And then *he gives the bread,* he hands it back to the disciples who brought it to him in the first place, only now it has been changed:

- *It has been blessed* so that it will really give life, health, and joy;
- *It has been broken* so that it is no longer available for its old uses;
- It now *belongs to the coming rule of God.*

And the disciples receive it; in the end they find joy and well-being through the bread as a gift of God.

This act in four moves is that *he took, he blessed, he broke, he gave;* it is a parable of the Christian life. The reason the church regularly enacts this drama in four moves is that this is the truth of our life in evangelical faith:

Jesus takes our life and we gladly yield it to him;
Jesus blesses our life and infuses it with power, meaning, and joy;
Jesus breaks our life so that we are not our own but we belong to him;
Jesus gives our life back to us but now in a way that is wholly transformed.

So imagine, First Church has been doing this drama of faith in four acts for two hundred and seventy-five years: *he takes, he blesses, he breaks, he gives.* And First Church will keep doing that for many more years to come:

- *yielding* its life to Christ;
- *receiving* God's blessing for its life;
- *having its life claimed* for the good purposes of the gospel;
- *receiving* life back from God in a completely changed form.

It is this claiming, feeding, empowering, yielding act that is at the center of new life in the church. And when we do not practice this drama in four moves, we go under our own steam. And when we go under our own steam, that leads to weariness, cynicism, despair, apathy, and maybe quarreling.

III.

Do I need to tell you that life in these *four moves* is profoundly countercultural? These moves run against the grain of American capitalism. They run against the grain of affluent self-competence. They contradict a technological capacity to have life on our own terms and therefore when the church does its regular dramatic act of yielding and receiving, it does something peculiar that gives joy and power that the world cannot plan. Consider:

- He takes. Cultural resistance to such an act is immense. We would rather say in our culture, "My life is my own. It belongs to me and I will live it the way I want, without being accountable to anybody." And against that, we Christians have a life taken by Jesus.
- He blesses. He infuses life with a gift while the world says, "I don't believe in such gifts, I don't believe that there are such gifts, and I don't need them anyway. I am perfectly capable and sufficient on my own."
- He breaks. He claims our life for his purpose of living in the world in compassion and forgiveness and generosity, but the world says, "I will not surrender my life, I will keep it for myself."
- He gives. And the world says, "I don't want anything from him because my life belongs only to me and I do not want it intruded upon."

When it is faithful, the church is profoundly countercultural. We refuse—we liberal Christians and we conservative Christians—we refuse the self-oriented, self-sufficient life of the world that inevitably ends in alienation and violence. We meet regularly to declare together in each other's presence that we are not our own, but we belong to our faithful savior Jesus Christ.

So First Church will continue the struggle about its downtown location, about its aging membership, about access to the basement, about the shelter for the homeless, about all sorts of things that preoccupy the congregation. Our kind of a church is not a hot option here or in many other places. As First Church thinks of its future as the people of God, we will inescapably fall back on these four evangelical moves. By making these moves, we declare to ourselves and to those who watch us that we are a *different people*, living a *different life*, engaged in a *different purpose*, trusting a *different story*, eating a *different kind of daily bread* and *drinking a different wine*. The world is about to run out of its own resources; soon or late it will want to know if there is an alternative. We, through the practice of these four moves in worship and in life, attest that there is another life that regularly breaks into the world resources that are not our own with purposes that are well beyond us.

IV.

In Mark 6, Jesus fed five thousand people. And then in Mark 8, Jesus fed four thousand people. And then Jesus, good teacher that he is, holds a seminar for his disciples. He knows about "action-reflection" models of pedagogy. The narrative in Mark 8:14–21 goes like this. Jesus and his disciples are out on the lake in a boat. The disciples have forgotten the bread! They did not yet understand that Jesus and his companions were in the bread business and Jesus says to his disciples, "Watch out for the yeast of the Pharisees and the yeast of Herod." Watch out for the junk food of the world, for what you eat of bread, of wine, of pride, of hate, of violence, of selfishness, of greed, of self-indulgence, of cynicism—what you eat will define your life.

"So," he says, "What have you learned about the bread?"— Why did you forget the bread?

Do you not understand about the bread, about the five thousand
and about the four thousand?
Do you have hard hearts?
Do you have eyes and not see?
Do you have ears and not hear?

Do you not remember? He wants to shake them. He says to them, "I just did two big miracles, and you do not see yet that life and food are totally different with me." He waits for an answer and they avoid eye contact at all costs.

Then like a good teacher he pulls back his sophisticated curriculum to more concrete operational issues. He asks his students questions to which they already know the answers. Okay class let us begin again:

When I fed five thousand people with five loaves, how much was left over? How many baskets surplus? And they said with loud vigor, "Twelve! Twelve." When I fed four thousand with seven loaves, how much was left over? How many baskets? And they said loudly, "Seven! Seven."

They know the simple math. But that is all they know, because they are concrete operational and cannot grasp the wonder and the mystery of life as it happened in the presence of Jesus. And then, after the feeble answer of the disciples, Jesus says one of the saddest things in all of scripture:

"Do you not yet understand?" (v. 21)

No, they did not get it. They did not get it that daily life and daily bread are transformed by the power of God so that whoever eats this gift from Jesus will live differently. They did not get it! The world does not get it yet. But we—dear people of First Church— imagine that in the next two hundred and seventy-five years First Church will indeed get it. This is the place where *he takes, he blesses, he breaks, he gives.* And the people depart to new life—life of joy, life of generosity, life of forgiveness, life of praise, life of neighbor, life of joy. Two hundred and seventy-five years or more of that! We are not our own. The one to whom we belong blesses and breaks . . . and *gives* and *gives* and *gives* and *gives!*

November 13, 2005
This sermon was preached at the 275th anniversary of First Congregational Church in Concord, New Hampshire.

51

The Peace Dividend

(Peacemaking)

ISAIAH 11:1–9

When peace comes, it does not come from business as usual, so we need not look for it there. When peace comes, it does not come from the sources from which we might expect it. Peace, when it comes, whenever it comes, *requires odd action from unexpected sources.* Without odd action from unexpected sources, the world will continue to go its uneasy, self-destructive way. I do not recruit you to be a peacemaker. But at least the church should have its head clear and its eyes focused, so that it knows where to look and for what to hope. I make no urging to you, but invite you to consider this poem in Isaiah as a portrayal of odd action for peace from an unexpected source. The poem concerns one who comes from God, a human agent, for peace depends on human agents who break vicious cycles and create space in which peace becomes a possibility.

I

The peacemaker is *an odd human agent.* This one really is human; peace will not be done by God from heaven. The agent is called "stump": There shall come forth a shoot from the *stump* of Jesse, a new person from a broken, burned out family, one who is cut off, who has no sign of life, from whom we expect no sign or gesture of newness. But it is a *shoot,* i.e., new growth that we did not expect, an utter surprise. The peacemaker is like an old potted flower, after a while you look and it has turned green with new life. If you make a list of peacemakers, you will see that they have arisen from unlikely sources, not

262

the official, visible heroes, but struggling people who refused to sit still any longer while death works its way in the world. There are the obvious ones, Gandhi, King, Tutu, Mandela, Havel, the ones who have stood so boldly for an alternative. If you come closer, there are also mothers in Argentina from whom we expected nothing, and Christians—Catholics and Protestants—in Northern Ireland who have said, "Enough!" Agents of reconciliation in family and in community, who act against business as usual, who put their bodies on the line, and say, "Stop!" They begin in another way, a way we would not have thought of until they make a move, and we notice an alternative out beyond our horizon. Peacemaking will be done by *new shoots* from *old stump*s that seemed to offer no new chance.

II.

Peacemakers are people who boldly choose *a "more excellent way,"* a way that breaks with convention and explores alternatives:

> He shall not judge by what his eyes see [not impressed by appearances], or decide by what his ears hear, [not swayed by rumor and gossip and pressure], but with righteousness he shall judge the poor, and decide with equity for the meek of the earth . . . righteousness shall be the belt around his waist, and faithfulness the belt around his loins. (Isa. 11:3–5)

Isn't it strange that in this poetic vision of peace, issues of justice are put on the table, this odd, unexpected agent of newness intervenes in situations of inequity, intervenes with power and advocacy and courage, to redress injustice. The poet knows that the issues of peace are essentially issues of justice: some have too much, more than their share, others have not enough, less than their proper amount. People notice the peacemaker because he dresses funny. You know how the people who make war dress, dressed in uniforms and medals, or dressed in computers and clipboards, or dressed in absoluteness and severity and greed and cynicism. But this one is dressed in righteousness and equity and peace, dressed for the work that is to be done.

The poet knows that if there is to be peace, economic domination must be reversed, economic disadvantage must be corrected, and that requires sharing goods, redeploying resources, reassigning land, and reimagining the norms of adequacy. It is telling that in the great overthrows of recent time, the powers of war, when their offices and homes and pantries are invaded, they had more than their share, embarrassingly hoarding and usurping, building *bigger* barns and more security to keep all the surplus, and now comes *the stump* to intervene with equity on behalf of the poor. Peacemaking, so the poet imagines, is not just good intentions and friendly feelings, but it is policy review and the hard work of breaking the patterns of distribution that are so destructive.

III.

This oddness, I imagine, is not an oddness taken up by just anybody. Who wants to be a stump dressed in equity? The task is too dangerous, too abnormal, too unthinkable. I could not imagine doing that, nor would I ask you to do it. Not only would most of us not risk such a vocation; we would not even think of it, because the present war-making injustice seems too normal and predictable and anyway, it has always been this way. So how could it be that ordinary people who would never think of it find themselves taken up into the drama of peacemaking?

The poet knows:

> The spirit of the LORD shall rest upon him,
> the spirit of wisdom and understanding, the spirit of council and might,
> the spirit of knowledge and the fear of the LORD.
> His delight shall be in the fear of the LORD. (vv. 2–3a)

Peacemakers are powered and driven and authorized *by God's spirit.* That sounds like a large and peculiar notion. Indeed, we have such misinformed notions of "God's spirit." We may think of Pentecost and speaking in tongues, experience, or even charismatic people who are an embarrassment to us.

That, however, is hardly what is happening here. The spirit, the wind of God, is the inscrutable, inexplicable, irresistible force of God's purpose and power that blows, uninvited, into our lives. What it does is to destabilize and decenter and disorient, and cause us to break with all our normalcies. We are indeed blown away when the wind of God blows, strangely filled with power, with resolve, with daring, with imagination, and we take a move outside our long established routines.

The coming of the spirit leads us to a staggering awareness: In order for things to be different, something has to change. Nothing will ever be different if everything is kept unchanged. That of course is true among the nations. We have watched things change recently, and now we notice the difference with its possibilities. Peacemaking, however, applies not just to the nations, but to communities, and churches, and our marriages, our families, and our lives. You want it different? Then think what peacemaking changes have to happen for the war to end.

The community of faith, and this poet, have noticed from time to time, that people get blown outside themselves to commit uncharacteristic acts of generosity and daring and freedom. So a neighbor, at the risk of losing face, forgives a neighbor and peace breaks out. A hurting member of an estranged family commits an act of honesty or generosity, and permits the family to begin at a new place. A teacher breaks out of the old, tired curriculum that bores everyone and asks the kids to reimagine the world, and peace is kindled. A businessman, believing deeply that "profit is not a dirty word," finds some allies and makes an investment in the health of the community that some stockholders would regard as a waste of resources, a political operative moves beyond the conventional, and carries hard-nosed people into new possibility where "no man has ever been." A church gets its mind off itself and its survival and its budget, and moves against normalcy to let the newness of peace permeate its life.

When asked about the strange departure from the old predictabilities, the explanation is often not very clear or illuminating. "It seemed the right thing to do." "I didn't plan it; I just took a step and then another, and found myself in a new pattern." Or, "I couldn't help myself; suddenly it all seemed clear to me and I knew what I had to do." "I decided that I wanted to make a stand and run one risk that would leave a healing mark on the world." Or this, "I don't know what got into me."

Well, the poet knows what gets into people. The poet knows what got into "stump" that caused new "shoot." *It is the wind.* It is the spirit. It is the spirit of God. It is the force and energy and authority and permit of God to push us outside of ourselves, to give ourselves over to the purposes of God that are larger than our tired, controlled selves. We cannot program or summon that wind. But our community knows that when risks are run, energy is strangely given, and power and joy, none of which we can have until we move. It is a peculiar wind that is given to stump, a wind of wisdom and understanding in which we notice for the first time what is in fact going on. It had all been so mystifying and immobilizing, but now the wind makes clear. It is a spirit of council and of might, good discernment and a strange energy for courage, old selves blown away, old fears overcome, old patterns broken open. Peacemakers are not business-as-usual people, but people who have the energy and the freedom to act against normalcy to let God's healing operate. The poet concludes: the peacemaker delights in the fear of the Lord. It seems so right, and it is so satisfying, for once in my life I had a match between my real self and my actions. I found a place in my life with a true and proper work, for the first time. I am astonished at what I did, and I know it was right, and I have a sense of new innocence and sureness that I never imagined. I made things uncomplicated and I acted, and I know God smiled with me in the newness. I find I am no longer tired or fearful, because the new gifts around me are gifts from God.

IV.

Then the poet makes a radical shift in rhetoric. When the stump, powered by the wind acts for the needy, not only is the actor blessed and the poor rescued. *The world is changed.* This is the real dividend of peace action. You know the words:

> The wolf shall dwell with the lamb,
> the leopard shall lie down with the kid,
> and the calf and the lion and the fatling together,
> and a little child shall lead them. The cow and the bear shall feed; . . .
> the lion shall eat straw like the ox.
> The suckling child shall play over the hole of the asp,
> and the weaned child shall put his hand on the adder's den.
> (vv. 6–8 RSV)

This is a lyrical vision of renewed creation. The poet takes a long look back to Genesis, back to the garden of paradise when it was messed up, and hate and fear and death entered into creation. Since that beginning point, the big ones have eaten the little ones, wolves have eaten lambs and snakes have poisoned children, whites have bondaged blacks, males have damaged females, and the world has become a tired drama of destruction, and hostility. It has been so from the beginning. And without the stump and the wind, it will continue to be so.

The peace dividend is that the cycle is broken. There is a vision and a glimpse of a new creation, a world made new. The one filled with the wind of God begins a chain effect against hurt and fear and hate and violence. The poet dares to imagine that an act toward a poor neighbor has a cosmic ripple effect. Skewed neighbor relations contribute to an unhealthy, deathly creation. Our greed guarantees hostility and our selfishness creates fear. Our lust for surplus ruins forests, which evokes droughts. Our chemicals upset the thermal patterns of the world. Of course, the poet is pre-scientific; but he is not stupid. He knows that one act of hate contributes to a hate-filled creation, and one bite of fear builds large reservoirs of resentment . . . and conversely, one neighbor act will impinge upon creation. One less gesture of greed will let one tree live, and one live tree begins the healing of creation. Human stuff matters to the whole of the cosmos.

The peace dividend is not just federal money reassigned here or there, important as that is. The real peace dividend is that the deathliness of the universe, in which we are all enmeshed, can be reversed. The world could become an hospitable place in which to live, because determined acts of justice unleash power for life.

You see, we have let the wrong people define the issue of peace. The peace issue depends not primarily on great budgets and secret policies and large weapon systems and treaties and deterrence. Those are mostly mystifications. The peace issues are a people-to-people matter reflected to be sure in policy, because acts and policies of injustice sow acres and acres of violence in the world.

It has taken other crises than our own, other daring people than us, other places than ours, for us to begin to notice and imagine and venture out of our tight patterns of control which we cherish but which are about to do us in. The question of peace in recent days has been reshaped for us so that we really can have access to it.

We have been witnessing:

- *odd people*, people we never heard of, not the big visible stars, but exhausted people like us who make newness possible;
- noticing that *new actions* have been made modestly, bravely, inventively against injustice and inequality in ways that evoke and insist upon change where no change seemed possible;
- powered by *a power beyond human conjuring* . . . surely the wind of *God*, a special plus given beyond human capacity, so that after the acts of human intervention, one can say, "I don't know what came over me," and we know, *it is the wind*;
- a *dividend of a new world*, new policy, new food distribution, new dignity, new politics. Both the fearful children and the awesome snakes have a new chance.

This is an odd poem that proposes that we think about peace in very different terms. I say this to you, because you are baptized. This poem in Isaiah 11 belongs to you because you are baptized. We baptized have received gifts and made promises. We have sworn in faith that we will not view the world in the old reductionist ways. We will view it through the faithfulness and power of God. Some of us have neglected peacemaking because we have grown accustomed to old tired fears and hates. We have become sated in our weary despair. Nonetheless, the wind blows newness, and shoots come out of stumps, interventions are made, and the dividend of peace spills over.

Think what would happen if this peacemaking, baptismal community with this poem moved beyond itself one gesture a week, little gestures that become a passion and a topic, and then a dividend, and we watch while that little gesture is made large and multiplied by God, until the conclusion . . .

> They shall not hurt or destroy
> in all my holy mountain;
> for the earth shall be filled with the knowledge of the LORD,
> as the waters cover the sea. (v. 9)

It is promised and it will come. But it starts in little acts of newness. "Knowledge of God" is the awareness that the power for new life is available and given to those who act. There comes in this process the discovery that God is good, a good friend, who invites us to friendship. The earth is not yet covered with that knowledge, but there are patches of newness performed by odd people like us, powered by the wind. And as there are patches of peace and justice, there is less hurting and less destroying . . . all over the earth.

So consider, our vocation is not being safe, being big, or being secure and in control, but for the newness of God. People like us, odd, unexpected, empowered:

> people to people,
> power to powerlessness
> new ways against old habits
> wolves and lambs.
> kids and snakes,
> a little child and all of us safe.

For things to be different, something must change. It is promised and we are invited.

April 1, 1990

52

Good Days in the Neighborhood

(Wedding)

MARK 12:28–34

Living a Christian life is not complicated, only demanding: "love God and love neighbor." Fashioning a Christian marriage is not complex, only difficult: "love God and love neighbor." They asked Jesus which of the commandments of Judaism is the most important. It was a favorite question among reflective rabbis, sort of a game that evoked careful, tricky answers. Perhaps they expected him to answer, "The most important commandment is to love God with all your heart and mind and soul." He answered well and they nodded in agreement. But he did not pause, not even for a comma, but added: "The second is this: 'You shall love your neighbor as yourself.'" They asked for only one and they got two, because the two conditions of Christian life and Christian marriage are to *love God* and *love neighbor*.

I.

The second commandment is in fact: "You shall love the life of your neighbor as though it were your own life." The command pertains to marriage because in marriage one finds one's supreme neighbor, the one whose life we love as much as we love our own life. That is what these vows mean about "plenty and want, in sickness and in health, as long as we both shall live." It is, as every married person knows, an endless burden of marriage to keep remembering that the life of this neighbor is as treasured and valued and honored and important and at risk as is my own life; the pledge taken is to treat this neighbor in order that the life of this neighbor may be more deeply joyous and more fully safe.

269

II.

The great threat to marriage in a therapeutic, consumer society, I propose, is that one imagines one has only this one neighbor, so to seek to build a private relationship of romantic Utopia that notices nothing else. Newly married persons are permitted that unreality for a few weeks or months. And then it is time to notice that marriage is a quite public matter, which is why we do weddings in this public way. Christian marriage, the finding of that supreme neighbor, is a way of living in the neighborhood generatively and generously toward all the other neighbors.

Thus Christian marriage requires looking beyond this first neighbor to many other neighbors who live all around the marriage and who count on that marriage as it matters for them. Jesus was asked about the neighbor whom we should love, and he answered that the neighbor is the one in need. Christian marriage looks with and through and beyond that "supreme neighbor" to many other neighbors, most especially the poor, the needy, the powerless, the victims. It should be clear to anyone who looks that our society is going to hell in a hand basket, because there are not enough neighbors who care about the neighborhood. And so we mark on this occasion that Christian marriage is a process of finding that "supreme neighbor," and then many other neighbors who wait to have their lives loved as we love our own life.

III.

Some of you do not know that in the South where we live that the "War Between the States" is sometimes called "The Recent Unpleasantness." I bring up the phrase because after romantic utopianism, every neighborhood, including marriage, is marked by many "recent unpleasantnesses." It cannot be helped or avoided; it happens. That recent unpleasantness may be,

- a sick child, or no child when you wanted one;
- a financial failure or less success than you thought;
- a bad medical diagnosis that shatters health and reminds us of the phrase, "in sickness and in health";
- the way of in-laws, and one never knows ahead of time . . .
- disappointments that we receive and that we enact, small utterances that cannot be taken back.

When the unpleasantness looms, one finds that even the supreme neighbor of your marriage (who seems adequate at the outset for everything) is sometimes less than helpful and not up to the crisis. And then the truth of Christian marriage is that one has recourse to that Holy Neighbor, God, who is our best and final neighbor. I think that is why Jesus linked "love God" and "love neighbor," because God is the ultimate neighbor to whom one goes for generosity and forgiveness, because we cannot live well without more forgiveness and more generosity than we ourselves can muster. Much as we might imagine otherwise, even our marriage neighbor will lack sufficiency in generosity and forgiveness, and we turn to that Holy Neighbor.

In Christian marriage, when we turn to this Holy Neighbor for what we must have to live, it is not to a stranger that we turn, but to one with whom we have practiced neighborliness, obedience, and worship. And then in the unpleasantness, recent as it always is, we find our life given afresh in generosity and forgiveness . . . without which we cannot live. And we return to our other neighbors, able to be generous, able to forgive.

IV.

Like Christian life, Christian marriage is a neighborly thing. There is the *supreme neighbor* whom we embrace as our own life. There is the *neighbor in need* just beyond our marriage, but a true neighbor. And there is the *Holy Neighbor* present to us in generosity and forgiveness. It is not true, as Mr. Rogers pretends, that every day is a beautiful day in the neighborhood. But it is true that every day is a better, more nearly beautiful day, when we love God and love neighbor in generosity and forgiveness.

July 13, 2001

53

The Impossible Self as Steward

(Stewardship)

ISAIAH 55:1–11
PSALM 92:1–4, 12–15
COLOSSIANS 3:5–17
LUKE 18:18–27

The recurring crisis of stewardship is not about money. It is not, as we used to say, about "time, talent, money." That crisis, rather, is about *the self* who gives or who does not give, how the self is constituted, identified, perceived, presented, and situated. Because a self—wrongly constituted, wrongly identified, wrongly perceived, wrongly presented, wrongly situated—will not ever be able to be generous or grateful.

Paul states the problem and possibility starkly:

> Do not lie to one another, seeing that you have stripped off the *old self* with its practices and have clothed yourselves with the *new self* which is being renewed in knowledge according to the image of its creator. (Col. 3:9–10, emphasis added)

Thus it is "old self/new self"! As I talk, consider how you yourself are clothed in identity, and then in your stewardship work consider someone whom you find most resistant to gratitude and generosity.

I.

In these readings we are given four case studies in the competing claims of old and new. I will first consider the four cases of the old self:

1. Paul in Colossians. The old self is a practitioner of the ways of greed, anxiety, and alienation:

> Put to death, therefore, whatever in you is earthly: fornication, impurity, passion, evil desire, and greed (which is idolatry) . . . anger, wrath, malice, slander, and abusive language from your mouth. (Col. 3:5, 8)

This self is unsettled, out of sync, having bought in on the anxious self-definition of the world, responsive to the fearful aggressiveness all around.

2. The Psalm does not speak much about the old self and certainly not in the verses of our reading. Just this in what we have predictably skipped over:

> How great are your works, O Lord!
> Your thoughts are very deep!
> The dullard cannot know,
> the stupid cannot understand this:
> though the wicked sprout like grass and all evildoers flourish,
> they are doomed to destruction forever.
>
> (Ps. 92:5–7)

The problem with the old selves is that they are too bored or too dull or preoccupied to notice the greatness of God's steadfast love. And when we do not notice that, we are on our own.

3. The point is a bit clearer in Isaiah 55. The poem addresses Jews in Babylon who have signed on for imperial values and requirements. First the poet reminds his Jewish listeners that there is free water, free milk, and free bread from the generous hand of YHWH. But then a hard question is put to them:

> Why do you spend your money for that which is not bread,
> and your labor for that which does not satisfy? (Isa. 55:2)

Why do you pursue a way of life that never satisfies? Why are you caught in the endless game of accumulation and control that never has good outcomes? Why do you give your time and energy, your very life, for the empty offers of the empire?

4. And finally, the Gospel reading offers this guy whom we call "the rich young ruler." He is punctilious in keeping the law, obeying orders, remembering the old mandates of his mother, meeting quotas, playing by the rules. He knows that is not enough for a good future. But it is all he can do; he is boxed in and cannot yield, much too fearful of a free fall. It is all quid pro quo for him. He cannot imagine gifts given to him or gifts given by him, because, says Luke, "he was very rich." Another rendering, of course, is that "he had great possessions." He had a big zone of control to manage that he hoped would let him "inherit eternal life," even though he knew down deep it would not.

What a fast company, the old self at Colossae in greed, the dullard in the Psalm who does not notice, the rat-race of Isaiah in Babylon, and the rich man in the Gospel. Be glad you are not their stewardship officer! Beyond them, of course, these several texts describe folk among us, maybe us on a bad day, smitten as we are by the narrative of anxious greed that propels our consumer society. Even as we pursue the rat-race, we know, down deep, like the rich guy, that this is not the truth of our lives.

II.

So the news is that there is another way of generosity and gratitude:
   1. In Colossians:

> [A]nd having clothed yourselves with the new self, which is being renewed in knowledge according to the image of its creator. (3:10)

And what follows for the new self?

> As God's chosen ones, holy and beloved, clothe yourselves with compassion, kindness, humility, meekness, and patience. Bear with one another and, if anyone has a complaint against another, forgive each other; just as the Lord has forgiven you, so you must also forgive. Above all, clothe yourselves with love, which binds everything together in perfect harmony. And let the peace of Christ rule in your hearts, to which indeed you were called in the one body. And be thankful. (vv. 12–15)

The new self is ready for sisters and brothers, and begins the day with forgiveness, which primarily means the forgiveness of debts. The new self enters a new economy of generosity.
   2. In the Psalm, the new self overflows with gratitude:

> It is good to give thanks to the Lord,
> to sing praises to your name, O Most High;
> to declare your steadfast love in the morning,
> and your faithfulness by night,
> to the music of the lute and the harp,
> to the melody of the lyre.
>   (Ps. 92:1–3)

And like a tree well watered, such a one flourishes, stays green, produces fruit, not crimped or fearful or anxious or calculating.

3. In Isaiah 55, the new self is on a journey home, away from the grip of the empire:

> For you shall go out in joy,
> and be led back in peace;
> the mountains and the hills before you shall burst into song,
> and all the trees of the field shall clap their hands. (Isa. 55:12)

The road home is one of hope-filled joy!

4. And in the Gospel reading, the new self is one who sells all, distributes to the poor, has treasure in heaven, and follows. The new self is the one who relinquishes enough for an easy life in the world, without anxiety.

III.

The tension in each of these readings is an either/or:

> in Colossians, either old self or new self;
> in the Psalm, either flourishing or stupidity;
> in Isaiah, either unsatisfied or on the way rejoicing;
> in the Gospel, either go away sad or follow.

The lessons state it starkly. The issue surely is to arrive at a rooted self that does not give in to the narrative of consumer capitalism with its military fearfulness. The task of stewardship is to be reclothed in a self of generosity and gratitude, categories that are a foreign language to the old self. So consider:

1. The language of "old self reclothed as new self" is most likely a reference to the drama of *baptism*. It is in baptism that the self is radically redefined. That is why affluent babies wear such fancy, traditional clothes at baptism. All of a life of following then is a "perfection of our baptism," a wondrous phrase from the Calvinist tradition.

2. The *Eucharist* is the meal of generosity that breaks the vicious cycles of fearful scarcity that make us anxious and selfish. We may do much more, as stewards, about the practice of the Eucharist in order to exhibit the generosity of God . . . more bread, more wine . . . called in my church "the welcome table." What a table, because the table of consumer capitalism is not welcoming; that table is grudging, calculating, and controlled by scarcity. That table generates fear; it thrives on scarcity; it keeps us moving toward an unreachable quota. It keeps us vigilant and on guard, being sure that we keep our stuff and get yours if we can. There is no generous stewardship at the unwelcome

table. But now, you prepare a very different table before me in the presence of my enemies, in the presence of my fear and my anxiety. A very different table!

3. I have appealed to baptism and Eucharist, signs that all of life is a brooding sacramental gift. Without that sacramental rootage, life becomes a series of quid pro quo transactions. So imagine that the folk with whom you do stewardship . . . and you . . . and I . . . are all finally hoping for another way beyond our old grim, tired selves.

You may think, as I often do, that to be resituated in and redefined by the mystery of generosity and gratitude is impossible, because I know my deep old self too well. But what the Lord of the narrative said to the rich guy he also said to his followers:

What is impossible for mortals is possible for God. (Luke 18:27)

Imagine stewardship as moving toward and living in the impossibility that is God's good gift. Before God finishes with us, we shall be new selves, praising our savior all the day long, going out in joy, walking in the light of *shalom*, no longer petty or calculating or grudging. We try on the new clothing of generosity, in order to see what it feels like to be newly situated, newly identified, newly perceived, newly presented,. . . not going away sad but heirs to the kingdom. It is indeed impossible . . . but possible!

July 31, 2010
Episcopal Stewardship Consultation, Indianapolis

54

Old/New . . . Tell/Sing

(Ordination)

ISAIAH 42:10–13
ACTS 16:25–40

I have been making a list of the kinds of people who do not sing very much:

> Angry people do not sing much;
> Anxious people do not sing much;
> Self-sufficient people do not sing much;
> People in despair do not sing much;
> Tired people do not sing much;
> Overindulged people do not sing much.

Indeed people who run with the rats in order to win the rat-race do not sing very much. They do not have the energy or the freedom or the courage or the patience to reach beyond themselves to that which is hidden and awesome and magical.

And then it struck me that our society, in its main accents, is designed to keep people from singing. It does so by keeping us overfed (indulged), overworked (tired), and surely anxious, always on Orange Alert. It does so by seducing us into thinking that shopping or television or big-time athletics are important, when in fact they are mostly narcotics in our society to keep us from noticing. And the outcome, predictably, is a society of one-dimensional people focused on an ideology, liberal or conservative, without freedom to reach beyond ourselves in wonder, love, and praise. And this, I believe, is how our dominant society wants it to be.

I.

In the midst of that mono-culture, God has set down a company of singers who refuse to give in to the culture of anger, anxiety, self-sufficiency,
despair, fatigue, and overindulgence. Of course, you know before I tell you
that I am not talking about any old singing, but rather about singing that
testifies to and continues to imagine the reality of the God of glory and
grace as the defining character in the world. We are indeed singers of praise
to God!

   The silence was first broken by our sister Miriam. Just as we got to the
other side of the Red Sea and looked back at Egypt and its slave camps, sister
Miriam took a tambourine, and with the other women she sang defiantly,

> Sing to YHWH,
> for YHWH has triumphed gloriously;
> horse and rider he has thrown into the sea.
>   (Exod. 15:21)

They broke the silence of bondage and fear, and sang what had not been permitted. They sang that God has defeated the claims of Pharaoh and the claims
of the National Security State, and we are in fact free at last; and they shook
their tambourines in astonishment!

   The song was picked up by mother Hannah who never doubted that the
birth of her special son would change the world. She sang:

> The Lord makes poor and makes rich;
> he brings low, he also exalts.
> He raises up the poor from the dust.
>   (1 Sam. 2:7–8a)

   The lyrics of mother Hannah are picked up by mother Mary who sang, as
Luke tells us,

> He has brought down the powerful from their thrones,
> and lifted the lowly;
> he has filled the hungry with good things,
> and sent the rich away empty.
>   (Luke 1:52–53)

   These sisters and mothers of ours sang revolutionary songs. They imagined and expected and trusted that the world will, by the power of God, be
healed and made right, even for the poor.

II.

So consider the way we have been singing. In Isaiah 42, the poet (or God) summons Israel:

Sing to the LORD a new song! (Isa. 42:10)

That phrase "new song" likely means that they had commissioned a new anthem for their choir in order to sing about the new reality of homecoming. They break the silence of exilic displacement; they knew that the reality of God is stronger than the power of bondage. They sing about YHWH, the God of restorative freedom:

Let them give glory to the LORD,
and declare his praise in the coastlands.
(v. 12)

All are invited to sing, because the world is changing by the power of God:

Let the desert and its towns lift up their voice,
the villagers that Kedar inhabits;
let the inhabitants of Sela sing for joy,
let them shout from the tops of the mountains.
(v. 10–11)

What all of us know, those singing, is that the Lord is no nice uncle or some cuddly therapist. The Lord is one who will make a difference:

The LORD goes forth like a soldier,
like a warrior he stirs up his fury;
he cries out, he shouts aloud,
he shows himself mighty against his foes. (v. 13)

They sing because they know that the God of Easter is stronger than the deathly power of oppression.

This forceful agent of newness is the God of the Exodus who had broken the grip of the Egyptian National Security State, in order to let God's people live freely and obediently in justice for the neighborhood.

III.

But what caught my eye is this story in Acts 16. Paul and Silas were preaching the Easter God who had freed them from the power of death. They are arrested by the authorities as troublemakers, and they are put in prison. And then, in prison, we are told:

> About midnight Paul and Silas were praying and singing hymns to God, and the prisoners were listening to them. (v. 25)

They were singing! Their singing was contagious; it attracted the other prisoners to the music. They are singing hymns to God. They are singing and praying. And their singing eventuated, we are told, in an earthquake, "so violent that the foundations of the state prison were shaken and the doors were immediately opened and their chains were unfastened." Free at last, free at last!

But they did not run. They stayed in their cells. And from that, two things happened quickly:

> The warden is invited to the gospel and is baptized;
> The authorities who had arrested them apologized for the way they had treated them, and sent them on their way.

The narrative, to be sure, does not explicitly connect the singing and the earthquake. But I would not bet against such a connection. The singing refused to give in to the authorities who wanted them to conform and to deny Easter. But they sang anyway!

IV.

Take that whole company of singers . . . Miriam, Hannah, Mary, the new song people in exile, Paul and Silas in prison. In their passion they kept the song going. But surely Pharaoh wanted to silence Miriam, and the Philistines wanted to silence Hannah, and the Babylonians wanted to silence Israel's singers, and Jerusalem wanted to silence Mary, and Rome wanted to silence Paul and Silas. Because the authorities are on edge about the danger of such singing. Unleashed power for something other.

There are lots of ways to silence the singing church. Turn the church into entertainment and pretend there is nothing at stake. Turn the church into a continuing quarrel about a lot of side issues. Turn the church into an echo of the consumer society. Have a conservative ideology as a one-truth mob. Have a liberal ideology with an uncompromising social agenda. Or get them to shop; or to become religious couch potatoes or get them to care the most about college or professional sports. Or just dumb down so that church can be on automatic pilot and faith becomes a drug of serenity. Do anything to siphon off the courage and the energy of the song.

But they sang and they kept singing in spite of that. And do you know why they were able to keep singing? Because they knew the old, old story behind the song. The learned it as kids; they cherished it as adults. They taught their children to cherish it. They memorized it into their DNA. They were baptized so that with good hearts and loud voices and tambourines they could not keep quiet.

> That old, old story
> > tells us that the world is God's good creation that requires environmental attentiveness;
> That old, old story
> > concerns miraculous new births to old folk without possibility, because it is never too late in the mercy of God;
> That old, old story
> > is about emancipation from the coercive requirements of Pharaoh and the pressures of quotas for more bricks;
> That old, old story
> > is about being at the mountain and always again making new covenant that redefines the world as a neighborhood;
> That old, old story
> > is about being in an arid place without resources, and watching bread being given in ways we do not understand;
> That old, old story
> > is about life in a world where gifts are given and neighbors are trusted and the poor are protected and given dignity, where power is kept under the discipline of truth, and war is not learned any more.

It turns out, would you believe it, that the old, old story becomes the new, new song. It is no wonder that they tried to stop the singing. Because it threatens the status quo; it challenges the old economics of greed; it exposes the politics of exploitation; it questions the church as narcotic. It unleashes the power of life into a world too much in love with death. The new, new song about the world is the old, old story of Easter. The new song they are to sing in Isaiah is about emancipation. The new song of Mary is about the old story of resurrection. Paul and Silas in prison sang a new song because they had not forgotten the old story of Jesus and his love.

When the old, old story becomes the new, new song, people become free and courageous and dangerous and high energy, and filled with joy. The powers always want to encourage amnesia, because if we cannot remember, we will not be able to sing, and if we cannot sing, we shall die.

VI.

So consider this calling that we acknowledge today. Robert, the church desig-nates you today as a teacher of the church or, if you like, a teaching elder. The church does that because it knows that it must have faithful teachers. It must have teachers to teach the old, old story. For unless there are teachers of the old, old story, there will be no singing of new, new songs. The church in our society, of late, has nearly forgotten. That is why some good church folk are shocked and scandalized to discover what a dangerous song is put on our lips by the spirit, and what a dangerous life is that of our baptism.

Before you finish, you will be expected to hone your critical skills and to embrace the large horizon of learning out beyond your discipline. You will be expected to acquit yourself as a good teacher and as a learned person who can do critical research. At the center of your call, however, is the narrative that defies all of our critical work and that sits oddly in the skeptical community of our world. I propose that your ordination today is primarily so that the church does not lose itself in numbness, despair, or fatigue. It turns out that when the church tells the old, old story well and faithfully, it can sing the new, new song. Such singing:

- gives energy for mission;
- gives generosity in stewardship;
- gives passion for evangelism;
- gives courage about social justice.
- gives us the essential resources for a life of glad obedience.

This ordination that we enact today is a bet that numbness, despair, and fatigue are not the wave of our future. We make this trade-off when we can, giving up *numbness, despair, and fatigue* for the sake of *wonder, love, and praise*. That liberating trade-off depends on singing new, new songs that depends on telling the old, old story that depends on having teachers to remind us. We situate you at this pivot point between story and song, between old and new. We commend you to God in thanksgiving and will continue to pray for your well-being, your courage, your wonder and your tenacity. Imagine that the singing you make possible will evoke more than one emancipatory earthquake!

January 9, 2011
At the ordination of Robert Williamson at Clemson Presbyterian Church,
Clemson, South Carolina

Scripture Index

CPSIA information can be obtained at www.ICGtesting.com
Printed in the USA
LVOW11*0117070415

433526LV00003B/76/P